BAKING IN AMERICA

Economic Development

VOLUME I

BAKING IN AMERICA

Economic
Development

BY

WILLIAM G. PANSCHAR

Assistant Professor of Business Administration
University of California, Berkeley

VOLUME I

NORTHWESTERN UNIVERSITY PRESS
EVANSTON, ILLINOIS · 1956

NORTHWESTERN UNIVERSITY STUDIES IN BUSINESS HISTORY

Gulf to the Rockies: The Heritage of the Fort Worth and Denver, Colorado and Southern Railways, 1861–1898, by Richard C. Overton. University of Texas Press, 1953.

Designed for Digging: The First 75 Years of Bucyrus-Erie Company, by Harold F. Williamson and Kenneth H. Myers, II. Northwestern University Press, 1955.

Baking in America: Volume I, *Economic Development,* by William G. Panschar; Volume II, *Market Organization and Competition,* by Charles C. Slater. Northwestern University Press, 1956.

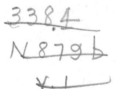

PREFACE

Since the beginnings of civilization bread has been the staff of life. The flat breads of ancient times, grandmother's old-fashioned home-made loaf, and today's precision-controlled product have all vitally contributed to the world's food supplies and have made baking a basic economic activity in all societies. While scholars have long been interested in the history of baking as household and industrial arts, no one attempted to carry forward the evolution of baking as it operates in a modern industrial society. It was to make a contribution to a better understanding of this neglected phase of the history of the industry that this study of the growth of baking in America was undertaken.

This history of American baking and its companion volume, covering the industry's current market organization and competitive behavior, are the result of a joint industry and academic interest in the economic analysis of one of the major industries in the United States. The original impetus for the studies came from industry leaders who, under an agreement with the Center for Social Research at Northwestern University, arranged for the American Bakers' Association to make a grant to the University to cover the costs of preparing the manuscripts. Under the terms of the agreement, the authors were assured of complete independence in evaluating and presenting their material.

In the preparation of the manuscripts many have taken part and many have shared the problems involved. The greatest debt is owed to Dr. Harold F. Williamson, Professor of Economics at Northwestern University. From the many vexing administrative problems, through the time-consuming tasks of helping to organize and rewrite several disjointed manuscript drafts, to the final details of publication, he was the co-ordinator who policed the job. Moreover, he marshalled a small army of people associated with him to speed up the process: Kathleen S. Hines, who assisted in too many ways to enumerate; O. A. Smalley, Arnold R. Daum, and Gilbert C. Klose, who contributed both ideas and sharp blue pencils; and several others who joined in the work.

I am deeply grateful to Dr. Richard B. Heflebower, Chairman of Northwestern's Economics Department, who, as my teacher and adviser, first called my attention to the meaning and significance of industry studies. Thanks are due also to Dr. Howard F. Bennett of the Business History Department at Northwestern University and Dr. Elmo P. Hohman of the Economics Department for their constructive criticisms of the manuscript, and to Dr. Virgil B. Heltzel for his painstaking services as editor of the Northwestern University Press.

Charles C. Slater, the author of Volume II, was my closest working associate; we shared ideas, problems, and responsibilities from the very beginning. His knowledge of the baking industry formed the basis for much of the organization of the history. Norman Byers, our research associate, ably performed as researcher, writer and critic. Most of the statistical data were gathered and organized by Helen Twedt, who showed a keen appreciation of the necessity of meeting deadlines. Albert Haase of Bolinas, California, patiently did most of the editing during the final stages in preparing the manuscript.

Without the keen appreciation of the research problems faced and the data, time and counsel contributed by the American Bakers' Association and individual members, this study could not have been completed. Special thanks are due Harold Fiedler, Secretary of the American Bakers' Association, and to the co-chairmen of the Association's co-ordinating committee with the University, Daniel Uhrig, President of the Purity Bakeries Corporation, and George Faunce, Jr., Vice-President of the Continental Baking Company. The leadership, guidance, and understanding of these busy men will always be remembered.

To my wife, Mary, who did so very much, I can but give thanks and advise marriage to all.

Finally, despite all assistance, responsibilities for presentation, organization, and analysis remain mine.

William G. Panschar

Berkeley, California

CONTENTS

[ix]

Part **FOUR:** BAKING THROUGH
DEPRESSION AND WAR,
1930–1950

LIST OF TABLES

LIST OF FIGURES AND CHARTS

INTRODUCTION

With the discovery, more than 10,000 years ago, that applying heat to cereal grains made them more edible for human consumption, bread baking became a part of a technical heritage shared in common by all societies in the world, from the earliest known records of prehistoric man through the civilizations of Egypt, Greece, Rome, the Middle Ages, and to our own society. Yet it has been only within the last century that this production process has changed from a simple home and bakeshop system to an advanced industrial activity. The history of the development of the modern baking industry in the United States is therefore in large part a story of the effects of the nation's industrialization on an age-old craft.

In chronicling the history of baking in America, there have been two major purposes. The first was to show how, why, and when the market structure and competitive pattern in the industry evolved. In this sense, history becomes a kind of laboratory for observing market structure and behavior in the past and for showing how historic changes in the organization of the industry have influenced the shape of its modern organization. This is shown to be an evolutionary process rather than a revolutionary one in that changes in the structure of the industry are part of a continuous and cumulative action. The second purpose was to get at the very heart of the process of economic change in the development of a modern industry. By describing the changes in the baking industry and by analyzing their causes and the reactions to them, the historical treatment centers attention upon the economic forces that make for change in an industrial economy.

These forces are seen to be not only those of a physical and technical sort, but also those operating in the larger social and economic environment.

In attempting to accomplish the stated objectives, the history of the baking industry has been divided into four broad time periods: from ancient times to 1850, 1850–1900, 1900–1930, and 1930–1950.

The years before 1850 serve as a broad introduction to the growth of the modern industry. Built upon an Old World heritage dating back to antiquity, an organized baking trade in America began with earliest settlements and remained little changed until the beginning of industrialization about 1850.

The half century from 1850 to 1900 served as an incubation period for the modern industry. During these years, in response to changes in technical, social, and economic conditions, baking began to move from the home to commercial bakeries. By 1900 relations among a few large establishments in urban centers were already foreshadowing an era of large scale production, distribution, and competition.

Over the next thirty years these characteristics became widespread in the industry as baking responded to sweeping changes in American life, a shift from rural to urban living, from an agrarian to an industrial economy, from railroad to automotive transportation. These forces led to the domination of the industry by large commercial establishments, and an industrial structure and a market behavior that remain essentially unchanged down to the present.

How the industry adjusted to this structure and to the depression and the turbulent war and postwar periods forms the main story of the period ending in 1950. It gives a setting for the analysis of the current behavior of the industry that is presented in Volume II of this study of baking in America.

BAKING IN AMERICA

Volume I

Economic Development
by
William G. Panschar
Assistant Professor
School of Business Administration
University of California
Berkeley, California

PART

ONE

THE EARLY HISTORY OF BAKING

CHAPTER 1

BAKING IN THE OLD WORLD

THE BAKING INDUSTRY in America today (1954) is a four and one-half billion dollar industry. It supplies 95 per cent of the nation's bread consumption and a major portion of all other baked goods. In American industry, baking ranks sixth in the value of products produced, tenth in number of wage earners employed, and eighth in value added by manufacture. In several respects, baking is the top-ranking industry among all of America's food processors. From the standpoint of number of establishments, value added by manufacture, number of employees, and size of payroll, it is second to none. The only food industry larger in dollar volume of business done is the meat packing industry.

The baking industry in America did not attain its present stature overnight. It grew slowly from small beginnings, dating from the earliest settlement on the Atlantic seaboard. And back of that lies a history in the Old World, a history involving centuries of a long and checkered evolutionary process. The story of baking, in fact, is almost as old as man himself.

It began, perhaps, when man first added cereal grains, the raw materials of baking, to his diet of fish and game. Such grains, in fact, have fed the world for 10,000 years. Millet, oats, barley, rice and wheat have been eaten from the dawn of time; rye since the days of Rome; and corn, in the New World, long before the arrival of Columbus. Grains are, and have been, man's most economical source of food. Once their value was recognized, it remained for some unknown benefactor to complete the "staff of life" by converting grain into bread by baking. Numerous improvements, of course, have been introduced since that epochal discovery, but the nub of his idea—the application of heat—has changed none since that time. Now for a closer look at early man and his bread.

A Prelude to Civilization

Our knowledge of the origins of baking is rather meager. The history begins long before man had become conscious of the written word. And, for this reason, it is a matter of conjecture only. Sometime in the far distant past man found that grass seeds satisfied his hunger. They were simply chewed whole and must have been a difficult fare. But they formed a hardy supplement to a skimpy diet, largely of meat. More important, perhaps, such grains could be stored without spoilage— an impossibility with meat, fruit or vegetables.

Thousands of years must have passed before it occurred to anyone to grind the grain between stones. Such milling also led to the screening of the indigestible seed coverings. This was a notable step forward. These two operations—grinding and sifting—formed the basic processes of milling which, except for refinements, are still in use.

The next step forward by ancient man was probably the tending of wild grains, which must have eventually suggested the possibility of cultivation. With this discovery, it was no longer necessary for man to wander about for his food. It made possible a more settled way of life with occasional forays for game. As can be imagined, the conscious cultivation of grains went a long way toward taming man himself.

Among the early peoples taking to such sedentary ways were the Swiss Lake Dwellers who lived during the Late Stone

Prehistoric Man Pouring Dough on Heated Stones

Baking Process in Ancient Egypt

Age, some 8,000 years ago.[1] On their marsh lands the Lake Dwellers had found and cultivated several kinds of grain. Millet was probably the first used, but barley and early varieties of wheat were also cultivated.[2]

It was perhaps by accident that the Lake people discovered that the ground seeds were more palatable if they were moistened. And, perhaps, it was by accident again that the moistened coarse meal was left in a fire to bake. Whether by accident or design, the Lake Dwellers had discovered bread—the first the world had known. It was man's first systematically prepared food and the end of an orderly process of gathering, grinding, sifting, and baking.[3] By modern standards, it would have been very unsatisfactory. The bread was hard on the outside, sodden within, and covered with dirt and grit.

The discovery of bread tended further to domesticate man. Together with cultivation of grains, it had the effect of changing society from small family groups into larger agricultural communities. During the Late Stone Age communities and towns emerged, based on the stabilizing influence of agriculture and its end products.[4]

For some 3,000 years the tough, hard sheet of baked meal continued to serve as man's primary food and as a basis for organized society. This was not only true for the Stone Age, but also for most of the ancient civilized world for an astonishingly long time. Baked meal, for example, was the only type of bread known to the Babylonians, Assyrians, and early Egyptians.[5] Then about 3,000 B.C. the pattern of baking was radically altered by a series of events occurring in the Valley of the Nile.

---

[1] James H. Breasted, *Ancient Times, A History of the Early World* (Boston: Ginn and Company, 1916), p. 20.

[2] H. E. Jacob, *Six Thousand Years of Bread, Its Holy and Unholy History* (Garden City: Doubleday, Doran and Co., Inc., 1944), pp. 13-14.

[3] J. Storck and W. D. Teague, *Flour for Man's Bread* (Minneapolis: University of Minnesota Press, 1952), p. 35.

[4] Breasted, *op. cit.*, pp. 26-29.

[5] Jacob, *op. cit.*, p. 26.

Bread in the Ancient World

In ancient Egypt the cultivation of grains, primarily barley, was practiced on an extensive scale. The climate and soil of the Nile Valley were ideally adapted to agriculture. Indeed, farming had become the major occupation of the Egyptian civilization. Its organization, however, was an affair of the state. In effect, all the cultivated lands belonged to the Pharaoh and were administered for him by the priests and nobles and to a smaller extent by peasants. For the most part the land was split into vast estates, tilled by slave labor. Each holder had to turn over a portion of his harvest to the royal household and another portion to the public granary. What was left to the land holder was available for his own use or for sale in the market place.

Baking itself had also become a highly organized activity, with official bakers and slaves in the royal household and on the estates of the great lords. In the beginning, the bakers were familiar only with the flat breads of wheat and barley which were baked in the coals of fire or in thick earthen jars. About 3,000 B.C. the routine of the Egyptian baker was upset by a momentous discovery, the art of leavening.[6] This discovery may have occurred in the royal household where a not too attentive baker set aside some dough and forgot about it. It soured and expanded, due to the growth of yeast cells, and accidentally perhaps, was added to the regular batch, with amazing results. The aerated loaf was unlike anything that had ever been known before. Nearly like our corn bread, muffins or biscuits, it was medium light and of good texture. Such loaves found immediate favor. They were a luxury and not a part of the daily diet of the common people, however, for leavened bread could be made only from wheat and it was far more expensive than barley.

The new bread led to another innovation, the invention of

---

[6] *Ibid.*, p. 27.

the oven, which gradually replaced the open fire method. Like raised bread, the oven was probably a creation of the royal bakery. It was not an oven in the modern sense. It was a cylindrical clay structure with a top narrowing to a cone and a flat partition dividing the interior. In the lower part there was an opening for a fire box; in the upper, a large opening for the breads and for the drawing off of gases.[7]

The oven was fired an hour or so before baking time. Then the soured dough was salted and kneaded thoroughly once more. Bran was sprinkled over the bottom of the oven to keep the dough from sticking. The oven not only produced a far better loaf than the open fire method, but its much greater capacity more adequately met the household needs of the upper classes.

With leavened bread and the oven, Egyptian baking gradually took on the airs of a fine art. Loaves appeared in a multitude of shapes—round, cubical, braided, in bird, animal and fish shapes, or in the pyramidal forms of the royal tombs. They were sprinkled with poppy seed and sesame and camphor added for a biting touch. Over fifty varieties of bread graced the Egyptian table. Raised bread and the oven formed the first important changes in the history of bread making.

The Hebrew shepherd folk, who had been taken into captive slavery in Egypt around the fourteenth century B.C., were among the first to acquire the Egyptian discoveries. When they were successfully led out of Egypt by Moses, they took their new found knowledge of bread making with them. In flight, the cumbersome ovens were out of the question and the Hebrews had to resort to the earlier flat breads. "Manna from heaven" was such an unleavened product. Once in Palestine, however, every housewife had her own small oven, and shortly, as life took on an urban look, a regular baking trade appeared.

By the time of Christ every city in Palestine had its own

---

[7] Ibid.

baker. In Jerusalem all the masters of the trade set up shop
on a bakers' street. According to the Bible the city had a modest "bread factory to which the master bakers brought their
flour to be baked into the breads they later sold in their
shops." [8]

Rather like our modern rolls, Hebrew breads were round
and slightly raised in the center. Scarcely thicker than a finger,
it took at least three breads to satisfy a man at mealtime.
When Abigail entertained David and his men, two hundred
breads were consumed, but only two jugs of wine. The ban-
quet bespeaks the size of the breads rather than any temper-
ance on the part of David.[9]

The Hebrews were thus among the early peoples who
helped spread the basic innovations of Egyptian bread making. Their religious rites required that the flat breads of their
wandering past be eaten at certain periods, but their daily
fare consisted of true leavened breads prepared and baked
the way their captors had taught them.

Like the Hebrews, the early Greeks probably learned of
leavened bread and conical ovens from the Egyptians. While
it is possible that this craft may also have been introduced by
the Phoenicians who carried on trade between Egypt and the
Aegean Islands as early as 1,000 B.C., it was not until roughly
600 B.C. that the Greeks employed the Egyptian methods to
any appreciable extent. Prior to that time very little wheat
had been cultivated and the Greeks of necessity had to eat the
flat barley breads of earlier times. But with the introduction
of better growing methods and wheat imports from Sicily and
Egypt, the wealthier classes at least took to leavened breads.

In time the Greeks improved upon Egyptian techniques.
One major improvement was the bee-hive oven, a closed oven
built in the shape of a hemisphere with a rather low ceiling.
It handled a greater number of dough pieces and its low,
rounded dome afforded much better retention of heat than

---

[8] *Ibid.*, p. 36.
[9] *Ibid.*

the earlier conical ovens. Because of its size, its use was confined to patrician households and to public bakeries. This
Greek oven was the forerunner of the famous peel oven
which was to be the baker's basic piece of equipment for the
next 2,500 years.

The Greeks' greatest contribution to bread making was in
milling, however; the finer the flour, the better the texture
and lightness of the bread. Since the days of the Egyptians
wheat had been ground by means of the primitive "saddle
stone," the grinding being done by rolling a smaller stone
over the wheat which was held in the trough of a large con-
cave stone. But the process was slow and limited to small
amounts of grain. It produced little more than a rough coarse
flour. Through a series of experiments with various mill-
stones, the Greeks developed the continuous rotary motion
hourglass and quern mills.

In the hourglass mill, two stones were fitted together as a
mated pair of self-centering orbits. The upper stone was enlarged into a hollow, or hopper, to feed the grain. The mill
was of such a size that men or animals could be harnessed to
it to provide steady rotation. The hand quern was developed
for use in the home, and was, in effect, a home appliance
based on the same principle as the larger hourglass mill. It
was constructed of two circular stones, one of which had an
opening for the grain and a hand crank. In performance the
Greek mills offered the miller two major improvements over
the "saddle stone." They increased the speed of grinding and
provided a steady flow of grain. Their flour was both finer
and whiter.

The Greeks were able to turn out a loaf so light and of
such fine taste and whiteness that it brought them deserved
honors as the most skillful breadmakers of the Mediterranean
world. It has been said that they produced as many as seventy-
two different kinds of bread.[10] Some were mixed with "the

---

[10] "Bread in the Ancient World," *Baking Industry Magazine,* XCVII (April 12,
1952), p. 8.

milk of grass feeding cows." [11] Others were seasoned with poppy seeds, oil, wine, cheese or honey. Cheese cakes and honey became the principal confectionery of the Greeks. In time, bread also took on religious overtones for pious Greeks. In the worship of Apollo at Delphi and of Zeus at Athens, loaves of all sorts were offered in great quantities. "There is little doubt that our hot cross buns go back to some symbol of the pagan worship." [12]

Public bakeries became common. Bread was said to have been more frequently bought in the Athenian market place than made at home.[13] The owners of bakeries were probably freedmen, but bakers as a class were usually slaves. An owner may have owned or hired his help. Wealthy households had their own baking facilities attended by skilled slaves of high value. In Athens an ordinary baker might be bought for $100; a specially skilled one might bring twenty times that amount.[14]

While baking had its roots in Egypt and Greece, it was in Rome that baking reached its greatest development in the ancient world. For several centuries after the founding of Rome, "porridge" (the baked meal of earlier times) not bread was the staple of the Roman diet.[15] It was probably about 200 B.C. that the Roman patricians were introduced to the bread and ovens known earlier in Egypt and Greece. Shortly, public bakeries made their initial appearance. As Rome grew in power and wealth, the bakeries increased many fold. During the reign of Augustus (30 B.C. to 14 A.D.) there were over 300 bakeries in Rome, an average of about one shop for every two thousand inhabitants.[16] As in Greece, each shop was a combination mill and bakery. Some mill-bakeries like that of the famed Latini brothers were extremely large. The brothers

---

[11] "Sixty Centuries of Bakers and Baking," *Bakers Weekly Magazine*, XXXII (December 17, 1921), p. 51.

[12] *Ibid.*, p. 52.

[13] *Ibid.*, p. 74.

[14] *Ibid.*

[15] Jacob, *op. cit.*, p. 26.

[16] Storck and Teague, *op. cit.*, p. 84.

had a daily grind of 1,000 bushels of flour, and a daily baking of between 100,000 and 150,000 round loaves.[17]

On a somewhat smaller scale public bakeries flourished in many other Roman cities. In Pompeii, for example, about twenty mill-bakeries—one for every thousand inhabitants— are known to have existed. Incidentally, these bakeries have been found in a fairly well preserved state and undisturbed for many centuries after the eruption of Mount Vesuvius in 79 A.D.[18]

Both in Greece and Rome, the public bake-shop was necessarily an urban enterprise since the daily production and distribution of a perishable product like bread was wholly dependent upon concentrated groups of consumers. In outlying rural areas, where hamlets and villages thrived, there were no public bakeries. And even in the cities it is doubtful whether such bakeries produced more bread than was made in the homes.

The owners of the Roman bakeries were considered among the most skilled of craftsmen; people commonly spoke of the *ars pistorica,* the art of baking.[19] By the reign of Augustus, the "art" had progressed to the point where many members of the baking trade had become specialists; besides the bread bakers, there were bakers of pastry, milk bakers and honey bakers making fancy sweet goods. In Rome the city's bakers had even established guilds whose rights were upheld by the government.

While many may have begun their careers as freed slaves, the professional bakers, for the most part, were highly respected men who had fair opportunities to rise to public office and wealth. One Pompeii baker, Paquius Proculus, became the mayor of his city. Another, Vergilius Eurysaces, was one of the most prosperous men of Rome, employing several hundred slaves. Appropriately, his tombstone was made up of

---

[17] *Ibid.*
[18] *Ibid.*
[19] Jacob, *op. cit.,* p. 78.

stone mixing troughs bearing inscriptions of his milling and baking operations.[20]

The Romans were the first to make breads comparable to our own. They were round and stood about two inches high. They looked more like large rolls than like our modern loaves, but they were far superior to the breads of the early Egyptians and Greeks. Besides these loaves, the most commonly used by the Roman, the bakers also produced a wide variety of breads and cakes in a profusion of artistic shapes and forms. There were milk breads and cakes, those whose dough had been mixed with eggs, and many others spiced with flavorings of rice, nuts, almonds, peppers, anise and laurel leaves. A particular delicacy, known as Parthian bread, was light enough to float. The wedding cake had its origin in Rome, where the most solemn form of marriage was made binding when the couple sacramentally consumed a "cake of far." [21]

The superiority of Roman baking was primarily due to the excellence of the wheat and flour, and the miller-bakers devoted much time and effort to grinding the variety of wheat that flowed in from all corners of the empire. It is said that they achieved a 75 per cent extraction from the wheat: one grade of fine white flour and two of meal in addition to the 25 per cent bran.[22] Their extensive use of the Greek hourglass mill and their sifting and blending made Roman flour the finest and whitest yet known.

Wheat and flour were not the only factors contributing to the excellence of the Roman baker's bread. A number of original leaveners or fermenting agents were introduced which produced a lighter and more aerated product. One ferment was made by soaking wheat in sweet wine for three days and allowing the mash to dry in the sun. Another made use of the froth or the foam from beer. Other leaveners were

---

20 *Ibid.*
21 Storck and Teague, *op. cit.*, p. 87.
22 *Ibid.*, p. 88.

modifications of the old Egyptian sour dough. One form was prepared from cakes which were baked and left to sour, while still another was prepared by boiling dough to a porridge and leaving it to sour. In most Roman homes the leaven used was simply unwarmed sour dough.[23]

The Roman bakers improved upon the bee-hive oven which had been inherited from the Greeks. By the end of the first century A.D., however, this oven was being replaced by the Roman peel oven, named for the long-handled peels used to handle the hot loaves. Essentially, it was a bee-hive oven enclosed within a brick structure. It retained the dome or arched baking chamber, but its walls were thickened to store greater heat and a brick chimney was added to carry off the smoke. The oven was still heated by a wood fire built directly in the baking chamber. In the homes of the plebeians much baking was done, as it had been for centuries, over an open-hearth fire. In some households bread and cakes were baked in a small oven, probably an earthenware jar.[24]

Oddly enough, while the rapid growth of Roman power was instrumental in creating a flourishing baking trade, it eventually led to its nationalization. The state control over baking came about through a series of events wherein grain, flour, and bread became a part of the food dole for the appeasement of the great Roman proletariat. The dole had its beginnings as early as 200 B.C., while Rome was being overrun by idle farmers who had lost their farms to wealthy nobles. To win their favor, the Senate in 123 B.C. adopted the policy of "bread and circuses." [25] "Circuses," frequently the bloody bouts of gladiators, were staged for their entertainment, and "bread" was the food dole inaugurated to help feed them; both were powerful political tools which were subject to wide abuse.

---

[23] "Sixty Centuries of Bakers and Baking," *Bakers Weekly Magazine*, XXXII (December 31, 1921), p. 57.

[24] Jerome Carcopine, *Daily Life in Ancient Rome*, trans. E. O. Lorimer (New Haven: Yale University Press, 1940), p. 37.

[25] Storck and Teague, *op. cit.*, p. 88.

Initially, the dole was a full ration of grain sold monthly to every adult citizen at about half the prevailing price. In 58 B.C. free grain was regularly distributed. In Julius Caesar's time, for example, there were over 320,000 Romans, out of a total free population of roughly 600,000, on the dole. By the end of the first century A.D. flour was substituted for grain. Finally, near the close of the third century, the dole became bread itself. Some 200,000 people received two breads daily.[26]

With free bread, bakeries became "places of State" in which the bakers and their apprentices were mere civil servants. The state, of course, paid a fee to the bakers, but they were, in effect, industrial serfs bound to their work. A baker was unable to sell his shop or leave his trade, and his son had to follow in his father's footsteps. In the 4th century bakers were put under tighter state control when the Emperor Diocletian passed rigid laws regulating the weights and prices of all baked goods offered for sale.[27] The free artisan tradition of bakers became a thing of the past. A Roman painting illustrates the new position of the baker. It shows a baker "standing at a table and holding in his left hand the symbol of the guild, the modius (bushel measure). His right hand, however, is holding a basket of bread toward the *plebs frumentaria* (the recipients of the national dole rather than paying customers)." [28]

While state control of the baking trade persisted, the emperors found it increasingly more difficult to maintain the dole after the third century A.D. Miller-bakers, like other craftsmen, continually deserted or evaded their obligations to the state as the social fabric of Rome slowly decayed. By 600 A.D. all vestiges of the power of the Empire were completely destroyed. The downfall, so one writer contends, was primarily due to the bread dole, although there seems to be little justification for such a claim.[29]

---

26 Jacob, *op. cit.*, p. 88.
27 *Ibid.*, p. 87.
28 *Ibid.*
29 *Ibid.*, pp. 75-89.

Roman Mill and Bakery Showing Peel Oven and Hour-glass Mill

Baking in Medieval Times

Medieval Baking

Contrary to popular belief, the Teutonic invasions did not totally disrupt the commerce and urban life of the Roman world. Many institutions, though modified by the barbarian, lingered on in many parts of the former empire, especially in its cities. Details are lacking on the baking trade; but with the duration of an urban economy, kept alive by the commerce and trade of the Mediterranean, baking undoubtedly persisted as a commercial activity for another century.

The real decline of Western European commerce, and hence of an active baking trade, came in the seventh century, when the Mediterranean became a Moslem sea through conquests of its eastern, southern, and western shores. The Moslem triumphs turned back the clock for Western Europe. By the end of the next century the Christian world had reverted to a purely agricultural state, devoid of its former commerce and trade. Merchants all but disappeared, and with them the exit of most urban ways of living. What cities survived were little more than church centers with feeble economic power. Europe gradually withdrew into a closed estate of feudal economy.[30]

The withdrawal had a marked effect on baking. Wheat became scarce. No longer accessible were the bountiful harvests of Egypt and North Africa.[31] Rye and other grains served as the principal raw materials of baking. Dark and unleavened breads became the daily fare of the peasant and serf; only the wealthy nobility were able to afford wheaten breads. In the decline of city and town, commercial bakeries virtually disappeared. Almost all baking was done on the hearth or in a skillet and on occasion in a small oven. What baking was done on a large scale was confined almost solely to the manors of feudal lords and to monasteries.

---

[30] Henri Pirenne, *Economic and Social History of Medieval Europe*, trans. I. E. Clegg (New York: Harcourt, Brace and Company, no date), pp. 5-7.

[31] Wheat was only grown in Italy and in northern and western France. William Ashley, *The Bread of Our Forefathers* (Oxford: The Clarendon Press, 1928), p. 135.

Feudalism, for all of the damage it dealt a once flourishing industry, left a significant mark on the future of the baker's trade. It witnessed the permanent separation of milling and baking. In large part this change stemmed from the widespread use of water mills, known to the Romans but little used until Medieval millers found them more efficient than the old hourglass types. Their operation, of course, depended upon water power which, in most instances, lay beyond the border of the feudal town. As a result, milling was removed from the bakery which remained behind feudal walls.

By the end of the eleventh century the economic revival of Europe got under way. The Crusades, beginning in 1096 A.D. and following one after another for two centuries, stimulated commerce. This revival began in the Mediterranean but soon spread to the shores of the North Sea. Its carriers, the traveling merchants or trader-capitalists, completely altered the feudal economy. They set up their trading centers, or burgs, as they were called, outside the feudal fortresses and ecclesiastical towns; and by the beginning of the twelfth century these burgs were challenging the older towns in a most disrupting fashion.[32] They drew artisans by the droves, many of whom were former peasants and serfs who had escaped from the bondage of their feudal lords; "City air makes a man free" had taken on a real meaning for thousands.[33] There, weavers, metal workers, and masons found their materials and markets. Millers, bakers and butchers found customers demanding their services. All in all, an economic revolution was in the making. This was a change common to Western Europe.

While accurate figures are lacking, all signs indicate that towns increased ten-fold in number between the opening of the twelfth and the beginning of the fourteenth century. At the same time, the urban population in nearly every town was

[32] Pirenne, *op. cit.*, pp. 35-43.
[33] *Ibid.*, p. 52.

growing. In many towns it doubled and even tripled during this period . . . there was now a virtual 'town renaissance.' [34]

The growth of cities and towns, new and old, touched off a revival of commercial baking. Bakeries reappeared on a scale reminiscent of Roman times. They grew in number as the urban population grew. Every town of any size supported at least one bakeshop; the larger towns and cities, many more. In 1573 the city of London had sixty-two "white bakers" and thirty-six "brown bakers." [35] Paris and Rome must have had a comparable number.

What were the characteristics of this rebirth of commercial baking? What did it represent in the way of change from the well organized craft of the Roman Empire? There were few changes in technology. From the mixing and kneading of the dough to the final baking of the loaves, commercial baking remained a handcraft utilizing the ancient methods of production. The Roman peel oven—although a little larger and with better retention of heat—was still the baker's basic item of equipment. The leavening agents were also much the same as those used by the Romans—sour dough and the fermenting barm of wine and beer. Similarly, home baking remained relatively unchanged. The poorer classes continued to bake over an open-hearth fire. Oftentimes they brought their dough to be baked, for a fee, in the baker's ovens. Some towns even provided a common oven for their folk. The well-to-do families, as in Roman times, had their own bakeshops in their kitchens, complete with peel oven and servant baker.

Techniques did not depart from the Roman model for a number of reasons. The Medieval towns were small, no larger than those of Roman times; their needs, as limited.[36] The

---

[34] Harry E. Barnes, *An Economic History of the Western World* (New York: Harcourt, Brace and Company, 1937), p. 157.

[35] These refer to bakers of white bread and bakers of dark bread. Ashley, *op. cit.,* p. 151.

[36] "It should, of course, be kept in mind that medieval towns were not large cities judged by our present-day standards. Most of them were not larger than our villages or lesser cities. A third-class American city today would rank in population with a medieval metropolis in western Europe." Barnes, *op. cit.,* p. 157.

demand for commercial bakery products was relatively light
and could be met with the old methods. The great majority
of all bread consumed was baked in the home rather than in
the public bakeries, because Europe remained essentially
rural, and the poorer classes, the great mass of the population,
were simply too poor to be good customers. Probably less
than 15 per cent of the population lived in towns at the
beginning of the seventeenth century.[37]

The varieties of baked products in the Middle Ages were
not much different from those of the Romans. Bread, of
course, was the major product; in many places nothing other
than bread was produced. The most common varieties, small
oval-shaped and cone-like breads, were more like the Roman
than like our modern loaf.[38] Some bakers did specialize in
cakes and pastries, but only for the tables of folk with a heavy
purse.

In contrast with Roman baking, almost all of the home-
made bread and much of the bakery bread (as much as 50
per cent) was dark rather than white. Wheat itself was still
none too plentiful; rye and, to a lesser extent, barley remained the principal grains for most of Western Europe.
Even much of the bread made from wheat was dark or whole
wheat because of the expense of milling white flour. In fact,
white bread was considered as much a luxury as fine handmade cake is today.[39]

Probably the most distinguishing feature of the baking
trade in the Middle Ages was its craft guild organization.
Guilds, of course, were not peculiar to bakers. They encompassed almost every artisan group in Western Europe. To
ward off the competition of newcomers, craftsmen had early
initiated the guild movement which town authorities willingly endorsed for the sake of regulating the different trades.

---

[37] *Ibid.*, p. 163.

[38] Jacob, *op. cit.*, p. 143.

[39] In England, ". . . a complete transition to a wheat bread diet on the part of
the mass of the people was only affected during the eighteenth century." Ashley,
op. cit., p. 132.

Their endorsement came in the form of licenses or charters for the various craft guilds within their city. The result was mutually advantageous to both the craftsmen and the public authorities. Each particular guild had to submit to public control over product quality, weights and prices but in return received a legal monopoly over its trade in the city.[40] Baking was among the first of the crafts organized into guilds. In the eleventh century Parisian bakers formed a guild; and in London one was organized in the year 1155. By the end of the twelfth century bakers' guilds were a common feature in most Western European towns.[41]

The controls of both guild and town were such as would drive a modern baker to despair. The guild required an apprenticeship of from three to seven years. The apprentice received his room and board at the bakery and only a few dollars a year for spending money. Initially, entry as an apprentice was free but by the fourteenth century it required both a fee and influence. At the end of his service and upon the payment of a small fee, the apprentice joined the ranks of the journeyman. Here he received regular wages and was permitted to go from one town to another to learn the fine points of his trade. After spending three years in this fashion, he did not automatically move up to the position of a master baker. He had to await a vacancy in the guild, pay an initiation fee and, in many places, produce a masterpiece to demonstrate his skill.[42]

The master baker worked in a tight little world. He was protected from the competition of all except those who were members of his guild. No one but a guild member was allowed to bake bread for sale. Tavern keepers were not permitted to bake for their own guests. Hucksters or peddlers could only obtain bread from the bakers, and frequently such retailing was not allowed at all. On the other hand, town au-

---

[40] Pirenne, *op. cit.*, p. 182.
[41] "Sixty Centuries of Bakers and Baking," *Bakers Weekly Magazine*, XXXIII (January 7, 1922), p. 52.
[42] *Ibid.*

thorities demanded a high price for the monopoly the guild enjoyed. If a baker's bread tasted poor, he was tried by the town council and fined.[43] Moreover, inspectors frequently visited the bakeshops to check prescribed weights and prices. Bribery on more than one occasion turned an inspector's head. If that failed, the guilty baker was led to the pillory or given a public whiplashing.[44]

The English statute of 1266, the Assize of Bread, is probably the most famous of the Medieval laws regulating the baking trade.[45] A later variation of this law is as follows:

It was taken for granted that a loaf of bread should be sold at the customary price of one penny. The baker was required to make his loaves of a definite weight, and to sell 418 pounds of bread, out of every quarter of wheat (eight bushels). The weight of the loaf was so fixed as to enable the baker with ordinary skill, to make in addition, out of the quarter of wheat, two peck loaves (or 24 lb. 14 oz.) of 'advantage bread' for himself. He was, moreover, to be allowed a sum of money every quarter, according to the following quaint table of 1497:—

'The Baker was allowed

'Furnace and wood .... 6d.
'The Miller .... 4d.
'Two journeymen and two apprentices...... 5d.
'Salt, yeast, candle, and sack bands........ 2d.
'Himself, his house, his wife, his dog and his cat 7d.
                                          ——
                                 'In all .... 2s. 0d.

'And the bran to his advantage.' [46]

Despite the regulations, the bakers' lot was not an unhappy one. Like other craftsmen, they were free men, not subject to

---

[43] Jacob, *op. cit.,* p. 137.

[44] Some countries even today still uphold rigid bread laws and still impose such crude forms of punishment for bakers. In 1954, an Egyptian baker was given ten lashes for selling bread at more than the maximum price. *Chicago Daily News,* December 30, 1954.

[45] This statute remained unrepealed for six centuries. Cf. Sidney and Beatrice Webb, "The Assize of Bread," *Economic Journal,* XIV (June 1904), pp. 196-218.

[46] *Ibid.,* p. 197.

the whims and caprices of a feudal lord. As guild members they were small-scale entrepreneurs, with a chance for wealth and position. "The leading men in the guilds and town offices were often one and the same persons." [47] A few became prosperous enough to become entrepreneurs in a modern sense; they did no labor themselves but hired other masters and journeymen to work for them.

Baking had come a long way by the close of the Middle Ages. In simplest terms, it had started by accident, perhaps, near the dawn of civilization. It was to undergo no radical change until the Egyptians and, later, the Greeks and Romans turned their genius to the making of bread. With the more settled ways of living, with new techniques, the commercial baker made his initial appearance. Then, for centuries, town life and commercial baking fell and rose together as feudalism advanced and, then, retreated from Western Europe. In its wake stood the baker, using techniques which differed little, in essence, from what they had been when the Roman baker practiced them.

---

[47] Barnes, *op. cit.*, p. 187.

CHAPTER 2

BAKING IN EARLY AMERICA

Baking was a part of the European heritage brought by the colonists to North America. But unlike their old homeland, the New World was a sparsely settled pioneer area which offered very few opportunities for commercial baking. It was not until the emergence of city and town that professional bakers, known for so long in Europe, became firmly established in America. As towns grew in size and number and as the frontier moved westward, commercial bakeries multiplied accordingly. But as in Europe, the techniques of baking underwent no significant change.

In Colonial Times

While the frontier of the New World had to be tamed by civilized ways before commercial baking could take hold in any firm way, within a few decades of the founding of Jamestown, Plymouth, and New York, several commercial bakeries sprang up in the colonies, as early as 1640 in Plymouth and 1645 in New York.[1] Other early settlements, scattered from lower Maine to Virginia, were supporting professional bakers by the end of the century.[2]

---

[1] See Storck and Teague, *op. cit.*, p. 149, and "Sixty Centuries of Bakers and Baking," *Bakers Weekly Magazine*, XXXV (July 1, 1922), p. 41.
[2] *Ibid.*

At that time, their number was small. For one reason, the total colonial population was only about 250,000—less than that of the large European cities in that century. Moreover, there were only three colonial centers of sufficient size to be classified as cities. Boston claimed 7,000 settlers; New York, 5,000; and Philadelphia, 4,500.[3] At this time, Boston listed six bakers, New York and Philadelphia each had seven.[4] In general, the ratio of bakeries to population in the urban centers appears to have been about twice that reported in the Roman era—roughly one for every thousand inhabitants.

By the time of the American Revolution the colonies had grown to an estimated 2.5 million people.[5] But that population was widely scattered with perhaps about 5 per cent of the people living in large towns or cities.[6] There were scarcely ten cities that could be called urban centers. The largest, Philadelphia, had about 28,000 inhabitants and New York had over 21,000. Boston was third with perhaps 16,000. The only large city in the South, Charleston, may have had 10,000 and Newport nearly as many, while such places as Baltimore, Salem, Providence and Albany ranged from 3,000 to 8,000.[7] Obviously, the opportunities for growth in the baking trade were meager ones. At best, its expansion was very slow. Indeed, in 1776 New York bakeries numbered only twelve compared to seven for the year 1700.[8]

The colonial baking trade differed little from its European prototype. Among the several similarities were local bread laws regulating the size, price and quality of bakers' bread. In 1640, only twenty years after the landing at Plymouth, the Massachusetts Bay authorities formulated an assize of bread.

[3] F. A. Shannon, *America's Economic Growth* (New York: The Macmillan Company, 1940), pp. 18 and 61.

[4] "Sixty Centuries of Bakers and Baking," *op. cit.*, XXXV (July 15, 1922), p. 63.

[5] H. F. Williamson (ed.), *Growth of the American Economy* (New York: Prentice-Hall, Inc., 1951), p. 83.

[6] C. W. Wright, *Economic History of the United States* (New York: McGraw-Hill Book Company, Inc., 1941), p. 79.

[7] *Ibid.*

[8] "Sixty Centuries of Bakers and Baking," *Bakers Weekly Magazine*, XXXIX (July 14, 1923), p. 69.

It was ordered "that no bread shall be made finer than to af-
foard at 12 ounces the two penny white loafe, and whosoever
selleth lighter weight to forfeit his bread." [9] Compliance was
assured by a regulation requiring each loaf to carry the trade-
mark of its maker. As in Europe, the price of bread was usually kept constant and the weight of each loaf varied with the
price of grain. In November of 1646, for example, Plymouth
required that "When wheate is ordinarily sold at their several
rates, the ld. white loaf shall weigh 11 oz. 1¼, when wheate
is sold at 3s. per bushel." [10] New Haven in 1650 directed that
when wheat was six and one-half shillings a bushel, the one-
penny white loaf should weigh six ounces. In addition, the
profits of bakers were regulated. In 1685 the Massachusetts
Bay authorities fixed the bakers' return at four shillings for
baking up each quarter of wheat.[11]

Unfortunately for the bakers, these town regulations were
not offset, as they were in Europe, by a guild monopoly. The
guilds simply did not exist in any strong fashion in colonial
America but were rather loose associations without the powers
of the Medieval guilds.[12] The municipal authorities did protect the bakers to some degree, however, by recognizing the
general rules of apprenticeship and by prohibiting peddlers
and middlemen from selling bread products.

Throughout the colonial period the baking trade continued
to be regulated, although the bread laws became less severe
both in scope and impact as the 18th century drew to a close.
The rise of a wage-earning class together with a growing
spirit of free competition tended to make such measures
obsolete.

---

[9] "Sixty Centuries of Bakers and Baking," *Bakers Weekly Magazine,* XXXV (July 15, 1922), p. 41.

[10] *Ibid.*

[11] *Ibid.,* p. 42.

[12] Even in Europe by the end of the seventeenth century the guilds were rapidly becoming obsolete. They still existed, but they were becoming merely formal, social or honorary societies whose powers were being assumed by government authorities. "Sixty Centuries of Bakers and Baking," *Bakers Weekly Magazine,* XXXV (July 29, 1922), p. 51.

Like the bread trade in Europe, colonial baking was still the difficult century-old handicraft operation. The baker worked from sunrise to sunset, mixing and fashioning the dough, firing the huge brick oven, and baking by its searing heat. Quality was a test of his skill and his experience alone. In general most bakers lived up to both, turning out a remarkably good loaf of bread.

Nor did marketing differ from the pattern established in Europe. The baker sold his wares in a shop in front of his bakeroom. The earliest colonial bakers, in fact, were custom bakers, baking only on order. As the colonial period drew to a close, an increasing number of bakers began to produce for the market rather than on order.

The colonial housewife was no less a baker than the craftsmen of the bakeshops. Indeed, it was generally accepted that the homemade loaf was superior to anything that the baker could turn out. Although on a smaller scale, the housewife's equipment and methods were not unlike those of the commercial baker. Her great kitchen fireplace had a separate oven chamber with a smoke intake into the chimney and an ash pit below. Like the oven of the bakeshop, the oven in the home was fired with wood until its brick walls were thoroughly heated and it was then swept of coals and ashes before the baking began. Along with the oven the long-handled peel was a treasured piece of equipment. "A universal gift to a bride, it was a symbol of domestic utility and plenty, and was held to be luck-bearing." [13] Sometimes bread was baked in pans; sometimes it was baked on cabbage leaves or oak leaves. In early colonial days bread was also baked in a "Dutch oven," placed directly in the fireplace among the hot coals.[14] Occasionally, the housewife used a so-called roasting kitchen, a raised box-like affair with an open side turned toward the fire.

---

[13] A. M. Earle, *Home Life in Colonial Days* (New York: The Macmillan Company, 1899), p. 67.

[14] *Ibid.*, p. 66.

The traditional white loaf was not the only bread made in the colonial homes. One long-time favorite, especially in the North, was brown bread, an Indian bread commonly referred to as "rye and Injun." [15] Corn pone and johnny cake were also popular items. In the South there was a strong preference for hot breads, hot biscuits, and corn breads.

Hard breads, known first as pilot or ships' bread and later as hardtack, appeared in the colonial period. This large, round, dry crisp wafer was made from plain, unleavened and unsweetened dough. Unlike ordinary bread, it could be kept for a prolonged period without growing stale. It was, therefore, in great demand by ship and boat provisioners and others who had great need for a bread that remained edible on long voyages and overland treks.[16]

The baking of ships' bread was, from the start, a full-fledged commercial operation because of the relatively simple processes involved in its production and because it was ordinarily sold in large quantities. Essentially a cracker product, the sturdy ships' bread involved little more than the baking of a flour and water mixture without the attendant problems of fermentation and perishability. The development of ships' bread baking was closely associated with the flourishing export trade in grain and flour which began about the middle of the 17th century. A fine wheat supply from the Middle and Southern colonies, together with a ready market in West Indies and Southern Europe, had provided the basis for the grain trade and had stimulated the development of the flour milling industry.[17] It was a natural step for the flour millers along the coast to include the baking and export of hard bread in their operations during the latter half of the 17th century. The trade became so marked during the next fifty to

[15] Storck and Teague, *op. cit.*, p. 148.

[16] Seamen's complaints were nonetheless strongly voiced. They complained of the poor quality of the product and the fact that it was as "hard as flint" requiring a good soaking in tea before it could be eaten. E. P. Homan, *The American Whaleman* (New York: Longmans, Green, and Co., 1928), p. 131.

[17] Williamson, *op. cit.*, p. 53.

seventy-five years that the middle colonies were commonly referred to as the "bread Colonies." [18] It was a trade that ranked second only to tobacco. The forerunner of the modern biscuit and cracker industry, the baking of ships' bread was a distinct and separate segment of the baking trade. Nevertheless, its story, down to 1900, weaves in and out of the history of American baking, providing sharp contrasts to what was taking place in the bread industry.

A Background to Change

From 1800 onward there was a marked expansion in the baking industry, in both the bread and cracker segments, in order to meet the demands of a great population movement. Americans in this era were on the move, pushing back the frontiers from plain and prairie. The westward trek of commercial baking was especially apparent in the Midwest, where, as people swarmed in from the Atlantic seaboard, frontier trading posts began to become towns.

When Cincinnati was little more than a village of less than 2,000 in 1780, it was served by one or two bakeries; forty years later fifteen bakeries were serving a population of approximately 12,000. By the mid-century the number of bakeries had risen to 140 and the population to almost 120,000.[19] Cleveland, which contained one bakery at its incorporation in 1814, had fifteen bakeries and a population of about 40,000 by 1853. Columbus, with 500 inhabitants and one bakery in 1815, contained 6,000 people and seven bakeries by 1843. Similarly, Detroit rose from a small colonial outpost to a city of 21,000 population with twelve bakeries by 1850. Milwaukee, with but one bakery shortly after its founding in 1835, grew to be a thriving urban community by the middle of the 19th century with over 20,000 people and at least a

---

18 Shannon, op. cit., p. 30.
19 "Sixty Centuries of Bakers and Baking," Bakers Weekly Magazine, XLIII (July 12, 1924), pp. 52-68.

dozen commercial bakeries. St. Paul, a mere village of 840 persons, had two bakeries in 1849.[20]

In the East older cities continued to support more bakeries. Philadelphia in 1857 claimed ninety-nine bakeries, nine of which were cracker plants. Similar increases took place in New York and Boston. Washington, D. C., provided a unique situation. In 1800 when it became the national Capital, the city had a population of only 3,200 and just a few bakeries; a half century later, when its population was over 40,000, the number of bakers totaled 123, a testimony of sorts to the city's transient population.[21]

While all this seems to represent an impressive rate of growth since colonial days, it is well to bear at least two points in mind. In the first place, home baking, despite the growing trade of the baker, was of infinitely greater importance in the life of the youthful republic. As we shall see later, the commercial bread bakers held a rather insignificant position as the suppliers of the daily bread for a population of some 23 million at mid century. In the second place, the basic techniques and overall scope of bread baking generally remained unchanged. Except for one or two attempts at developing mixing machines about 1810, no mechanical aids relieved the baker in his task, nor did he depart from the age-old methods of counter sales. Under such circumstances, it is not strange to find several cities retaining their local bread laws after 1850.[22]

During this same half century, on the other hand, the seeds of change were being actively sown by the biscuit and cracker bakers. In 1801, Joshua Bent, a ship's breadbaker in Massachusetts, introduced the celebrated "Bent's water-cracker," smaller and more compact than pilot bread. By 1840 three new varieties, the soft or butter cracker, the soda cracker and the round sugar-biscuit or cookie made their appearance. All

---

[20] *Ibid.*, XLIII, XLIV, XLV, pp. 53-76.
[21] *Ibid.*
[22] "Sixty Centuries of Bakers and Baking," *op. cit.*, XXXVIII (April 14, 1923), p. 57.

these differed from the earlier crackers in that they contained shortening and were products of a fermented dough. Of the three, the butter and soda crackers were most important; the sweetened biscuit was primarily an English import. By 1840, also, the cracker industry had achieved some degree of mechanization. In use were a hand operated mixer, a rolling machine to thin out the dough, and a stamp to cut the dough into the desired shape. They served to increase the scale of operations of cracker bakeries, which was already larger than that of bread bakeries.

Baking Industry in America in 1850

The year 1850 is a convenient vantage point to pause for a deeper look into the structure and operations of the baking industry. It marks the end of an old order and the beginning of a new order. In a way, it represents the autumn of an era of handicraft. Fortunately, this stage is reflected in the first body of statistical data we have of the industry, the *Census of Manufacturers of 1850*.

According to this Census, there were at that time 2,027 bakeries in the United States, producing over $13 million worth of baked goods and employing a total of 6,727 wage earners.[23] Although still operating on a small scale, baking held a respectable position among the nation's manufacturing industries. By value of product sold it ranked nineteenth, accounting for a little over 1 per cent of all manufactures. By number of establishments and number of wage earners it held the thirteenth place. Among all food processing industries, a group accounting for a little less than 15 per cent of the total output of all manufactures, baking was second in value of product, second in number of establishments, and third in number of wage earners.[24] Within this group, baking was outranked only by flour milling, the most important single in-

---

23 U. S. Bureau of the Census, *United States Census of Manufacturers: 1850.*
24 *Ibid.*

Early 19th Century Bakeshop

A Bakery in 1842

dustry in the United States as measured by the dollar value of products produced.

The Census figures do not distinguish between bread and cracker bakeries, but one estimate indicates that 95 per cent, or roughly 1,900, of the nation's bakeries were bread bakeries.[25] Quite likely, however, they accounted for no more than 70 per cent of the over $13 million output of the industry. They were mostly one-man shops, each with an annual output well below $5,000. Cracker bakeries, on the other hand, had an annual product as high as $50,000.

As had no doubt been true since the early colonial period, meats and flour products constituted the bulk of food consumed in the United States at the middle of the nineteenth century. In 1830, for example, the per capita consumption of wheat flour was 170 pounds per year; meat consumption was slightly higher, amounting to 178 pounds per year. By 1850, the per capita consumption of wheat flour had risen to 205 pounds and was greater than that for any other food or food group. With the exception of meat at 184 pounds, the consumption of no other food group exceeded fifty pounds per year.[26] Consumption of fruits, vegetables and dairy products was especially limited because of transportation and preservation difficulties.

Although bread constituted a large part of the American diet, eating tastes, conditioned by environment, differed in various parts of the country. In the North the staple diet was cured pork, white bread and other flour and grain products, potatoes, and corn and apples, supplemented with small amounts of fresh beef, fruits and vegetables. The staple diet of the South was simpler; it was made up of cured pork—mostly bacon and salt pork—and corn bread with a few vegetables and fruits. For Southerners corn was the principal grain, corn meal serving in the same way as wheat flour in the

---

[25] Letter to the author from Mr. W. E. Long, formerly head of the W. E. Long Company, a bakery service organization. April 4, 1953.

[26] R. O. Cummings, *The American and His Food* (Revised ed.; Chicago: University of Chicago Press, 1941), Appendix B, p. 258.

North. In the West regions that were well served by transportation and maintained close contact with the eastern states, had dietary tastes that differed little from those of the East. But in the frontier areas of the West tastes were much simpler. Bacon and corn bread were the day-in-and-day-out "vittles." [27]

There was good reason for the important dietary status of grains and grain products. They were the lowest in cost and highest in energy yield of foods available to the typical working class family of the 1850's.[28]

Despite the overriding importance of breadstuffs in mid-century diets, only a small percentage of bread was supplied by the commercial bakers. Their annual output topped nine million dollars, but it represented less than 10 per cent of total bread consumption. For one thing, baking was confined to the city. The question of whether to buy or bake simply did not arise for those rural Americans who made up 85 per cent of its total population. Even in the urban centers most bread making was a home activity. It appeared cheaper for the housewife to bake her own bread and other perishable bakery products. She did not take into account the cost of fuel or her own time and labor, which were costs to the baker. Moreover, with the prevailing low incomes of most American families of the day, half of which went for food, any savings were real savings.

Most people, probably on real as well as fancied grounds, preferred home baked bread to that of the baker. Unlike many other manufactured goods, the quality of his products was generally no better than those of the housewife; and it would remain so as long as baking was still a trade with no systematic insurance of perfection. The idea that homemade bread was superior was accordingly still widespread, and com-

---

[27] Edgar W. Martin, *The Standard of Living, 1860* (Chicago: University of Chicago Press, 1942), Chapters II and III.

[28] *Ibid.,* p. 393.

mercially baked bread, if offered to guests, was usually served with an apology.

The fact that the baker continued operating indicates that such considerations did not apply to all consumers. The precise make-up of his demand at this time is far from clear. Part of his sales no doubt represented supplementary or convenience buying on the part of many who still baked the bulk of their needs at home. It is quite possible that a considerable portion of the working class, who lived in tenements where good ovens were lacking, patronized the neighborhood bakery. Many such people called on the baker for a considerable amount of baking of cakes, pies and even meats that were prepared in the homes. And it appears likely that the baker's talent in baking fancy bread, pies and pastries had some appeal to an upper income clientele.

It was clear at mid-century, however, that two major production problems would have to be overcome before the commercial bakers could hope to supply a major portion of the demand for bread and other perishable baked goods. One was to cut costs. The other was to improve quality. A brief review of the production processes in use at the time will indicate the formidable task that lay ahead.

Bread baking in 1850 was still plagued by age old difficulties. Bakeries were for the most part one-oven and one-man shops in which craft traditions still had a tight hold. There was no mechanized equipment. There was nothing but the baker's skill to determine the quality of his products. His loaf was not always uniform, nor did it always taste the same. Sometimes his entire output was ruined by conditions beyond his control. These were some of the risks which had long harassed the baker and which were considered as normal to his business.

Baking involved many arduous tasks. Foremost among these was the firing of the peel oven. The brick oven, still fired with wood, was basically a Roman oven except for improvements in size, its thicker walls and better dampers. The oven was usually fired in the evening of the day before the products were baked. When the arch of the entire oven turned white, the fuel bed was brought forward to the oven door and withdrawn and the oven swabbed clean to remove all ashes and dust. Once the oven hearth was clean, the damper and oven door were shut tight, and the heat allowed to spread over the entire hearth area for about two hours. This was the "equalization period," and not until its end was the oven ready for baking.

Meanwhile the baker was at work preparing his ingredients. He had to sift the flour carefully to remove any foreign material and had to blend several types or shipments of flour in order to get a mixture that would suit his particular shop conditions. These operations were not easy tasks. Flour in wooden barrels, containing 196 pounds, or in 140-pound jute bags, was dumped into one end of a wooden trough. The flour was then shoveled into the sifter placed over the other end (as well as onto the baker).

Another task before baking was the preparation of the yeast mixture or brew. The baker had to make his own yeast mixture because compressed yeast was still unknown. There were almost as many brews as there were bakers, since each had secret recipes which he thought superior to those of other bakers. Actually, the baker merely cultivated the growth of yeast cells in a fermented brew made from flour, sugar, malt, water, potatoes or old stock yeast. The original stock yeast might be brewer's yeast or barm, the so-called patent yeast, or other forms of fermented materials. Brewer's yeast was a frothy liquid from the top of ale. Patent yeast was made from malt, hops and water.

The last step prior to actual baking was the mixing of flour and other ingredients into dough. This could be done by the "straight dough" method, mixing all of the ingredients at one time. But it was an infrequent practice, for the baker had less control over the fermentation of the yeast. Instead, practically all yeast-raised doughs were made by the

sponge dough method. From a half to three-quarters of the
required flour and other ingredients were mixed with the
yeast, and sufficient water (about 55 per cent) was added
to form a moderately stiff dough called the "sponge."
Mixing the ingredients in a trough by hand until the sponge
reached the proper consistency was no mean task. It took a
strong man to perform this job, and quite commonly the
baker climbed into the trough to do the mixing. When the
sponge was "set," it was allowed to ferment and rise for the
proper length of time, being timed with the heating of the
oven.[29]

A variety of yeast-raised products could be made from one
master sponge. The sponge was "broken" by adding a required amount of water until it was down to a semi-batter or
semi-fluid condition. The baker then dipped out so much for
sweet yeast dough, so much for rye, so much for other special
bread. The rest of the necessary ingredients were then added
to the remaining mixture, and the dough was again tediously
hand-kneaded. While the various dough batches were matur-
ing, pie fillings and various toppings for coffee cakes and
other products were made. When the dough matured, the
various shapes were formed. Rye and white bread were
moulded into loaves and placed in the oven. Next came the
sweet rolls and coffee cakes, with doughnuts the last to be
processed. Finally, after the early morning breakfast goods
were well on their way to the sales room and consumers'
tables, the cakes were make. They could be made last because
they did not require the oven to be as hot as did the other
products. In fact, jelly rolls and sponge cakes could be baked
with a spot fire without heating the entire baking chamber.

The entire process was a test of the skill and experience
of the baker, especially on controlling the quality of his prod-

---

[29] A principal reason for the use of the sponge dough methods of mixing was that
the fermentation periods were less critical when this method was used. Sponge doughs
had the advantage of standing longer without marked deterioration of the quality
of the final product should the baker fail to make the right decision on the proper
fermentation time.

uct. Estimates on timing, for example, always had to be conditioned by temperature and humidity conditions, for adverse weather conditions could ruin the entire production. (It was not uncommon, even as late as 1900, to find weather vanes in the bakeries.) For setting or breaking the sponge cold water was used in warm weather and warm water in cold weather. Temperature and humidity were also important in determining the proper proofing periods, for if the weather was too warm, the bread might rise and fall before it could be put in the oven, causing a "sour" product. The mixing time and the fermentation time of the sponge and dough were also affected.

Furthermore, the baker could not depend on obtaining uniform types of flour. Different localities, crops, weather conditions, mills, or mill-runs gave wheat different baking characteristics. Proper mixing and fermentation times and the size, color and flavor of the resultant product varied with the particular flour used. The baker reduced his problem somewhat by blending several purchases of flour. It was also possible to stagger purchases so that only a portion of the blend would have to be changed as one type of flour was used up.

Other sources of difficulty for the baker sprang from the nature of the yeast mixture. Even with secret or favorite recipes, the baker never could be sure of the strength of his stock, especially if it was not used right away.

The oven also presented several problems. For example, the heat was never perfectly uniform throughout the entire oven, so that the doughs had to be placed in the oven accordingly, those requiring more heat in the hottest areas and those requiring less heat in the cooler areas. Baking temperatures could not be controlled closely nor adjusted rapidly to the requirements of particular products. Even the type of wood used for firing the oven might result in poor products if the baker did not know its heating qualities.

In the light of these difficulties, it is a tribute to the skill and patience of the professional baker that he was able to bake as well as he did. The craft tradition remained strong because of these difficulties which only ability and skill could handle. One became a baker literally by growing up in the trade, first as a young apprentice, then as a journeyman and, perhaps, finally as a master baker. What, therefore, may seem to have been daily trial and error was really the result of constant watchfulness on the part of an experienced craftsman.

Distribution of perishable bakery products other than at retail was virtually unknown in 1850. There may have been some wholesale selling of pies and cakes to hotels and other institutions, but, in the main, bakers sold at retail in their own shops or distributed direct to the consumers' homes.[30] House-to-house delivery by the baker in 1850 was really a part of his function of being a retail bakery operator; delivery to the home was done more to give satisfaction to certain customers than to establish a home delivery trade. On occasion bakery goods were sold by street vendors in the larger cities, but they were more common in Europe than in the United States.

Actually the perishable goods baker of the 1850s had few marketing or distributing problems. His shop was a community fixture, and he maintained a strong personal relationship with his customers. The customers knew his wares and entered his shop by personal choice. Little advertising was needed to build up the trade. Bread was sold unwrapped across the counter, and there was no necessity for the baker to identify his bread or sweet goods.

The Biscuit and Cracker Industry

In all phases—demand, production and distribution—the biscuit and cracker business presented a sharp contrast to the bread business. The relatively non-perishable nature of

---

[30] "Sixty Centuries of Bakers and Baking," *op. cit.*, XXXIX (September 1, 1923), pp. 49-50.

cracker products determined the extent of contrast. Their keeping quality occasioned purchases in great quantities by ship provisioners and suppliers for the long, overland westward treks. Although there was some demand on the part of general stores, hotels, and restaurants, ships' bread and crackers were basically the staple of travelers, much as bread was for the more stationary family.

Less perishability also meant less difficult processing requirements and, therefore, more chance for mechanization than in the case of bread and other perishable baked goods. Unleavened cracker doughs did not have to go through a fermentation process. Even leavened cracker doughs did not require thorough stretching and kneading. Kneading machines which were hand operated thus found an early use in cracker plants. And in contrast to bread dough which was divided, rounded, proofed and then moulded, the shaping process in biscuit and cracker production consisted merely of rolling the dough into flat, thin sheets, and cutting it to desired shapes. By 1850 a series of hand-rolling machines were in use to thin out the dough sheets, which were the shape required by an automatic stamp.

Finally, in contrast to perishable bakery products, wholesaling was the principal channel of distribution of ships' bread and crackers. In a limited way the biscuit and cracker bakers sold direct to nearby general or grocery stores, hotels, restaurants and other institutions; but because of their keeping qualities, cracker products were sold mainly to jobbers and wholesalers, or to general provision houses. These dealers in turn sold to general and grocery stores, to wagon trains for overland trips and to ship owners. As a result, the control and the function of maintaining reputation and service were shifted to the wholesaler or jobber, whose brand the products carried.

While the biscuit and cracker industry exhibited many features of industrialization, the bread baking industry in the United States in 1850 was still a craftsman's trade. It was a trade of limited dimensions and of small handicraft shops not much different from its European antecedents. As with most artisan crafts, skill based upon years of experience in the trade was the dominant factor insuring the baker's success. Bread was an extremely important food in the diet, but the economic conditions of the time were such that commercial baking had little place in the economy.

TWO

FROM A CRAFT TO AN EMERGING INDUSTRY

1850–1900

CHAPTER 3

THE RISE OF COMMERCIAL BAKING, 1850–1900

THE STRUCTURE of the American baking industry, as it was to emerge in the twentieth century, was foreshadowed by major changes that occurred between 1850 and 1900. Led by the trend away from home baking, new developments during the latter half of the 19th century set the basic patterns for the industry as we know it today. To be sure, home-baked bread and pastries were still held in high esteem by the end of the century, but a greater percentage of the population depended on the professional bakers to supply their needs than had been true fifty years earlier.

Primarily as a result of increased demand, the baking industry at the turn of the century was a study in contrasts. At one end of the spectrum, and still by all counts the largest segment of the industry, were the small-scale retail bakeries, little different from their counterparts in the colonial period. At the other end were the industrial bakers using large-scale baking techniques and distributing their products in ways that would be familiar to their successors half a century later.

The Expansion of Demand

In a broad way, this half century was an age of massive experiment. Decade after decade rang up new advances in industrialization. In industry after industry, the factory displaced the home in turning out consumer goods. The pattern of change varied endlessly, of course, by industry and according to demand. Some industries were pace setters; others lagged far behind. Yet, even among the laggards, there was no resisting the forces which the massive experiment had set afoot.

In the vanguard of pace setters were the textile and clothing industries. By 1860, for example, the New England cotton and woolen mills had virtually displaced household spinning and weaving. In another forty years the ready-made suit, mass produced in the factory, was the stock and trade for the Main Street merchant. By 1870 the factory had taken over the making of shoes. Collars, cuffs, gloves and hats were carrying factory labels by the turn of the century, in testimony of the fact that the age of the homespun garment had drawn to a close.

As for the food processing industries, these, too, were marked by change. Flour milling, as noted earlier, had begun the move away from the home early in the colonial era. Sugar refining had acquired a highly mechanized look by 1860. The canning industry was booming by 1885. Meat packers of the Midwest by the turn of the century had virtually supplanted local butchering. In their wake the baking industry began to weaken the hold of the housewife on bread-making, although baking was the last of the major food processing activities to be removed from the home. Nevertheless, in absolute terms, the overall expansion of commercial baking from 1850 to 1900 was impressive—the number of bakeries increased sevenfold and the value of their products, thirteenfold.

Breadbaking was responding to changes in demand that were, in the main, associated with an expanding economy and an emerging industrial society. One basic influence that affected demand for all products was a growing population. Between 1850 and 1900 the number of people in the United States rose threefold, from twenty-three million to over seventy-five million.[1] Such a phenomenal growth meant greater bread consumption, part of which the baker could be expected to supply. But since his industry expanded at a rate greater than that of the population, it is obvious that the increase in population is only a partial explanation for the rising demand.

The growing output of the bakers, in part, reflected a relative decline in home baking. In 1850 they accounted for less than 10 per cent of all bread consumed, but by 1890 their share climbed to 20 per cent; and in 1900, to 25 per cent.[2] For other perishable bakery products—cakes, pies and pastries —the bakers' contribution to total supply remained negligible.[3]

The trend away from home baking was largely accelerated by two characteristics of an emerging industrial society— urbanization and increasing real income. In 1850 the American economy was predominantly rural, with less than 15 per cent of the people living in cities or towns of 2,500 or more inhabitants. There were, in fact, only six cities which claimed a population of a hundred thousand or more. By 1900 America boasted an urban population of over thirty million people representing 40 per cent of the total population. Compared to 1850, the urban population had multiplied over eight and one-half times, while the rural population experienced little more than a twofold increase. In each decade the urban population had increased approximately 45 per cent compared to about 25 per cent for the entire population.

Urbanization was important in the decline of home baking for several reasons. First of all, it provided the concentration of people so necessary to the mass distribution of perishable bakery products. Urban centers also facilitated the delivery

[1] U. S. Bureau of the Census, *Historical Statistics of the United States: 1789–1945* (Washington: Government Printing Office, 1949), p. 25.

[2] "Study of the Flour and Baking Industries in the United States" (A Report Prepared by the Research Department, J. Walter Thompson Company, Chicago: January, 1924), p. 20.

[3] *Ibid.*

of bread to grocery stores, making it easier and more convenient for the housewife to purchase bread along with all of her other groceries. City life had also cut into her baking time, for she was drawn into a neighborhood community with its varied activities—church, school and social.

Then too, American industries were hiring an increasing number of women, especially in the urban districts. By 1900 17 per cent of the nation's labor force was comprised of women. Moreover, married women constituted approximately 6 per cent of all employed persons in 1900.[4] The fairly high percentage of single women regularly employed might be expected to mean a decrease in the number of future wives trained in the art of baking bread.

Illustrative of the degree to which bakeries in 1890 were located in urban centers, seven states with about 60 per cent of the urban population contained 69 per cent of the nation's bakeries and accounted for 68 per cent of the total value of bakery products. Ten years later these same seven states again had close to 60 per cent of the urban population, 66 per cent of all bakeries, and produced 69 per cent of the value of products produced. It is of interest to note that these seven states in both 1890 and 1900 contained only 41 per cent of the nation's population, indicating that urban population growth was more important for commercial baking than the overall population increase. Moreover, none of these seven states were in the southern areas of the country; they were all in the North, and only one state was west of the Mississippi. The sparse population in the southern states and the long standing preference of southern communities for hot breads tended to retard development of commercial baking in the South.

Urbanization was not of itself a sufficient factor in the decline of home baking. People had to have the means, as well as opportunity, to take advantage of the services of the commercial baker. The industrialization that swept through

---

[4] Historical Statistics of the United States: 1789–1945, *op. cit.*, p. 63.

America in the last half of the 19th century formed the basis for a steadily rising income. As shown in Chart 1, real income per capita rose from less than $250 in 1850 to more than $450 by the turn of the century and exhibited no tendency to reverse itself.[5]

CHART 1 *

REAL INCOME PER CAPITA, 1849–1899

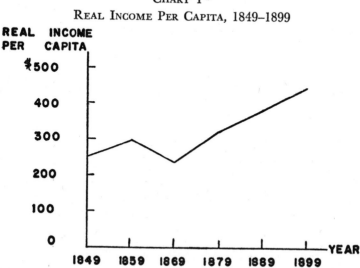

* Monetary income figures have been deflated by an index of the general price level in terms of 1926 dollars. Robert F. Martin, *National Income in the United States, 1799–1938* (New York: National Industrial Conference Board, 1939), p. 6.

With increased income, more and more families patronized the commercial baker. They were able to pay for the ease and convenience of buying bakers' bread. Moreover, with the increase in real income social values changed. More women could get out and do more things. Skills tended to shift from making things to buying things. A good loaf of homemade bread became less of a mark of distinction for homemaking.

While at the end of the century three-fourths of all bread was still being baked in the home, there was every reason to suppose that population increases, industrialization, urban-

---

[5] Robert F. Martin, *National Income in the United States, 1799–1938* (New York: National Industrial Conference Board, 1939), p. 6.

ization, advances in real income and a greater confidence in bakers' products would continue to operate in the half century that lay ahead. The prospects for further expansion of commercial baking were bright.

Bread and Diet Changes

While home baking was on the decline, American dietary habits began to change. More varied and more costly foods began to appear on the American table. Bread was still there, in no less quantity, but Americans were simply eating more; they were eating more of the foods rich in vitamins and minerals—lean meat, milk, fruit, and leafy vegetables.

The urban table, in particular, was marked by the change. Behind it was more than a matter of appetite. The grocery list of the housewife lengthened as the abundance of the field began pouring into the city on rail. The decade following 1850 had marked the beginning of an era of railroad expansion, an expansion that continued apace throughout the rest of the nineteenth century. Railroads helped to spread meat packing, commercial dairying, market gardening and horticulture which had been previously confined to the environments of urban centers, thereby increasing the perishable food supply of the city.

In addition, refrigeration and better methods of food preservation assured larger supplies of out-of-season goods. Fresh meat, for example, supplemented the traditional diet of locally cured pork. The up-and-coming canning industry brought a year-around supply of fruits and vegetables. In 1860 canners had only put up about five million cans; by 1870 the output had reached thirty million cans; and by 1900, over 800 million cans.[6] After 1850 a safer milk supply increased rapidly. Fresh milk from the country supplanted "swill milk which came from cows fed with distillery mash and stabled within city limits."[7] In the late 'seventies the

---

[6] Cummings, *op. cit.*, p. 69.
[7] *Ibid.*, p. 53.

bottle-delivery of milk first began in Brooklyn, and soon spread to other areas. And by 1900 pasteurization was firmly established in several cities.

The weekly food budget for a typical working-class family in 1851 illustrates the early lack of variety in the diet. It was basically a diet of bread, meat and potatoes.

TABLE 1 *

WEEKLY FOOD BUDGET FOR A FAMILY OF FIVE,
PHILADELPHIA, 1851

Butcher's meat, 2 lbs. per day at 10¢ per lb.	$ 1.40
Barrel of flour, $5.00, will last eight weeks	0.62½
Butter, 2 lb. at 31½¢ per pound	0.63
Potatoes, ½ bu.	0.50
Sugar, 4 lb. at 8¢ per pound	0.32
Coffee and Tea	0.25
Milk, two cents per day	0.14
Salt, pepper, vinegar, starch, soap, soda, yeast, cheese, eggs	0.40
Amount for food	$ 4.26½
For shelter, clothing, and other expenses	6.11
	$10.37½

* Cummings, *op. cit.*, Appendix F, p. 264.

Additions to the American diet were not long in appearing, however. A food expenditure budget for 1864 illustrates the change. Vegetables and fruits were now a part of the food expenditure.

The trend toward more varied foods continued throughout the last half of the 19th century. Witness the following comment on a survey of food habits of New York City families in 1895. "The diet of an Irish truckman's family, which may be taken as fairly typical of the group, included during a period of about two weeks a variety of meats and dairy products and about fifty-six pints of milk. Though proportionately less potatoes were used than in the 1851 and 1864 budgets, onions, beets and dried peas and beans were served.

TABLE 2 *

WEEKLY FOOD BUDGET FOR A FAMILY OF SIX,
NEW YORK CITY, 1864

Meats for the week (being a half ration supply)	$ 3.50
One bag of flour	1.80
Four pounds of butter	1.60
Small measure of potatoes, daily, at 17¢ per day (7 days)	1.19
Three and a half pounds of sugar	1.05
One pound of coffee (mixed or adulterated—can't can't afford better)	0.35
One quarter of pound of tea	0.38
Milk	0.56
Vegetables	0.50
Dried apples—to promote the health of children	0.25
Two pounds of lard	0.38
Soap, starch, pepper, salt, vinegar, etc.	1.00
Amount for food	$12.56
For shelter and other expenses	5.94
	$18.50

* Cummings, *op. cit.*, Appendix G, p. 265.

Fresh and canned tomatoes, strawberries, turnip greens, string beans and canned peas also appeared on the table." [8]

Increased income provided the means for people to buy and consume more food than they were doing earlier. That total food consumption was going up is known by the fact that the proportion of income families spent for food remained constant at about 50 per cent.[9] (Cf. Table 3)

People were, therefore, using their increased income to consume more food, especially the newer foods that were rapidly becoming available. And with increased total food consumption, flour and bread no longer dominated the family food budget. The per capita consumption of these products remained fairly constant between 1870 and 1900, but in con-

[8] *Ibid.*, p. 78.

[9] This is contrary to the generally held theory (Engel's Law) that the percentage of income spent for food tends to decline as income increases.

trast to earlier times, they were no longer the sole mainstay of the diet.

TABLE 3 *

PERCENTAGE OF THE LOW-PAID WAGE-EARNERS' EXPENDITURE
GOING FOR FOOD AT VARIOUS PERIODS

Date	Description	Per Cent
1851	Budget, laborer, Philadelphia	41.0
1864	Budget, printer, New York	68.0
1874	Survey of Massachusetts workers, annual income $300–$450	64.0
1890	Survey of Massachusetts workers, annual income $300–$450	50.0
1901	Survey of Massachusetts workers, annual income $300–$450	56.0
1901	Survey of Massachusetts workers, annual income $450–$600	54.8
1901	Survey of Massachusetts workers, annual income $600–$750	53.3
1901	Survey of Massachusetts workers, annual income $750–$1,200	53.1

* Cummings, *op. cit.*, Appendix J, p. 268. Only a part of his table is reproduced here.

The Demand for Biscuits and Crackers

In contrast to the bread-baking industry which derived its impetus from a decline in home baking, the increased demand for biscuits and crackers took the form of a demand for newer and different products which, except for cookies, had never been baked in the home to any great extent. During the Civil War, the biscuit and cracker bakers benefited from the need of the field armies for a bread that would not deteriorate rapidly. Consequently, many bakeries in the North began supplying the Union Armies with crackers, ships' bread and hardtack. This call for a "portable" bread stimulated the growth of the biscuit and cracker industry in a way that the so-called "traveling" market for overland and ship travelers had earlier. After the Civil War, however, the development of better and faster modes of transportation caused "portable" bread sales to dwindle. Travelers had to worry less about imperishable food supplies, as railroads increasingly replaced slower wagon, canal and river transportation in domestic trade, and steamships supplanted sailing vessels on the high seas. In parts of the Far West there was still a need for the "portable" breads, but the peak demand had passed.

Fortunately, yeast-raised crackers and English sweet crackers, or cookies, caught the public fancy. Leavened crackers had been made as early as 1800, but until compressed yeast became available about 1870 their production was not attempted on a large scale. Sweet biscuits had previously been imported from England. When such sweets achieved a measure of popularity in this country, Belcher and Larrabee, cracker bakers of Albany, New York, imported machinery and methods for baking them shortly after the Civil War.[10]

The change in the demand for biscuit and cracker output was clearly a shift from staple to "luxury" products. Unlike the demand for bread, there was little opportunity for cracker bakers to benefit from a home to factory movement. But like the expanded demand for food in general, the boom for the cracker industry was made possible by increased incomes and the willingness of people to add new foods to their changing diets.

---

[10] H. F. Eggert, in a privately printed pamphlet entitled, *Interesting Facts about Nabisco—National Biscuit Company.*

CHAPTER 4

CHANGING TECHNOLOGY—THE EMER-GENCE OF LARGE-SCALE PRODUCTION

THE LAST HALF of the nineteenth century marked the beginning of the end of the traditional handicraft ways of baking. Shortly after 1850 the age-old artisan methods began to falter as the demand for bakers bread grew stronger and stronger. At first the challenge was met by an increase in the numbers of bakeries; but, by the 1870s that was not enough. Bakers had to find easier and faster ways to meet the demand, and in finding them, they broke abruptly with the past. In swift succession came a whole host of innovations that were to give the larger bakeries a factory look. Ovens, fuel, and firing; flour and yeast; and mixing, dividing, and moulding—all were affected. The bread industry, which had lagged behind the biscuit and cracker industry, began to take on a more modern appearance. By 1900 it was clearly demonstrated that factory methods, although accepted by only a handful of bakers, were not to be stayed by tradition. In this half century baking technology experienced its first significant change in over 1,500 years.

Oven Improvements

Basic to the new technology were the changes in the construction and operation of ovens. With increases in demand, the ancient peel oven, long the mainstay of the baker's trade, proved gradually to be a production bottleneck. Increased output was not easy to achieve because the oven was not adapted to continuous baking; after each baking period a new fire had to be started, the equalization time allowed for the fire removed and the oven swabbed clean of fly ash and other dirt. It was a laborious, time-consuming task. Moreover, unless the fire was evenly distributed throughout all parts of the oven, heat inequalities resulted which made for variable baking temperatures.

An early attempt at oven modification came when some enterprising baker built a fire box on one side of the baking chamber door. Rather than being gradually pushed into all parts of the oven, the fire remained stationary and greatly simplified heating and cleaning. Other bakers took another approach to reduce time and labor. They constructed fire boxes on both sides of the oven. This improvement yielded a further advantage: it overcame heat inequalities that often resulted from a left- or right-hand fire box. Neither improvement, however, eliminated the necessity for refiring after each baking period.

In the 'seventies, the problem was solved through the introduction of indirect continuous firing, an innovation paralleling the importance of the invention of the oven itself. The fire box was removed from the baking chamber and placed behind the oven or below it. Heat from the fire box was conducted through a series of flues running above and below the baking chamber and out through the chimney stack. A proper baking temperature could be maintained indefinitely in the oven simply by adding more fuel. More important, the fire did not have to be removed or put out while baking took place. Continuously fired, one peel oven could do the work of three of the older types with considerable savings in labor.

Still another improvement was the replacement of the flues and baffles above and below the baking hearth by water filled pipes so installed that a short portion of each protruded into

The Horse and Wagon Era

Brick Peel Oven, 1900

the fire box. There the direct heat from the fire vaporized the water into high pressure steam, which, in turn, heated the oven.

With the introduction of a separate combustion chamber came the use of more efficient fuels. Coal and coke were the most common replacements for wood. By the turn of the century the use of oil and gas became more widespread. By that time also electricity was being experimented with, though its application was limited by cost considerations.

Continuous baking set the stage for a series of pioneering attempts at further oven improvements. First among these was the draw-plate or deck oven introduced about 1880. Essentially a standard peel oven, it had as a distinctive feature a baking surface on wheels that could be withdrawn from the baking chamber. Some models were made with double-deck construction to facilitate the handling of a greater number of dough pieces. The draw-plate oven had the advantage of easing the loading and unloading chores of oven tending, but at the same time was limited in use because of the intense heat given off by the baking plate when it was removed from the oven.

Another variation of the standard peel oven was the rotary oven also introduced about 1880. Instead of the stationary hearth of the peel, it contained a circular revolving hearth, supported on a mechanically driven axis. Like the draw-plate oven, it shortened the loading and unloading periods, since the baking plate could be rotated mechanically, making all parts of it easily accessible at the oven door. It also yielded some advantage in the equalization of heat during baking because the baked goods moved horizontally through the entire baking chamber.

A totally different principle was employed in the revolving reel oven, the forerunner of the modern type. It had been introduced and widely adopted in the biscuit and cracker industry during the Civil War, but was not thought practical for bread baking until about 1880. The reel oven operated much like a ferris wheel in that the hearths were trays pivoted between vertical discs revolving in a large baking chamber. Power was furnished by a simple system of counterweights; later models were driven by steam and in some cases by electricity. As with the peel ovens and their modifications, the reel oven was indirectly fired with coal or coke and built of heavy refractory construction materials. Its principal advantage lay in easier loading and unloading, since each tray could be brought directly to the door. It was contended that by providing for baking in more than one vertical heat zone, more efficient baking would result, but this advantage was not proved before 1900.

While these new ovens held great promise, their early performance did not sufficiently exceed that of the peel. The continuously fired peel oven remained by far the most popular. It provided baking conditions traditionally regarded as ideal, "namely solid bottom heat and a properly proportioned top heat obtained by radiation from the low ceiling which was seldom more than one foot above the hearth." [1] This idea in turn rested on an almost universal assumption among bakers: peel ovens gave satisfactory performance because they were constructed of brick or refractory materials with great heat-storing properties.

In the case of the draw-plate and rotary ovens, heavy brick construction limited their advantages to easier loading and unloading. Heavy construction in the reel oven actually brought a disadvantage. Higher baking chambers to allow for the vertical movement of the trays made the beneficial effects of radiated top heat more difficult to attain. And with the bake stuffs passing through vertical heat zones, which affected various baking products differently, there was less control over the uniformity of the finished product. Early mechanical ovens also had operating shortcomings. Reels, trays and motive power were relatively crude with the result that mechan-

---

[1] E. Pyler, *Baking Science and Technology* (Chicago: Siebel Publishing Company, 1952), 11, p. 703.

Rotary Oven, 1900

ical failures frequently offset any advantages of speed and efficiency. And in the reel oven also "coal, coke or wood, . . . were not suitable for fuel." [2]

The famed peel oven, to be sure, contained certain limitations. Its weight and requirements of floor space were both excessive and it permitted no close control of baking temperatures. If left idle too long, the oven was also subject to frequent flash heats which resulted in excessive baking temperatures. Nevertheless, it performed quite satisfactorily under the watchful eye of a skilled oven man. Moreover, once a peel oven was installed, it would give service for more than twenty years. Since it could be converted to bake continuously simply by installing flues or steam pipes, most bakers found little incentive to replace it with the new ovens—whether draw-plate, rotary, or reel.

The Development of Baking Machinery

Continuous oven operation was but the first step in meeting the production requirements of a rising demand. The baker who so converted his oven could perhaps triple his production, but only if he could provide sufficient batches of dough for baking. Dough-mixing, fermentation and dough-shaping, or make-up operations therefore had to increase in size and speed. With skilled labor relatively scarce, bakers sought to eliminate the age-old and laborious hand methods. Their first efforts were naturally devoted to developing a mechanical mixer to replace the most difficult phase of manual labor, one that was the most likely to slow the whole baking operation.

One or two models of mixing machines had been experimented with as early as 1810, but they did not come into general use until the 'seventies. The earliest model, forerunner of the present horizontal mixer, was nothing more than a small trough or bowl equipped with a curved shaft manually

---

[2] J. M. Albright, "How the Bakers and Equipment Manufacturers Cooperated to Build Better Bread Making Machinery," *Baking Industry Magazine,* XCVII (April 12, 1952), p. 112.

cranked to mix the dough. It fell so far short of efficient per-formance, however, that it was suitable only as an auxiliary to hand-mixing.

As the needs for a better mixing machine grew, gears were added to increase the power derived from cranking. By 1880 mechanical power eliminated the necessity of hand operations. Belt-driven through a system of shafts and pulleys from the central power plant of the bakery, some mixers even had two speeds and were equipped with a reversing gear. The design and power of the agitator arms were also improved; single and double spiral blades were increased to about half the size and strength of those in existence today. The capacity of such horizontal mixers ran as high as six barrels of flour. Vertical mixers of small capacity were developed for use in smaller shops and for mixing cake batters.

Despite the progress in mechanical mixers, by the turn of the century many bakers felt that the machines could not du-plicate the thorough mixing or desired consistency achieved by an experienced mixing hand. There were many com-plaints that machine mixing did not properly prepare the dough for the all-important fermentation process. Mechanical mixers, therefore, were still often supplemented with hand-mixing.

Another problem of machine-mixing was temperature con-trol. Heat developed by the friction of the mixing operation was a frequent source of trouble because it created too much gas in the dough. As a result, practically all of the mixers in use before 1900 were slow speed machines.

To counteract the difficulties of mechanical mixing, an-other machine—the dough brake—was introduced in the early 'seventies. Basically, it consisted of a set of rollers through which the dough passed upon coming from the mixing opera-tion. The rolling process squeezed much of the gas and air out of the dough and helped to give it the desired consistency. The first dough brakes were hand operated; later, they were power-driven. After the turn of the century the development of high-speed mixers reduced the use of dough brakes in all except the biscuit and cracker industry where they remain essential equipment for certain non-raised products.

Unlike other industrial operations, where the size of equipment could be increased to very large dimensions, there were some effective limits of scale as far as mixing was concerned. Only limited-sized batches of dough could be adequately mixed at one time, not only because of the defects of machine mixing itself, but because there were limitations to the amount of dough that could be fermented at one time.[3] In large plants, therefore, a battery of mixers had to be installed to provide sufficient batches of dough for baking at full capacity. But despite the difficulties of machine-mixing, mixers were an absolute necessity in the large bread bakeries of 1900. Their contribution to output was equal to that of continuously fired ovens.

Great as were the contributions of ovens and mixers to large scale production, their impact on the thinking of the commercial baker was still more important. They led to new inventions and, in a sense, they spelled defeat to those who said it could not be done—to those who stubbornly clung to handicraft methods. For ovens and mixers represented only the beginning of machine baking. There remained the challenge of many grueling hand tasks—cutting, scaling, shaping, moulding, manipulation of flour by brute force and hand-loading. These, too, were to be subject to Yankee ingenuity before the close of the century.

The first automatic dough divider appeared about 1895. Early machines were designed primarily for dividing rolls, but were quickly followed by a succession of bread dough dividers. These machines automatically cut the dough into pieces of the correct weight, a job previously done by bench hands wielding a simple cutting instrument and a small scale. The dividers were belt driven. They had only one set speed,

---

[3] It is still true that only limited-sized batches will ferment properly.

but performed well enough so that by 1897 "everyone seemed to be making dividers." [4]

A moulding machine was introduced about 1888 to replace hand labor in de-gassing the dough pieces and moulding them into shape for baking after the dough had been cut and scaled. Although its type and construction are unknown, this early machine moulded bread faster than bench hands, at a reported rate of 2,000 loaves per hour. [5] In 1892, Peter F. Bryce, a baker of Indianapolis, originated the forerunner of today's moulder. He invented a set of head rolls through which the dough pieces traveled to receive a loose moulding and dusting automatically. Seven hands could turn out up to ninety loaves a minute on this machine. [6] Modern machines, for all of their later improvements, are simply a refinement of Bryce's design.

Flour handling also came in for a change. By 1900 bakers in the larger establishments were making use of a gravity-feed sifting mechanism. From a second floor storage area flour was dumped into a hopper installed above an automatic sifter, given a thorough sifting and conveyed through a canvas chute directly to the mixer. A wooden box with a metal sieve on the underside comprised the sifting device. A brush mounted on a drive shaft extending through one end of the box gave the necessary agitation while clearing the sieve.

Mechanization in bread production had only a limited counterpart in the preparation of specialty products—cakes, pies and doughnuts. Such products required much handwork, but by 1900 small mixers and beaters and portable ovens gained modest footholds in commercial processing. Many shops also made use of a variety of special cutters and depositors. In addition, a host of small-job machines—egg beaters, doughnut stoves, small flour sifters, and apple corers—all found their way into commercial pastry production.

---

[4] J. M. Albright, "Bread Making Machinery," *op. cit.*, XCVII (April 12, 1952), p. 117.
[5] *Ibid.*, p. 120.
[6] *Ibid.*

An Early Mixing Machine, 1892

An Early Moulder, 1898

Improved Baking Quality of Ingredients

Mechanization alone could not have spearheaded the advance toward large scale production in the last half of the nineteenth century. The emergence of standardized machine output had to await the appearance of a more reliable yeast and a better, more uniform quality bread flour. The impact of these two rivaled that of the machine on baking, for they reduced operations to industrial routine by eliminating the unknown of inferior yeasts and flours.

In 1868 Charles Fleischmann began the commercial production of compressed yeast. Although his yeast was far superior to the older barm and other ferments commonly used, Fleischmann had no easy time of it in winning the acceptance of the baker. For one reason, the yeast was hard to keep fresh because of inadequate refrigeration. Distribution, too, was difficult and costly beyond metropolitan areas. And until Fleischmann began building up a system of regular deliveries for an improved product about the turn of the century, most bakers continued to rely upon their own ferments, merely using compressed yeast for their stock yeast.[7]

The advantages of compressed yeast for the baker were many. It had greater leavening power than the homemade yeast ferments yielding a more uniform dough fermentation. It had stability and dependability allowing a routine baking operation consistent with large-scale production schedules. It also made a better quality, better-tasting loaf. Finally, compressed yeast meant less work. For the baker who used it fully, it eliminated the cumbersome preparation of the old-fashioned brew or ferment.

Two years after Fleischmann's contribution to better baking, the millers of the Northwest in 1870 solved the problem of milling hard spring-winter wheat, a problem which had plagued them for years. Their "patent" flour was stronger,

---

[7] Personal communication, Mr. John T. Buckheit, Technical Service Department, Fleischmann Division, Standard Brands, Incorporated, New York, 1954.

whiter, and better keeping than the previously common, winter-wheat flour. For the nation's bakers, it meant a better all-around loaf of bread, whiter, lighter, and of superior grain and texture. It gave the loaves a rich brown color heretofore not obtained in baking. Of special significance, this flour yielded a greater amount of bread per barrel—some 12.5 per cent over the best winter-wheat flours.

With the advent of large scale milling about 1880, some millers were also able to assure their customers a consistently stable quality flour. By mixing wheats of different varieties and from different sources in the correct proportion, and by establishing wheat- and flour-testing laboratories, millers supplied bakers with a flour more suited to the needs of machine-handling and to large scale production schedules.

The Factory Bakery

Mechanization gave the nation's larger bakeries an output and an appearance commensurate with factory operations. Their scale and efficiency were much greater than had formerly been possible. Some bakers in the larger cities were able to turn out up to 15,000 loaves of bread per day. Most large-scale operations around the turn of the century probably averaged a daily production of well under 10,000 loaves, but this output was far in excess of the best in the days of handicraft baking.

Mechanical power destroyed the familiar picture of the small handicraft bakeshop. What greeted the eye now in the factory bakery was a battery of ovens—sometimes numbering up to fourteen or more—and mixers. Motive power for the machinery was provided by shafts and pulleys suspended from the ceiling and driven from a central steam plant. A few bakeries had direct drive electric motors. There was little semblance to the environment of the artisan baker!

Figure 1 shows a diagram of a wholesale bakery of 1895 in Dubuque, Iowa. Although the bakery was not one of the largest of the period, its layout illustrates the nature of factory operation. Including the basement, there were three floors for the operation of this bakery. The living quarters were at the front of the second floor. Adjacent to them were the stalls for the horses which were led up to the second floor by way of the ramp in the middle of the building. The first floor contained the wagon room, the flour and mixing room, and the retail and wholesale rooms. Baking was done in the basement.

Three ovens are shown, two large bread ovens and one

FIGURE 1
FLOOR PLAN OF MULGREW'S BAKERY, DUBUQUE, IOWA, 1895 *

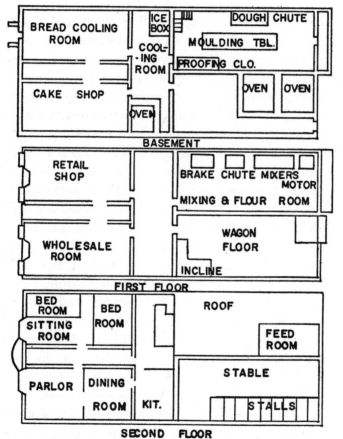

* J. E. Hopkins, "Design and Construction of Bakery Building," *Baking Industry Magazine*, XCVII (April 12, 1952), p. 132.

smaller cake oven. There is no specification of their type. Two mixers are indicated in addition to a dough brake which was used in conjunction with the mixing operation. The flour and mixing rooms were combined, although this was not true of most bakeries. There was a chute provided for delivering the mixed dough to the baking area below. Apparently there were no moulding machines in use in this bakery, since only a moulding table is shown in the bread room. Likewise, there is no indication of a divider or any flour-handling equipment. The only major pieces of equipment appear to be the ovens and the mixers with their dough brakes.

Of special interest are the proofing closet and the cooling rooms which were becoming more and more a necessary part of every large bakery. These were separate rooms removed from the baking and mixing areas where temperature and humidity conditions were more equable. Dough troughs were simply wheeled into the proofing closet at the various fermentation stages in the baking process. In the cooling room, bread was placed on racks immediately upon coming from the oven.

Note also that this baker was both a retailer and a wholesaler who had two stores on the street floor—one used for the retail business and the other used as a wholesale shipping room. While wholesaling was the main business of this baker, like many others he continued to operate a retail store. The records of this early bakery also indicate that electricity was used throughout for both power and light, although electrical power was not common among bakeries before 1900.

Another interesting point illustrated in this diagram is the fact that the final products were baked in the basement. Characteristic of the great majority of bread bakeries in the country, basement baking led to much criticism of the industry because it fostered unsanitary baking conditions. But basement baking was considered necessary because of the excessive weight of the huge ovens and the use of a gravity feeding system.

Contrast with Biscuit and Cracker Technology

The biscuit and cracker industry had long been characterized by large-scale operations due to the keeping qualities of its products. For all practical purposes, the industry had become technologically separate from the bread baking industry as early as 1800. The separation of the two branches became more pronounced during the period 1850–1900.

The great demand for ships' bread and hardtack during the Civil War taxed the capacity of the cracker industry—especially oven capacity. To meet this situation the cracker bakers developed the continuously fired reel oven. The daily capacity of a single oven jumped from the cracker equivalent of six barrels of flour to the equivalent of twenty-five or thirty barrels. By 1900 ovens had increased in size to the point where they baked the products from over fifty barrels of flour per day. Many such ovens were over two stories high. Mixers, dough brakes, rolling machines and automatic dough cutters and stamps also became a part of the attempt to meet the peak demand of the war.

After the Civil War, when the so-called "traveling" market for biscuits and crackers began to decline, the industry adjusted itself to the new conditions by importing the machinery and methods for making English sweetened biscuits and yeast-raised crackers. In addition, during the late 1890s the National Biscuit Company introduced wrapping and packaging machines for cracker products, which were quickly adopted by other industry members. By 1900 there was scarcely a cracker baker in the country who could exist without a mechanized operation.

The Extent of Large Scale Bread Baking

The emergence of large scale production methods in the bread-baking industry hastened the end of the handicraft system, but it did not eliminate that system. Much remained to be done in mechanizing the baking operation. Machines for making products other than bread, for example, were almost non-existent. Even in bread production, all equipment needed further improving. Moreover, many hand operations still had not succumbed to the machine even in the most modern plants. Nor had conveyor systems and mechanical loading and unloading of machines been devised to provide a continuous flow of production.

That the new technology had not encompassed more than a fraction of the industry by 1900 is evident from the following table:

TABLE 1

SIZE DISTRIBUTION OF BAKERIES BY NUMBER OF
WAGE EARNERS, 1899 *

Wage Earners Employed	Number of Establishments in Each Classification	Per Cent of Establishments in Each Classification
All Groups	14,917	100.0
None	1,889	12.7
1–4	9,769	65.4
5–20	2,834	19.0
21–50	258	1.7
51–100	89	0.6
101–250	66	0.4
251–500	8	0.1
501–1,000	3	Less than 0.05
Over 1,000	1	Less than 0.05

* Kyrk and Davis, *op. cit.*, Appendix Table XVI, p. 94. Only a part of their table is reproduced here.

Seventy-eight per cent of the bakeries in the United States in 1899 had four or fewer employees, indicating the continued existence of the small-family handicraft bakeshop. Most of them had only grown from their 1850 level to the extent of hiring an extra hand or two. In fact, 13 per cent of the bakeries in 1900 had no hired employees at all; they were the traditional one-man shops. Large-scale bakeries probably numbered no more than 10 per cent of the total number of bread bakeries.[8] They accounted, however, for a larger share of output than their number indicated—perhaps 20-25 per cent of industry sales.[9] This estimate is further supported by census statistics on the number of bakeries using mechanical power of one kind or another in 1899. Less than 10 per cent of the nation's bakers reported the use of such power.

One basic reason why more bakers did not take advantage of the technological advances is that the demand for commercial bakery products, while greatly increased, was still not sufficient to support a great number of large-scale producers. A large city, for example, might support two or three dozen small bakeshops, but only a handful of industrial bakers. Three-fourths of all bread consumed was still baked in the home, and most of those who did buy commercially baked bread preferred to do so in the small retail bakeshop.

Equally significant perhaps, in acting as a limitation to industrial baking, was the baker himself—in his resistance to change and in his devotion to the status quo. Imbued with what was probably the deepest of all craft traditions, the great majority of bakers simply did not wish to change their ways. Indeed, they actively fought any attempts to introduce mechanization. While perhaps difficult to understand today, their pride of craftsmanship and their belief in their ability to produce high-quality products were unshakable and inborn. This feeling for handicraft workmanship was strongest among the great number of foreign-born bakers who retained most of their Old World traditions.

These prejudices were specifically borne out in bakers' reactions to baking machinery. Regardless of the advantage involved, many bakers refused to have anything to do with any equipment that carried the taint of mechanization. Illustrative of the obstacles faced by equipment manufacturers is the

---

[8] This estimate has received support from various industry sources as being a good approximation.

[9] This estimate has also received industry support, specially from Mr. W. E. Long, formerly head of the W. E. Long Company, and Mr. Harold LeMar, Vice President of the P. F. Petersen Baking Company.

following comment by P. V. Connell, Vice-President of the J. H. Day Company of Cincinnati, Ohio. Speaking about selling mixers around the turn of the century, he says,

> The main task of the Day Company was to educate the prospective users of this equipment in the knowledge that power machinery could do a better job than processing by hand. . . . These bakers were so opposed to anything that even looked like a power machine that they would often refuse to use even a hand powered sifter or egg beater. There was even greater prejudice against the dough mixer and few bakers could be made to believe that bread dough could be made any other way than by hand. . . . More than 75% of the efforts of . . . (the advertising) department was devoted to showing the comparative value of machinery over hand labor. The remaining 25% of the time and energies were devoted to emphasizing the Day machinery.[10]

Such reactions even extended to journeymen bakers working in the employ of master bakers. A case in point is the employee who threatened to quit his job as oven man rather than tend a proposed mechanical reel oven. The expense of purchasing equipment and the fact that early machines lacked mechanical perfection were also important in deterring their use. These factors served only to strengthen the stubbornness built upon the craft traditions.

Nevertheless, handicraft baking was fighting a losing battle. The stage was set; for the next several decades were to bring forth the momentous impact of industrial baking.

---

[10] Personal letter discussing the history of the J. H. Day Company, from Mr. P. V. Connell, Vice-President, J. H. Day Company, 1954.

CHAPTER 5

THE EMERGENCE OF WHOLESALE
DISTRIBUTION

WITH THE EMERGENCE of industrialized baking by the turn of the century, the pattern of distribution changed markedly. The traditional sales over the bakeshop counter simply could not keep pace with the rapidly increasing demand for bread, which not only created new problems of supply but also called for new marketing techniques. In an effort to capitalize on the growing market, operators of the larger and more progressive bakeries pursued several courses. They inaugurated deliveries to grocery stores, by far the most important departure from precedent. Some carried their marketing efforts still further by carving out new channels of distribution—drop shipments, institutional outlets, house-to-house distribution, and multi-unit retailing.

To be sure, these innovations accounted for only a small share of the total industry sales by 1900, but they clearly set the selling pattern that was to become dominant during the next half century. These innovations, also, could not have been made in the absence of changes that were occurring in marketing generally in the United States, changes that contributed to the rise of the grocery store as the most important retail outlet for food and the mecca of the housewife.

In the 1850s the general store, with its wide variety of merchandise ranging from soda crackers to hardware and ready-made clothes, was the dominant retail outlet. It held this position because it adequately met the needs of the population at that time. America was predominantly rural and lacking in good transportation facilities and demand was limited for any particular line of goods. Single-line stores had made an appearance in urban centers, but they were limited in number and in the variety of goods sold. Grocery stores, for example, handled only non-perishable staples such as flour, crackers, salt, sugar and molasses. Fresh foods were sold principally by street vendors and in public markets where butchers, fishmongers, produce dealers and butter and egg men distributed their wares.

Increasingly, after the Civil War, the single-line retail outlet challenged the supremacy of the general store. Rising incomes, the continued farm to city movement and the increased availability of a greater number and variety of manufactured goods promoted the rise of single-line stores selling at prices which the general store could not meet. The latter continued to serve rural areas, but city dwellers preferred to make their purchases from stores that specialized in drugs, hardware, home furnishings, dry goods, tobacco, shoes or food products. By the turn of the century the general store had all but disappeared from the urban center.

The trend toward specialized retail outlets was enhanced by a growing interest in retail distribution on the part of manufacturers. In an effort to meet and influence the needs of consumers, they began making extensive use of brand names, small-unit packing, and direct consumer advertising. Jobbers and wholesale middlemen, long dominant in American marketing, quickly felt the growing independence of manufacturers.[1]

In the food field these changes were reflected in the growing importance of grocery stores. Of particular significance to

---

[1] F. Presbrey, *The History and Development of Advertising* (Garden City, New York: Doubleday, Doran and Company, Inc., 1929), p. 362.

their growth were the rise of the canning industry and better transport facilities, including the refrigerator car, which insured larger and more stable supplies of fresh fruits and vegetables. More and more the typical urban grocery store differed from the traditional country store with its "staples in bulk, doled out in brown paper parcels . . . fruits in barrels and casks, sugar in boxes, molasses in hogsheads," and its unforgettable odor compounded of "everything in general and nothing in particular." [2] Customers could now choose from a widening variety of staples pre-packaged in convenient quantities and bearing the manufacturers' brand names. Fresh fruits and vegetables drawn from nearby market gardens or shipped from the South and West were on display. These could be supplemented by a variety of canned goods.

Selling Beyond the Retail Shop

For large commercial bakers grocery stores offered an attractive opportunity for making their products more conveniently available to the housewife. Grocery store distribution meant a good chance to increase sales and at the same time encourage the substitution of bakers' bread for homemade products. The grocers were, of course, quite willing to add another money-making item to their growing line of merchandise.

To distribute beyond the confines of his bakery involved a radical departure from the bakers' long established pattern. He had to become more than a skilled craftsman. Like other industrial proprietors, he became a manager, confronted with the attendant problems of finance, industrial relations and marketing policies.

In the first place, the baker had to provide an organized method of delivery. Because of its perishability, bread had to be distributed to the stores at least every other day. Push carts and bread baskets—long used for occasional house delivery—were not adequate for larger volume and longer dis-

---

[2] Thomas D. Clark, *Pills, Petticoats, and Plows* (New York: Bobbs-Merrill Book Company, 1944), p. 22.

tances. Thus began the era of horse and wagon delivery. For the up and coming baker, it spelled larger outlays in plant investments. Not only was it necessary to buy horses, wagons, and accessory equipment, the animals had to be stabled and fed and space made available for the vehicles. Men had to be hired to drive the wagons, keep equipment in repair and care for the horses.

An effective delivery system further required careful planning of routes and sales territories. Each route driver was assigned a certain group of grocery stores. These he serviced either daily or every other day, depending largely on the grocer's needs. His route was limited by the distance his horse could cover in a day, not more than ten miles from the bakery.[3] Around the turn of the century, the average wholesale baker had from two to ten routes, and the average weekly sales per route were somewhat less than $150, or—on the basis of four cents per loaf, roughly 3,500 loaves.[4]

Secondly, the baker had the problem of devising a satisfactory financial arrangement with the grocer. A perishable product like bread was unsalable after one or two days on the counter. And since it was virtually impossible to estimate the exact wants of customers, the grocer was often left with a supply of unsold bread at the end of the day. Neither the grocer nor the baker could afford to alienate customers with leftovers. In dealing with this problem, the baker was at a disadvantage, for he had to satisfy the grocer who had the customers. He was forced to adopt a system of consignment selling by which the grocer was credited for any bread left unsold. Some bakers tried to offset this costly burden by securing an exclusive deal with the grocer whereby he would handle only their products. The most common arrangement, however, was one in which the grocer handled bread from several competing bakers.

---

[3] Letter to the author from Mr. Harold LeMar, Vice-President, P. F. Petersen Baking Company, Omaha, Nebraska, June 16, 1954.
[4] *Ibid.*

Finally, the baker who turned wholesaler had to change the size and production characteristics of his entire operation. He not only had to increase his output to meet the needs of widespread distribution, he had to lower his unit costs so as to counter-balance the smaller amount received on selling at wholesale prices. Volume increases and lowered costs were made possible, of course, by utilizing the recently developed technological improvements such as continuously fired ovens and mixers, dividers and moulders. He also had to become a specialist concentrating almost exclusively on the production of bread. The new equipment was designed for bread baking rather than the baking of fancy goods. At the turn of the century, "the wholesale distribution of cakes was almost unknown." [5]

For those bakers who had begun to increase the size of their operations through the early use of machinery, production requirements presented few major problems. Such changes often required, however, a larger financial outlay than most bakers could afford. A few simply refused to consider mechanized baking, no matter what the cost. Some retailers resorted to mergers for the necessary funds or equipment. Such was the case with the formation in Omaha in 1893 of the U. P. Steam Baking Company, forerunner of the present P. F. Petersen Baking Company. Four retail bakeries were merged in April of that year with paid-in capital of $15,000, and wholesale operations were begun shortly thereafter.[6] The success of selling through grocery stores prompted many wholesale bakers to search for additional outlets to support their productive capacity. Indeed, bakers probably began taking on supplementary modes of distribution at about the time grocery store deliveries began.

A few farsighted pioneers quickly recognized hotel and restaurant proprietors as potential customers. Wholesale bakers were in a fine position to service these outlets through their

---

[5] Letter to the author from Mr. Harold LeMar.
[6] *Ibid.*

already organized route system. A few found this new market large enough to become specialized institutional bakers. In most cases they made no provision for stale returns, but their prices were generally lower than those charged to grocers. The products also differed from those sold to grocery stores. Restaurants demanded steamed rolls and other hard crusted hearth products as well as the conventional loaf. They also bought cakes and pies which had not yet found their way to the grocers' shelves.

In the changing pattern of distribution regular house-to-house routes were also established by some bakers to deliver bakery products direct to the consumer's door. The Freihofer Company of Philadelphia, for example, was one of the pioneers in this direction, operating sixty-four routes selling to both wholesale customers and housewives.[7] But, like the institutional business, the home delivery market was relatively minor compared to grocery store delivery. It was found almost exclusively in the large eastern cities.

Some of the largest bakery operations were characterized by still another form of distribution, the so-called drop shipment sale. Under this scheme bakers sold to out-of-town grocers where no wholesale bakeries were located and delivered orders by rail shipment. By such methods bakers sold to grocery stores in towns as far away as 100 miles. Drop shipments were not very widespread and often sporadic, but they provided a welcome adjunct to local selling.

While wholesaling was the core of the changing distribution in the baking industry, retail operations also reflected the changed conditions of demand and production. Several enterprising retailers found a way to circumvent some of the limitations of the retail bakeshop by establishing branch stores. Similar to the average retail bakery, these branches differed only in that their products were delivered daily by horse and wagon from a main bakery. In this way the baker

---

[7] G. N. Graf, "The Years Teach Much Which the Days Never Know," *Baking Industry Magazine*, XCVII (April 12, 1952).

could achieve some of the advantages of large-scale production and still remain in the business to which he was accustomed. At the same time, however, the demand and production limitations inherent in producing and selling a wide variety of goods deterred the widespread adoption of multi-unit retailing.

Market Areas and Increased Competition

The changes in distribution removed baking from its neighborhood atmosphere and gave it a new kind of market of wider significance. The expansion and overlap of what were formerly isolated market areas, coupled with increased competition, were, to say the least, revolutionary in their impact on the industry. Prior to the expansion of distribution, the bread baking industry in a typical market consisted of a relatively large number of small retail shops, each of which was virtually confined, as illustrated in Figure 1, to a small neighborhood or community area. There was relatively little or no interference from other bakers because each baker was confronted with no more than one or two neighborhood competitors. And even here, because of the small degree of market area overlap, head-on competition was negligible.

The industrial bakers, on the other hand, found themselves faced with a completely different situation. Not only did their market areas overlap; they were almost identical. Isolated neighborhood market areas quickly became a thing of the past, for in most cases the entire city constituted the wholesalers' market. Moreover, many wholesalers sold beyond the city limits by means of drop shipments to nearby towns and communities. A typical market could therefore support only a few such wholesale bakeries.

The sale of bread by relatively few vendors, each serving the same territory, quickly gave birth to a different kind of competition. It was direct competition of a sort which forced the baker for the first time to think beyond mere production problems. Since consumers had a choice of products from sev-

FIGURE 1

EFFECTIVE MARKET AREAS OF RETAIL BAKERIES

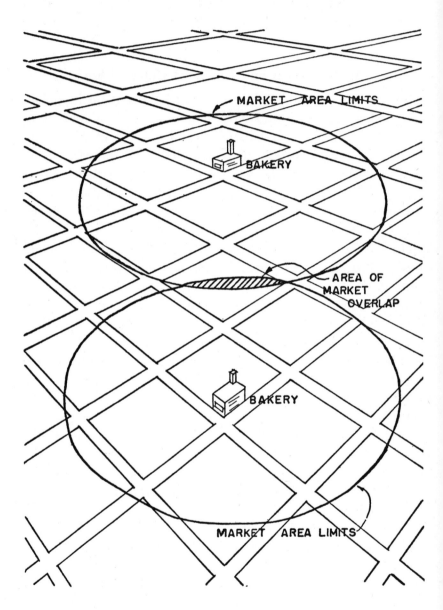

eral bakeries at their grocery stores, the baker realized he could no longer let sales take care of themselves as the earlier retailer had done. He therefore began devoting conscious effort to selling his products to insure himself an adequate share of the market.

FIGURE 2

EFFECTIVE MARKET AREAS OF INDUSTRIAL BAKERS

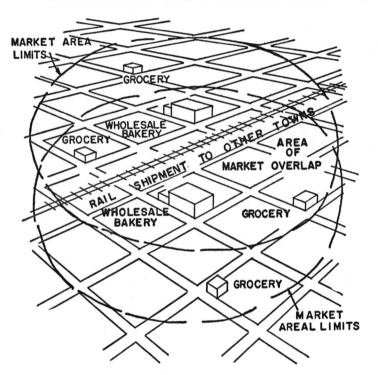

To this end the industrial baker embarked upon an entirely new experience. Unlike the retail baker, he had to distinguish his products from those of his competitors. Establishing a reputation for quality goods was an absolute necessity for getting repeat sales and increased market share. His first attempts represented a continuation of the earlier practice of branding his initials or trade-mark on the unwrapped loaves of bread. By the turn of the century he was making use of small labels affixed on the bread bearing trade-marks, prices or illustrations. He also advertised his products in local newspapers and magazines. Some enterprising bakers "rented space on the walls of buildings and advertised that their bread was on sale in places other than their own bakeries." [8] In experimenting with the tactics of direct competition, price-cutting was also used to promote sales. The technique of price manipulation was indeed quite simple and direct, but it often proved disastrous to the user; for with frightening regularity his competitors retaliated in kind, and a price war set in.

To a limited extent, other methods were also tried. Some bakers gave their customers secret discounts, probably in the belief that the price shadings would remain concealed. On occasion gifts and favors were passed out to grocers and their clerks in order to push the sale of the donor's bread. "Bread checks" good for a free loaf of bread were issued to housewives, and "jimcracks," story books and balloons were given to children.[9] Consignment selling also offered a unique method of competing for increased sales. Several enterprising bakers began displaying large quantities of bread in the grocery store—larger amounts than they actually expected to sell. They suffered a greater return of stale loaves, but they did so in the hopes that a larger display would suggest to the consumer that the bread had been delivered more recently and was, therefore, fresher. More aggressive bakers went a step further, installing glass cases, free of charge to the grocer, for a better display of their products.

It is important to note, however, that the use of these competitive tactics about 1900 was both limited in scope and experimental in nature. Not all wholesalers adopted them, and those who did, did so with little consistency; the typical baker was only partly aware of the changed competitive con-

---

[8] E. J. Sperry, "65 Years of Bakery Advertising," *Baking Industry Magazine*, XCVII (April 12, 1952), pp. 149-150.

[9] Letter to the author from Mr. W. E. Long, formerly of the W. E. Long Company, April 4, 1953.

ditions under which he operated. Moreover, he had not gained enough market experience to weigh their actual or potential effects. He did not know whether any one technique would prove successful, whether it would increase his share of the market, or how his competitors would react to it. He merely experimented with the competitive tactics available as he groped his way through the early experiences of industrial competition. The emergence of a definite pattern of competition had to await other advances in industrial baking after the turn of the century.

Contrast with Biscuit and Cracker Distribution

As wholesale bread distribution appeared, the biscuit and cracker bakers also began route deliveries to grocery stores. But by way of contrast, they were inaugurated via a different avenue and for different economic reasons. The biscuit and cracker bakers took on direct distribution only after a series of frustrating experiences with jobbers and wholesalers, who had secured a tight hold on the market before 1850. Through their superior contacts and ability to handle small accounts these distributors had maintained virtual control over the marketing of cracker goods. In the 'seventies and 'eighties they gained added strength. With improved rail transportation and a growing demand, cracker bakers had begun to penetrate one another's market area. In much the same way that wholesaling expanded the market area for bread bakers, such penetration extended the market for a single cracker baker to include the entire country. A baker was no longer able to call any particular market his own. A period of tense, cutthroat competition followed with bakers struggling to win the favor of the wholesalers.

In the hope of re-establishing stability and of gaining a better balance of power between buyers and sellers, the larger bakeries began to consolidate in the late 1880s. The principal plants in New England, New York, New Jersey, eastern Pennsylvania and Maryland joined together in a new concern, the New York

Biscuit Company. A number of large bakeries in the West and
South combined to form the American Biscuit and Manufacturing Company. Then followed the formation of the United
States Baking Company in western Pennsylvania and the Middle West, and the National Baking Company in Illinois and
Iowa.[10] Despite the mergers, however, the immediate situation
did not improve to any great extent. Competition to achieve
wholesale distribution still remained extremely severe.

Competition was not the only problem involved in selling
through wholesalers. For one thing, the biscuit and cracker
bakers, far removed from the final consumer, had no effective
sales appeal. In fact, their products were sold under the wholesalers' brands. Moreover, under the cumbersome machinery of
jobbing so much time elapsed between baking and consumption that it was very difficult to insure the freshness of the
crackers. The heyday of the open cracker barrel did not help
sales either. The bottom half of the barrel usually contained
soggy, broken crackers; and if the cat didn't sleep in the barrel, the mice did.

In 1898, as part of a far-reaching program to achieve a co-
ordinated system of production and distribution for biscuits
and crackers, the National Biscuit Company was formed by
merger of the previously merged companies and several other
smaller firms. Plants which were scattered all over the country
were brought into one huge firm—a firm so large that in its
first year of operation it had a sales volume amounting to
about 70 per cent of the entire industry.[11] While National Biscuit undoubtedly presented an effective counterbalance to
the dominant position of the wholesalers, its management
embarked upon an entirely new marketing program designed
to move closer to the consumer by selling direct to retailers.
This required national advertising and small unit packaging. Having devised a small container with an innerseal

10 Eggert, *op. cit.*
11 Personal communication from Mr. G. Tomlinson, Chairman of the Board,
National Biscuit Company (New York, New York), June 12, 1953.

wrapper for one of its soda cracker products, the company introduced it to the public with a carefully organized, direct advertising campaign centered around the now familiar name, "Uneeda Biscuit." [12] At the same time, N. B. C. began selling direct to the retail grocery and general stores through a system of route salesmen much as the bread bakers were doing. While the campaign was limited to a single product, its success was truly phenomenal.[13] Within a few years Uneeda Biscuit was a household name known to practically every man, woman and child in the nation. The cracker barrel was on its way out.

Although these changes in marketing were not fully realized in the industry until after the turn of the century, the National Biscuit Company had set the pattern for the future. Other biscuit and cracker firms tried to imitate not only the National Biscuit Company's methods, but their trade name as well. They tried such names as "I Wanta Cracker," "Taka Cracker," and "Hava Cracker," but with relatively little success. National Biscuit Company had been the first in its industry and among the first in the grocery field to take part in the fast growing national trend to direct retail delivery of a branded and nationally advertised product, and therefore gained the marketing initiative at the expense of its competitors.

As in most instances of radical departures from established patterns, it is altogether too easy to give the impression that the changes involved were far more sweeping than they were. In the biscuit and cracker industry it was clear that distributive changes had really just begun by the turn of the century. The transition to wholesale bread distribution is also illustrative of changes that were limited in their adoption.

Since large scale production was instrumental in providing the impetus to wholesale distribution, the bakers who turned

---

12 The development of the name "Uneeda Biscuit" is told in a remarkable series of letters written in 1898 and preserved by officials of the National Biscuit Company. Mr. Tomlinson, Chairman of the Board, was kind enough to put these letters at the author's disposal.

13 It was not until the 1930s that practically all products of the biscuit and cracker industry were made available in small unit packages.

to distributing through grocery stores were the same ones who had increased their plant capacities and decreased their unit costs by taking advantage of the improved methods of production. It was estimated that not more than 10 per cent of the nation's bakers were large-scale producers who accounted for approximately 25 per cent of total industry output. Another 10 per cent, perhaps, were doing some wholesaling, for many small-scale retail bakers did engage in a limited amount of grocery store trade. For that matter, most wholesale bakers continued retailing operations; it was not until after 1900 that the retail store disappeared from its place in front of the large-scale bakery.

Thus, even though wholesaling emerged as an integral part of the baking industry, some 75 per cent of commercial bakery products were still produced and distributed by the small craft shops in 1900. Demand limitations undoubtedly prevented an industry-wide adoption of wholesaling, but there is room for supposition that more bakers could easily have enlarged their businesses. Inertia was especially great in regard to distribution, for, as we have noted, most bakers were production men and not salesmen. Their craft traditions and prejudices may have been strong enough to deter them from changing their mode of operations.

CHAPTER | **6**

A SURVEY OF INDUSTRIAL GROWTH, 1850–1900

To UNDERSTAND the extent and nature of the great changes in the baking industry that had taken place in a half century, we must stop at 1900 and look about us—at the industrial scene in which the industry grew and at the growth of the industry itself.

During the half century ending in 1900, industrialism had advanced with mighty strides in the United States. The gains recorded by industry generally since 1850 were tremendous: the dollar value of products increased elevenfold, from $1 billion to over $11 billion; the value added by manufacture, tenfold, from $465 million to $4,869 million; and the number of wage earners, fivefold, from 961,000 to 4,703,000. In a real way Americans were confronted with a whole new world by 1900; industrialism had come of age.

In the broad sweep of industry growth the baking industry turned in a performance that was a creditable one, to say the least. Indeed, when compared with the whole setting in 1900, its growth more than matched the relative gains made by American industry in the five decades from 1850: the dollar value of bakery products rose from $13 million to $176 million, a thirteenfold jump; the value added by manufacture, from $5 million to $81 million, a sixteenfold increase; and the number of wage earners, from 6,727 to 60,192, a ninefold gain. The relative growth of the baking industry, compared to manufacturing as a whole, is shown in the table below:

TABLE 1

GROWTH OF THE BAKING INDUSTRY AS A PER CENT OF ALL
MANUFACTURING INDUSTRIES, CENSUS YEARS, 1849–1899 [a]

Census Year	Per Cent of Number of Establish- ments	Per Cent of Value of Product	Per Cent of Value Added by Manufacture	Per Cent of Average Number of Wage Earners
1849	1.65	1.30	1.06	0.70
1859	1.37	0.90	0.74	0.50
1869	1.41	0.87	0.84	0.69
1879	2.52	1.23	1.18	0.82
1889	2.95	1.37	1.33	0.91
1899[b]	7.15	1.54	1.66	1.28

[a] U. S. Census of Manufactures.
[b] Excluding neighborhood and hand trades.

In looking at the position of the industry at 1900, however, one must bear in mind that the rapid improvement in its status on the industrial scene was more than matched by that of other food processors, who, together with the baking industry, accounted for 20 per cent of the value of all manufactures in 1900 as against 15 per cent fifty years before. Among food processors, in fact, the baking industry had to give ground, falling from second to fourth place at the turn of the century.

Ahead of it, at this juncture, were meat packing, flour milling and sugar refining. Meat packing forged ahead of both baking and flour milling to lead the field among American food manufacturers. Sugar refining as early as 1860 had also bypassed the baking industry, which at that time was no match for this highly commercialized operation.

Now for a closer look at the baking industry itself.

TABLE 2

GROWTH OF THE BAKING INDUSTRY, A FEW KEY MEASURES,
CENSUS YEARS, 1849–1899 [a]

Census Year	Number of Establish- ments	Value of Product (000)	Value Added by Manufac- ture (000)	Average No. of Wage Earners
1849	2,027	$ 13,294	$ 4,927	6,727
1859 [b]	1,930	16,980	6,346	6,514
1869	3,550	36,908	14,696	14,126
1879	6,396	65,826	23,213	22,488
1889	10,484	128,422	55,914	38,841
1899	14,917	175,657	80,817	60,192

[a] U. S. Census of Manufactures. Data on both the perishable products, bakeries, and biscuit and cracker bakeries, are combined.

[b] That a few census measures for 1859 are listed as being less than similar measures for 1849 is due to the fact that the Census Bureau in 1859 made a less thorough canvass of the industry than in 1849. H. Kyrk and J. S. Davis, *The American Baking Industry,* 1849–1923, Miscellaneous Publication No. 2, Food Research Institute (Stanford, California: Stanford University Press, 1925), p. 24.

Manifestly, as the table reveals, the rate of growth turned in by the industry from decade to decade had been rather steady. Between 1860 and 1870 the industry more than doubled the value of its product, the value added by manufacture and the number of wage earners; the number of bakeries increased by 84 per cent. In the next decade the value of product and number of establishments jumped 80 per cent; the value added by manufacture and the number of wage earners, by more than 50 per cent. Growth during the 'eighties was even more impressive. Dollar value and value added by manufacture more than doubled, and the number of bakeries and employees rose by 70 per cent. Only in the decade ending in 1900 did the overall rate of growth begin to taper off.

These rates of growth reflected a truly phenomenal absolute

growth decade by decade, with the gains in each category becoming larger and larger. Between 1870 and 1880, for example, the payroll of the industry gained more than 8,400 new employees. In another decade the payroll was carrying an additional 16,400. In terms of value of product, the additions were correspondingly large: $36 million added in the 'seventies, and over $62.5 million in the following decade.

This tremendous growth was accompanied by a basic shift in the structure or make-up of the industry itself—that of the division of baking into two rather distinct parts, a small-scale retail segment and a large-scale wholesale segment. The break at 1900 was small, but clear-cut, nevertheless. It revealed two groups of bakers differing in almost every phase of the baking business.

The wholesale baker was an industrialized baker utilizing the latest equipment, concentrating on large volume bread production and operating on a factory basis. The retailer carried on his trade in the tradition of the craftsman of old, turning out a wide variety of handmade products. Less than ten per cent of the more than 14,000 bakeries could be classed as industrial bakers as we know the term today. But the typical industrial baker had annual sales of about $30,000; a few upwards of $200,000. The more numerous retail operators, on the other hand, probably averaged well under $5,000 a year.

What did this difference, $30,000 against $5,000, signify? First, that the wholesale baker had discovered the age of the machine which was to affect the working lives of both the baker and the housewife in a few short decades. Second, that the vast majority of his profession had yet to discard the ways of the handicraft baker. And one might add that their eventual abandonment did not come easy even when the logic of mechanization seemed inescapable.

At this juncture one final footnote should be added, perhaps, on the position of the biscuit and cracker bakers at the turn of the century. By this time, they accounted for approximately 30 per cent of total sales of both cracker and bread products.[1] Although their output was far less than that of the bread bakers, they were, nevertheless, a part of a highly mechanized industry, separate and distinct from the bread-baking industry. Cracker products were less perishable and characterized by more simplified production techniques than were bread, cakes, and pies. The industry therefore took on an entirely different structure from that of the bread industry. The history of the cracker bakers has been carried to the turn of the century to provide just such a contrast. Their story does not end here, but they have served their purpose of comparison to our main story—the development of bread baking.

---

[1] According to one of the officials of the National Biscuit Company, the company had an annual output around the turn of the century of $34 million, which represented approximately 70 per cent of the cracker industry sales. On the basis of these figures, the share of total industry accounted for by cracker bakeries becomes 28 per cent.

PART

THREE

THE DEVELOPMENT
OF INDUSTRIAL BAKING

1900–1930

CHAPTER 7

THE CHANGING PATTERN OF DEMAND

In 1900, only the most optimistic of prophets could have predicted the course that the baking industry was to take in three short decades. For here, an incredible growth took place that raised the industry to first place among food processors and made it a giant on the American industrial scene. This change—a change which, as we shall see, transformed both the kitchen and the bakeshop—did not come about abruptly. It could not. For it depended upon three things. First, the change in the pattern of demand. Second, the triumph of mass production. And third, the coming of the automobile age and mass distribution. All these had to come slowly, by degrees, each reinforcing the others. To tell this story, to trace each major development in detail, will be the task of the next three chapters. To begin, there was the all important matter of demand.

The Housewife Consents

No such startling change in the industry could have taken place without the consent of the housewife. Before 1900, as we have seen, more and more home-makers had begun to depend upon the baker for their family bread. To be sure, widespread acceptance of the baker's loaf, at the turn of the century, was still largely urban in character. But that perfect symbol of kitchen talent—a good loaf—had lost its glamor in many American homes.

With the spread of urban living after 1900, that symbol became more unattractive. In that year, less than four families out of ten lived in towns of 2,500 or more. The world for more than 60 per cent of American families was a rural affair. By 1930, however, a little less than 45 per cent of the people lived on the farm. More than 38 million people had been added to the urban population since 1900. In the shift, the home loaf went the way of the long skirt.

Associated with urban living were other changes, bearing the label of the 20th century, that pulled millions of American women out of their accustomed environment and gave them new ways of spending their day. The advent of the automobile, for example, ended the isolation in the home. Even for the farm wife, it brought the kitchen and the grocery counter closer together. The movies, radio, and phonograph as well as the increased role of social activities in the city brought further competition for the time of the housewife and her family. City apartment and tenement buildings with their lack of adequate kitchen facilities and space contributed more directly to a decline in home baking. Moreover, urbanization was associated with smaller sized families. For the nation as a whole, family size fell some 14 per cent between 1900 and 1930, with the decline being more pronounced among urban dwellers.[1] In keeping with the changing patterns, more women were also taking jobs. World War I was especially important in this respect. By 1930, married women accounted for about 12 per cent of the nation's labor force.[2] That represented a real gain over 1900, when roughly 5 per cent were so employed. To these examples one could add many more, all of which contributed to the trend toward commercially baked foods.

A survey made in 1922 of 3,000 urban and farm families gives a more precise picture of the relation between urbanization

---

[1] Statistical Abstract of the United States, p. 24.
[2] Historical Abstract of the United States: 1789–1945, *op. cit.,* p. 63.

and baking in the home. Farm families baked 94 per cent of their bread; in towns of 5,000 or less the proportion was 56 per cent; in centers of 5,000 to 25,000 inhabitants, 49 per cent; and in cities of 25,000 or more, the figure was 35 per cent.[3] This sample is confirmed by later census data. The ten most heavily populated states in 1929, while containing about half of the total population and two-thirds of the urban population, accounted for 72 per cent of the sales of the baking industry.

Higher incomes, too, had sparked the change in demand, for the American public had more to spend on comforts and conveniences. For instance, between 1900 and 1930, per capita income increased approximately 37 per cent.[4] With greater income, most families could easily ignore the extra cost of bakers' bread, which ran between two to five cents per loaf higher than the home-made product.[5] According to one survey, made of a middle income group in Chicago in 1924, the higher the income the better the customer for the baker. The upper third of this group, so the survey reveals, bought all their bread; about half of the middle third did also; and about 40 per cent of the lower third.[6]

By 1930, for the first time in the history of baking, commercial bakeries surpassed the home as the source of the nation's bread, supplying over 60 per cent of all bread consumed.

The Baker Takes a Hand

The bakers themselves played an active role in the shift from home to commercial baking by improving their product and making it more attractive and readily available to purchasers. This was no small accomplishment. According to one observer,

---

[3] Carl L. Alsberg, *Combination in the American Bread Baking Industry,* Food Research, Institute Miscellaneous Publication No. 3 (Stanford University, Calif.: Stanford University Press, 1926), p. 29.

[4] Robert F. Martin, *National Income in the United States, 1799–1938* (New York: National Industrial Conference Board, 1939), pp. 6 ff. Income is expressed in 1926 dollars.

[5] Margaret G. Reid, *Food for People* (New York: John Wiley and Sons, Inc., 1943), p. 143.

[6] "Study of the Flour and Baking Industries in the United States," *op. cit.,* Appendix, p. 3.

the typical urban home-maker at the turn of the century held
a none too favorable attitude toward bakers' bread.

> In the first place no baker ever knew how to make a loaf of
> bread. In the second place I can save about a penny a loaf
> making it myself. And in the third place, women who go
> running out to bakeshops are lazy no-goods who don't care
> anything about the health of their families. And, what is
> more, everybody knows them for what they are.[7]

Such an attitude suggests that before the baker could expect
a wider acceptance of his bread, he would have to convince
potential buyers that his loaf was as good or better than the
home-made loaf, that it was produced and distributed under
sanitary conditions, and that it was worth the extra pennies in
cost.

As a matter of fact, although few housewives in 1900 would
admit it, the quality of bakers' bread was at least equal to the
home-made loaf. Both contained essentially the same ingredients, but it is likely that the commercial baker maintained a
closer control over the baking process and, as a result, produced
a more uniform product. Over the next thirty years, the bakers'
advantage in this respect gradually became more pronounced.
With the widespread use of commercial yeast and uniform types
of flour and further perfection of machine handling of ingredients, bakery production became more routine and more reliable. The craftsman's art gave way to the precision of the bakery
engineer, and the housewife was hard put to match it.

The conditions under which baking was done and the product distributed were different matters, however. That they were
deplorable even the most ardent of baking apostles would
agree. They were indefensible, in fact. Bakeries were seldom
kept free from dirt and grime. Pest control was unheard of
and rats and mice were left to the skills of the bakery cat.

In 1902, New York sanitary inspectors reported that condi-

---

[7] Robert J. Casey, *Chicago Medium Rare* (Indianapolis: Bobbs-Merrill Book Co.,
1949), p. 107.

tions in their city were "beyond description."[8] Under such circumstances, it is not remarkable that a number of newspapers began to campaign vigorously for reform. As late as 1910, one enterprising editor, more zealous than accurate, charged that bread labels were being "licked with saliva."[9] While this particular canard was false, it is illustrative of the kind of press the baker of that day enjoyed.

Such was the temper of the times that leaders of the industry took up the fight for reform. The National Association of Master Bakers, forerunner of the American Bakers Association, was their forum. Organized in 1897, the Master Bakers led the crusade. Sanitation was a foremost topic on the agenda of their convention in 1901. Several speakers highlighted cleanliness as an avenue to larger and larger sales. A paper on the "Economical Methods of Keeping Bakeries Clean" was presented at the 1902 convention, and cleanliness became a recurring theme in later meetings of the association. Finally, in 1912, the convention adopted a standard sanitary code and made plans to cooperate with local public health officials for its enforcement.

Nonetheless, improvements within the bakeries themselves were not enough to allay the suspicions of consumers. Some means of protecting bread through the channels of distribution had to be devised if it was to be delivered to the consumer in wholesome condition.

A few bakers, as early as 1895, had begun to solve this problem of handwrapping bread in wax paper and tying the loaf with string. But the cost delayed widespread use of wrapping for a decade or more. As one baking industry veteran recalled: "when I came into the Baking Industry (in the early 1900's), I found . . . bakers' bread, unwrapped, unidentified, nondescript, . . . being produced and carted around to stores and homes with no regard for sanitation or pride of ownership." [10]

---

[8] *Baking Industry Magazine*, XCVII (April 12, 1952), p. 64.

[9] George N. Graf, "The Years Teach Much Which the Days Never Know," *Baking Industry Magazine*, XCVII (April 12, 1952), p. 197.

[10] W. E. Long, "Solving the Bakers' Advertising and Merchandising Problems," *Bakers' Helper*, April 17, 1937, p. 782.

But with the development of automatic machinery, wrapping after 1913 became general throughout the industry. The bakers did not let their efforts go unannounced. Their advertising brought home the point to consumers.

> So securely wrapped in neat waxed paper that it's impossible to find on it a particle of dust or a thumb or finger print.
>
> Wrapped in my bakery and not touched by anybody's hands from the time it leaves the bakery until you get it home.
>
> Placed in a Moisture-Proof, Germ-Proof, Dust-Proof, Waxed Paper Cover, Automatically Wrapped and Reaches you with all of its Original Freshness, Purity, and Cleanliness.[11]

Even the retail bakers, who sold from their own shops, took steps to make consumers aware of their precautions to provide a clean loaf. One common practice was the placing of a reel oven in the window of the bakeshop so that the public could see for themselves how the baking was carried on.

Industrial bakers also directed advertising campaigns to convince purchasers that home baking was not all it was cracked up to be. About 1908 this was the nature of their appeal:

> It's worry and work to bake at home.
>
> Take care of the Young ones in this weather and leave the baking to us.
>
> Your wife can run your household ever so much easier, more economically, and with infinitely less friction and domestic infelicity if you will only insist upon her buying our bread.
>
> Hot kitchen, exhausted patience with indifferent results— that's home baking.
>
> Can you make better clothes than your tailor? Then why try to bake your own bread?
>
> That pain in your stomach is frequently caused by eating sour and soggy bread.[12]

---

[11] E. J. Sperry, "65 Years of Bakery Advertising," *Baking Industry*, April 12, 1952, p. 156.

[12] *Ibid.*, pp. 154-155.

In publicizing the advantages of commercially baked bread, most bakers did not neglect to call attention to the particular qualities of their own product by brand advertising, which began as early as 1904 and became simpler through the growing practice of wrapping. It helped put bakers' bread on a par with other well known manufactured products which purchasers were accustomed to ask for by name. Undoubtedly, many a housewife gave up baking in the home because of a growing familiarity with the quality of particular brands.

World War I was particularly important in giving bakers an opportunity to capture more of the home baking market. As a part of the wartime effort to conserve food, the government inaugurated a program of controlling the nation's food supply. The grains, especially wheat, were of the utmost importance to the program. Mondays and Wednesdays were "Wheatless Days"; bakers and the public were asked to use "mixed flours" made of 75 per cent wheat and 25 per cent corn, rye, oats, and barley. The use of substitute flours required several adjustments in formulas and bread making processes and increased the difficulties of making a palatable loaf of bread. With their greater knowledge of and control over baking, bakers were better equipped than the housewife to turn out a satisfactory product. This fact was made known by no less an authority than the United States government when, as a part of the effort to avoid waste, the Food Administration urged people to buy bakers' bread.

> In the actual baking operations, there is very little waste in commercial bakeries. Their formulas are well worked out, the amount of ingredients accurately standardized, the temperature is regulated, the period of fermentation under control, the heat of the ovens properly maintained and very few batches go wrong.[13]

No doubt many housewives, discouraged by their lack of baking success, bought rather than baked their "Victory Bread" and soon became accustomed to purchasing their bread needs.

---

[13] Alonzo E. Taylor, *War Bread* (New York: The Macmillan Co., 1918), p. 95.

40 143

The Demand for Commercially Baked Variety Goods

At the time that the commercial bakers were capturing a large share of the bread market, cakes, pies, pastry, and cookies were becoming a significant part of bakery production. Unlike bread, however, the increased demand for such goods was the result of both a rising per capita consumption and a decline in home baking.

Increased consumption of luxury bake stuffs was part of a broad change in food habits generally. After 1900, there was a marked trend in America toward a more varied diet including, among other things, an increase in the consumption of desserts. By 1930, the per capita consumption of canned fruit had risen from 3.8 pounds in 1910 to 15.8 pounds; ice cream from 1.2 pounds in 1906 to 15.6 pounds, and sugar and syrup from 34 pounds in 1909 to 123 pounds. Specific information on the per capita consumption of variety baked foods is lacking, but even on a conservative basis, it probably doubled between 1900 and 1930.

The baker, of course, benefited from this trend only to the extent that he shared with the housewife in the baking of sweet bake goods. The very nature of these products made it difficult to effect a larger transfer from the home to the bakery. For long after the average housewife willingly served bakery bread, she continued to take pride in the quality of her cakes and pies. Compared to bread, these items took much less of her time and offered a greater opportunity to save money. Furthermore, individual tastes played an important role in keeping the baking of variety goods in the home. The commercial baker was limited by necessity to the production of a relatively few varieties which he hoped would have a wide appeal; nevertheless, between 1900 and 1930, he increased his share of total sweet goods production from roughly 10 per cent to an estimated 20 to 25 per cent.

But even this modest decline in home baking coupled with a rising population and an increasing per capita consumption of sweet goods provided a significant addition to the bakers' demand. Bread still remained the bakers' most important product, but measured in percentages of total industry volume, variety baked goods accounted for 35 per cent in 1930 compared to 30 per cent thirty years earlier. (Cf. Table 1)

The increased demand for baked foods other than bread did provide a broader base for commercial baking. Bakery operations became more diversified and specialized. Wholesale bread bakers, for example, were able to offer grocers a limited amount of variety goods which lent themselves to machine production methods. These included doughnuts, cup cakes, cakes, and pies. The demand for these goods was sufficient to permit some bakers to specialize in supplying a single line of sweet goods such as cakes or pies. In addition, it provided for the development of bakeries especially catering to the needs of the home delivery market and the institutional trade, formerly serviced by bakers selling to grocery stores. Even the retail bakers, both single and multi-unit, became specialists, in a sense, supplying the demands of those who wanted to select from the widest variety of baked goods available.

Declining Per Capita Consumption of Bread

It is paradoxical that the emergence of the modern baking industry in the United States occurred at the same time that the public was decreasing its per capita consumption of bread. This trend occurred as part of a broad change in American food habits, a change which bakers themselves were generally slow to recognize.

In contrast to the last half of the 19th century, Americans did not increase their total food intake after 1900. By that time, the limits of the average citizen to increase his consumption of food had apparently been reached. As shown in Chart 1, the total amount of food consumed by each individual varied by no more than 50 pounds around an average of 1560 pounds for the 1909–1930 period.

TABLE 1

PRODUCT BREAKDOWN OF PERISHABLE BAKERY PRODUCTS PRODUCERS
CENSUS YEARS, 1923–1929 [a]

Product Class	Millions of Dollars				% of Total Value			
	1923	1925	1927	1929	1923	1925	1927	1929
Bread, Rolls, and Yeast Raised Sweet Goods	630.7	729.9	803.3	849.8	69.2	71.3	70.1	67.9
Cakes, Pastry and Doughnuts	189.8[b]	206.8	259.0	299.1	20.8	20.2	22.6	23.9
Pies	76.4[c]	68.6	69.9	83.9	8.4	6.7	6.1	6.7
Other Perishable Products	8.2	7.2	5.7	13.8	0.9	0.7	0.5	1.1
Biscuits and Crackers	6.0	12.3	8.0	5.0	0.7	1.1	0.7	0.4
TOTAL	911.1	1023.7	1145.9	1251.6	100.0	100.0	100.0	100.0

ᵃ Percentages of total value were computed from Census of Manufactures "products" data for the "Bread and Other Bakery Products" industry. Since not all firms reported a product breakdown, these same percentages were applied to the total value of product of the industry on the assumption that these non-reporting firms had the same average product mix as those reporting a breakdown. As a result, the importance of bread and other yeast-raised products is probably overstated since most non-reporting firms were, very likely, small retailers who produce a high per-centage of non-yeast sweet goods. The percentages of the total value of product of the industry accounted for by those firms which did supply a breakdown of total value by products given in the census of manufactures or computed from it were 79.3% in 1923, 81.1% in 1925, 86.2% in 1927, and 89.5% in 1929.

ᵇ Does not include the value of output of pastry which was included with "pies" in the 1923 Census of Manufactures.

ᶜ Includes the value of output of pastry.

CHART 1

PER CAPITA CONSUMPTION OF ALL FOODS, 1909–1930*

POUNDS

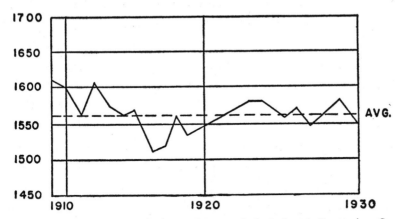

* U. S. Department of Agriculture, Bureau of Agricultural Economics, *Con-sumption of Food in the United States, 1909–52,* Agricultural Handbook No. 62 (Washington: Government Printing Office, September, 1953), pp. 137, 138, 144.

While the average quantity of food did not vary during these years, there was, nevertheless, a marked change in the composition of the items that went into the diet. Compared with the staple fare of the early 1900's, with its emphasis on bread, meat, potatoes, milk, with occasional additions of fresh fruits and vegetables, the typical diet thirty years later contained a much larger proportion of fruits, vegetables and dairy products. Table 2 illustrates the changing food pattern of the nation between 1909 and 1930.

The largest decline came in the low cost, high energy-yielding foods, chiefly potatoes and wheat flour. The annual consumption of potatoes showed a sharp decline from 202 pounds per capita in 1909 to 141 pounds in 1930, a drop of about 30 per cent. Per capita consumption of wheat flour, which stood at 210 pounds in 1909, fell to 165 pounds by 1930, a decline of about 21 per cent. Between 1900 and 1930, it decreased some 26 per cent, from 225 pounds to 165 pounds.

Figures on the per capita consumption of bread are unfor-

TABLE 2

PER CAPITA CONSUMPTION OF FOOD GROUPS AND MAJOR
INDIVIDUAL FOODS IN POUNDS, 1909 AND 1930[a]

	Lbs. per capita 1909	Lbs. per capita 1930	Difference between 1909 and 1930	
			lbs.	%
All Dairy Products[b]	360[d]	376	+ 16	+ 4%
Milk	262[d]	269	+ 7	+ 3
All Grain Products	295	226	− 69	− 23
Wheat Flour	210	165	− 45	− 21
Potatoes	202	141	− 61	− 30
Meat, Poultry, and Fish	175	151	− 24	− 14
Beef	58	38	− 20	− 34
Vegetables (except potatoes)	258	285	+ 27	+ 10
Tomatoes	44	43	. . . .	. . . .
Leafy Vegetables	63	103	+ 40	+ 63
Other Vegetables	150	130[d]	− 20	− 13
Fruits	131	148[d]	+ 17	+ 13
Citrus	15	34[d]	+ 19	+ 127
Apples	62[d]	38	− 24	− 35
Other Fruits	60	71	+ 11	+ 18
Sugar	73	108	+ 41	+ 56
Fats and Oils[c]	40	47	+ 7	+ 17%
Total Consumption of Above-listed Foods	1534[e]	1488[e]	. . . .	. . . .

[a] U. S. Department of Agriculture, Bureau of Agricultural Economics, *Consumption of Food in the United States, 1909–52*, Agricultural Handbook No. 62 (Washington: Government Printing Office, September, 1953), pp. 137, 138, 144.

[b] Excluding butter.

[c] Including butter but excluding bacon and salt side.

[d] These figures are not the actual figures but the trend values which have been used to give a more realistic picture of the changes involved.

[e] Represents over 95 per cent of total per capita food consumption in each of the years 1909 and 1930.

tunately not available and so must be inferred from those on wheat flour, the principal raw material of baking. The inference is a difficult one, however, for wheat flour statistics do not tell the whole story. For one thing, high speed mixing and formulas rich in milk, sugar, and shortening had raised the bread yields obtained from flour. One hundred pounds of flour in

1909 yielded an estimated 137.5 pounds of bread; by 1930, it produced over 150 pounds.[14] In addition, there is reason to believe that the utilization of flour by bakers was more efficient and subject to less wastage than that of the housewife; because of the rapid decline in home baking, the apparent decline in bread consumption may therefore be somewhat fictitious. On the other hand, since it is generally agreed that variety baked foods were being consumed in greater quantities by each person between 1900 and 1930, more and more flour was being diverted to their production. Furthermore, the increased use of stale returns as a competitive device may have increased the total amount of bread wastage.

Although these scanty data afford no direct answer, it is difficult to avoid the conclusion that the average American was eating less bread in the three decades following 1900. It is clear that the decline was not so great as that of flour, but bread consumption did face a loss of perhaps 10 per cent.[15]

With the exception of meat, poultry, and fish, all other food groups exhibited an increase in per capita consumption.[16] The major trend was clearly toward more expensive and varied foods such as fruits, especially citrus fruits, sugar and leafy vegetables.

These changes between 1900 and 1930 were primarily the result of increased family incomes. In meeting their energy requirements, people found that they could afford to substitute more expensive and varied foods for the low cost, high calorie staples. Thus one of the very factors which helped bring bread making out of the home and into the bakery was, at the same time, causing people to eat less bread.

The change in food buying habits was also accelerated by

---

[14] Arthur T. Joyce, "America's Changing Food Habits," *Bakers' Weekly,* September 17, 1954, p. 4.

[15] The assumption of a 10 per cent decline in the per capita consumption of bread should not be construed as an exact figure. The debate over the relationship between the figures on flour consumption and those of bread will wax hot for a long time. This study of the baking industry does not pretend to present anything more than the author's opinion.

[16] The decline in meats was, in fact, reversed after 1930 and has since risen above its per capita consumption value at the turn of the century.

an increased availability of fruits and vegetables. In terms of both quantity and quality, these foods became more abundant between 1900 and 1930. In 1900, the great national traffic in fruits and vegetables was in its infancy. Thirty years later, with better packing, grading, and inspection, control of temperature in transit, fast freight trains, and on-schedule deliveries, the marketing of these goods had assumed tremendous proportions. In addition, machine developments in the canning industry made available higher quality preserved fruits and vegetables at lower prices.

Vitamins and Minerals

While rising income was the major factor in the changing American diet, its effect was strengthened by forces that had both a scientific and emotional basis.

At the turn of the century, dieticians recognized only protein and calories as nutritional elements. In 1898, Dr. Wilber O. Atwater, one of the nation's leading nutritionists, declared:

> Fruits add little to the food value of the diet, although they undoubtedly are valuable for other reasons. . . . Wheat flour in the form of bread, macaroni, etc., is one of the most nutritious and at the same time cheapest foods.[17]

Within a few decades, however, the importance of minerals to human nutrition began to be understood. Calcium was found to be essential for bone development, iron for blood formation, phosphorus for the building and upkeep of bones and teeth and for generally regulating all body processes. The role of vitamins in the diet became more widely recognized with the discovery of Vitamin B in 1911 and Vitamin A in 1913. Fruits and vegetables were found to be the richest source of both minerals and vitamins.

Public attention was forcefully drawn to these new discoveries during World War I, when the United States Food Ad-

---

[17] Office of Experiment Stations, *Dietary Studies in Chicago, 1895 and 1896,* Bulletin No. 55 (1898), p. 72, cited in Reid, *op. cit.,* p. 184.

ministration urged the nation to eat more fruits and leafy vegetables, not only to conserve less perishable flour, meat, butter, and sugar (which could be shipped overseas), but to protect and improve the nation's health.

Following the war, and with the discovery of two more vitamins, C and D, the campaign for a "balanced diet" was carried on over a wide front: by women's magazines, in the schools, by agents of the Department of Agriculture, doctors and nurses, public health services, and welfare agencies. While the gap between the best nutritional advice and food habits was frequently wide, the high praise of fresh fruits and vegetables no doubt contributed to their increased prominence in the average diet.

Agitation to change diets was not always confined to the limits of scientific knowledge. There were many Americans who willingly accepted the claims of faddists that a particular food or foods held the key to health and happiness. As *Fortune Magazine* has observed, "More food notions flourish in the United States than in any other civilized country on earth, and most of them are wrong. The fearful United States adult is forever receptive to new trick systems of eating."[18] And in the opinion of one prominent nutritionist:

> There is no field of practical importance related to human well-being in which there is greater opportunity for dogmatism and quackery for pseudoscience and unwarranted prescriptions and proscriptions than in the domain of our daily diet.[19]

Among food faddists, white bread had long been a favorite "whipping boy." Despite the fact that since the days of Rome people preferred baked goods made from white flour, and the whiter the better, food faddists insisted that white bread should be eliminated from the diet. In a back-to-nature theme, they proclaimed that whole wheat bread was the superior bread.

"Artificial" bleaching of flour, introduced about 1904, was

---

[18] "The Wonders of the Diet," *Fortune*, May, 1936, p. 86.
[19] L. B. Mendel, "The Changing Diet of the American People," *Journal of the American Medical Association*, XCIX (July 9, 1932), p. 120.

hailed by the food faddists as proof of the poor qualities of white flour and bread. Some went so far as to claim that white bread was poisonous. Actually, the Alsop bleaching process for white flour achieved, in a few hours, what had formerly been produced only after months of storage.[20] It had no effect on the quality or nutritive content of the flour, but it appeared at a time when there was a general agitation against adulteration, mislabeling, and chemical treating of foods. The passage of the Food and Drug Act of 1906 was one result of this general clamor.

It took a Superior Court decision and a ruling by the Department of Agriculture to silence the critics of bleached flour. The government held that the Alsop process was not in any way injurious to people's health, although all bleached flour entering into interstate commerce had to be marked as such.

With the discovery of vitamins and minerals, the food faddists were given ammunition for a renewed attack upon white bread. As practical means of "enriching" bread with these elements was still to be discovered, the bakers were not in a very good position to defend their product. The flour milling process largely removed the wheat germ and bran (or husks) in which the mineral and vitamin content of wheat is chiefly centered; probably not more than a quarter of the nutritive value of wheat remained in the flour. On the other hand, some of this nutritious loss is fictitious because the bran is poorly digested by the human body and, consequently, the calcium, phosphorus, and iron of whole wheat are poorly utilized.[21]

All things considered, it is doubtful whether the nutritional difference between whole wheat and white bread warranted the extravagant claims frequently made for the former, and it is also doubtful whether these criticisms of white bread had

---

[20] Storck and Teague, op. cit., p. 303.

[21] The protein of whole wheat flour also has lower digestibility; this may also be true of the carbohydrates which supply the calories, although there are conflicting findings on this point. Bran is actually irritating to the digestive tract of some people so that it is impossible for them to consume whole wheat bread. See American Medical Association, Handbook of Nutrition (New York: The Blakiston Co., 1951), pp. 621-673.

any significant effects on consumption. As far as encouraging people to consume whole wheat bread was concerned, they had little effect whatever. Whole wheat flour sales remained at no more than 2 or 3 per cent of total flour production. Armed with the knowledge that fruits and vegetables provided their needed minerals and vitamins, most persons continued to enjoy white bread.

Probably a much greater influence on the consumption of bread after World War I was the concern over body weight. The age of the flapper with its "straight line" look, led to an outburst of dieting on the part of women. Considerations of health also started a trend away from starchy, high calorie foods. Excess weight had become a matter of increasing concern for many Americans. The mortality experience of life insurance companies showed that excess body weight was closely correlated with a reduction in life expectancy, and doctors generally began to advise their patients to pay careful attention to their scales.

Because bread was considered essentially an energy producing, high-calorie food, it was excluded from most reducing diets. This exclusion was often carried to an extreme and only corrected later when it was recognized that bread had a part in a balanced diet.

In keeping with the general concern over health, fancied or otherwise, producers of fruits, vegetables, and dairy products undertook well marshalled advertising campaigns which tended to convey the impression that they offered the major roads to healthful living. It is easy to overestimate the effect this advertising had on dietary habits, but the impact of its appeal cannot be ignored.

Marketing cooperatives were among the earliest food processors to catch the public eye. The California Fruit Growers Exchange, founded in 1907, began almost immediately to make "Sunkist" a household word. The California Associated Raisin Company, a few years later, did the same for *Sun Maid* Raisins.

These organizations were soon joined by others including the Florida Citrus Exchange and the Dairymen's League.

The co-ops used newspapers, magazines, posters, and the newly discovered radio. They flooded teachers, doctors, food editors, and social workers with nutritional advice. Their advertising themes appealed to health and appetite. Sun Maid Raisins were coupled with the slogan "Have you had your iron today?" The vitamin and rich calorie content of oranges was widely proclaimed by both the Florida Citrus Exchange and the California Fruit Growers Exchange. While particular brands were highlighted, much of this advertising was effective in getting people to eat more oranges or lemons or raisins or to drink more milk.

By the 1920's, processors of most other food products had accepted this new challenge to their market position. Meat packers, cereal millers, sugar refiners, and beverage manufacturers all joined the battle for a larger share of the consumer's food dollar. In 1929, food and beverage manufacturers spent more for newspaper space than any other group except the drug and toilet goods sellers, and more for radio time than any group other than the makers of radio and musical instruments.[22]

The nation's bakers lagged far behind on the advertising front. To a great extent, their battle was fought by their suppliers, who quickly recognized the dangerous effects of a decline in the general consumption of bread. In 1913, the Fleischmann Yeast Company began their "Eat More Bread" campaign which they publicized widely for several decades. They featured a Department of Agriculture statement: "Measured by actual nutritive power, there is no other complete ration which can compare with bread."[23] The Washburn-Crosby Company, producers of Gold Medal Flour, in 1923 started their "Eat More Wheat" campaign which was officially endorsed by the Millers' National Federation. Many bakers were encouraged to use the slogan in connection with their own brand adver-

---

[22] Cummings, *op. cit.*, p. 156.
[23] *Baking Industry Magazine*, April 12, 1952, p. 328.

tising. In the late 1920's the American Institute of Baking campaigned on an "Eat More Toast" program featuring the slogan "Make Toast Your Breakfast Food." They went further and enlisted the cooperative advertising of producers of butter, jam, jelly, and meat.

That bakers were slow to appreciate the decline in the per capita consumption of bread stemmed largely from the record growth of their industry between 1900 and 1930. It was the heyday of the industry, the "Golden Era" of baking, in which the demand for baked foods seemed never-ending. Demand for all commercially baked goods resulted in a 600 per cent increase in output as population rose by 60 per cent and as home bread making fell to 40 per cent of total bread consumption. These factors were more than enough to offset an approximate 10 per cent decline in per capita bread consumption. In addition, bakers enjoyed a significantly increased call for variety products.

It is not surprising, therefore, that the typical baker in 1930 was not unduly concerned about the broad changes in food habits and that he was concerned primarily with the competition from the housewife and rival bakers. "The 'Old' baking business never felt it had much to worry about—it just continued to live off the existing demand," George Graf observed. "As an industry it never felt the necessity for fighting for a market." [24]

It was apparent, however, that one day they would come to recognize that they "must militantly fight for markets competing with other groups for a reasonable share of the food dollar." [25]

---

[24] "Graf Attacks Complacency in Facing Decline in Baked Foods Consumption," *Bakers Weekly,* July 5, 1954, p. 53, reporting a speech by George Graf, Director of Quality Bakers of America Cooperative, Inc., before the Metropolitan Bakery Production Club of New York.
[25] *Ibid.*

CHAPTER 8

THE TRIUMPH OF TECHNOLOGY

IT WOULD HAVE BEEN impossible to satisfy the demand of the American public for commercially baked goods, between 1900 and 1930, without mass production. What Ford had done for the automobile industry, bakers had to do for their own industry, for two facts had caught up with them. One was that Americans wanted not only cheaper bread, but better bread. The other fact was that the housewife looked to the bake shop—and not to her own kitchen—to meet this demand. The situation gave the baking industry a tremendous lift from World War I. The result was breathtaking; the volume of production was terrific.

As early as 1900, the seeds had been sown for the new look of the industry. Although crude, by modern standards, the machine age had overtaken the bread bakers. They had learned to build machines for mixing, dividing, and moulding. They had converted their ovens to continuous firing. But they still had a long way to go. Mechanical equipment, for one thing, was lacking for the fermentation, rounding, and several proofing stages of the baking process. For another, baking had not yet been put on an assembly line. Its use was an old one for flour millers. Meat packers, too, had applied the principle to their operations.

From 1900, the baking industry began to catch up, first by

improved models of older equipment and, second, by a series of new inventions. The result of these developments was an integrated flow of production, which, for all practical purposes, revolutionized the industry.

Flour and Dough Handling Equipment

It had been discovered shortly before the turn of the century that moving the dough directly from the divider to the moulder resulted in a generally poor quality loaf of bread. To correct for this defect, bakers found that the dough pieces had to be "rounded-up" and then subjected to a ten or fifteen minute intermediate proofing period before being moulded into shape for baking. Rounding was necessary to give each piece of dough a skin or coating in order to retain the gases generated during the fermentation period. Proofing was necessary to give the dough a chance to recover from the punishment received in the divider.

At the turn of the century these operations were performed by hand and formed the basis of what was termed the "missing link" in bakery mechanization.[1] About 1906–1907 the "missing link" was completed, at least in crude forms, when B. Howard Smith of the Smith Baking Company, Kansas City, working with Fred Wolff, introduced a rounder and proofer. At the same time, William Fisch of the Highland Bakery, Birmingham, Alabama, devised and patented similar inventions.

The early rounding machines consisted of a long traveling leather apron against which a moulding board operated backward and forward, gently pressing and kneading the dough pieces, thus pulling a skin over them. By this method each dough piece received twelve kneadings over the length of the machine, the action having effects similar to those obtained by hand work. Connected with the rounder was the overhead proofer, a belt conveyor which carried the rounded dough

---

[1] Albright, "Bread Making Machinery," *op. cit.*, XCVII (April 12, 1952), p. 117.

pieces up near the ceiling where the warm air helped the dough to recover.

Over the succeeding years, rounding and proofing equipment improved by better engineering and design. Rounders, for example, were made more compact and incorporated a circular design and principle of operation much like those in use today. The dough piece now traveled spirally within a dough race over a revolving surface in such a way that all parts of it were exposed to the revolving surface. By this action, the dough received a uniform rounding. The revolving surface was variously shaped, sometimes in the form of a bowl or cone, sometimes like an umbrella, or even a drum. Each design proved popular and met with widespread acceptance.

The original overhead belt-driven proofer was modified shortly after 1907 with the addition of cups or trays to carry the rounded dough balls. Some machines also substituted a chain drive for the belt drive. By 1920, the entire overhead conveyor had been enclosed in a housing to protect the dough from dust, dirt, and air drafts. Since the proofer constituted one of the links between the divider and the moulder, the necessity of synchronizing its rate of travel with speeds of these units was obvious. By 1930, this was being accomplished with the use of a variable speed drive or transmission which permitted the regulation of proofing time within close limits.

For smaller plants of limited overhead space, box type proofers were designed. The first such proofer, introduced about 1910, was a revolving square case containing several sets of drawers which held the dough pieces. Suspended on a vertical shaft, it could be rotated to face either the rounder or the moulder where the dough pieces were hand received or hand fed. Later models eliminated all mechanical features, being simply enclosed floor cabinets where the dough could be stored during the short proofing period.

While the early development of rounders and proofers was a great step forward, two make-up operations, by far the most critical in the entire baking process, did not lend themselves to machine techniques. These were the fermentation and final proofing stages of dough preparation. Fermentation required over three hours time and proofing almost one hour, thereby imposing unique production requirements on baking procedure. Moreover, the fermentation process had to be carried out in multiple units because of limitations in the size of the dough batch that could be effectively fermented.

Prior to 1900, most bakers gave little attention to special equipment for fermentation and final proofing. After the dough was mixed, it was simply dumped into several wooden troughs and allowed to ferment, exposed to dust and dirt, and undesirable temperature and humidity conditions.[2] It was not unusual to have batches go wrong or to find dough that contained splinters and paint chips from the wooden troughs.

The final or pan-proof, as it is now called, was handled in much the same way. From the moulder, the dough pieces were placed in heavy steel pans which were then loaded on wooden racks and wheeled away. Again there was no attempt to provide for proper conditions under which the dough could be proofed.

Some bakers built separate fermentation and proofing rooms in an attempt to provide a better dough environment, but there was no attempt at what could be called controlled conditions.

Not until World War I were proper atmospheric conditions for dough rooms and proof rooms attained. After experimenting for several years, J. C. Gordon, President of the Gordon Baking Company, developed an air conditioning unit which represents the first known system of temperature and humidity control in dough rooms. While little is known of the details of his unit, it was probably not unlike those used in the middle 1920's. At that time the typical dough room was a pre-fabricated unit equipped with a humidifier

---

[2] In the sponge dough method used by most bakers at that time, two fermentation periods were necessary, a preliminary one after mixing a part of the dough ingredients and a second one after the sponge and remaining ingredients were mixed.

and a series of coils through which water was circulated. The humidifier kept the sponges and doughs from crusting, a major problem in the fermentation process, while the water coils controlled room temperatures.

Dough troughs were also greatly improved by this time. No longer made of wood subject to splintering, they were constructed of light steel and mounted on easy-moving steel casters.

By 1920, bakers were using pre-fabricated "steam boxes" for the final or pan proof. They were of wood construction and depended upon a crude hand operated steam mechanism. While they left much to be desired, they did provide proofing conditions superior to those attained earlier. Ten years later these "steam boxes" incorporated steel construction and automatic steam control, as well as an air conditioning unit. They were also provided with steel tracks over which bread racks containing the panned dough could easily be moved.

A number of major changes were also made in machine mixing after 1900. As early as 1905, high speed mixers were introduced, and in less than two decades such equipment was an important part of the industrial bakery. These machines eliminated the use of dough brakes for the thorough kneading and stretching required of bread doughs. The early high-speed mixers had one major drawback, however. They created a great amount of friction heat which resulted in an overly gaseous dough. Chipped ice was at first used to cool the doughs and later, about 1920, cold air blasts were applied. It was not until the late 'twenties that mixers were effectively refrigerated by built-in brine jackets.

After 1920, equipment manufacturers began building heavier and sturdier mixers, adding safety devices, and increasing the size, power and speed of mixing machines. Although their size had been practically doubled between 1900 and 1930, there were still effective limits to the size of dough batches which could be mixed at one time. It was difficult to get good results with doughs weighing over 1,200 pounds.

Thus, in the largest bakeries, a battery of mixers was still required to keep the oven continuously supplied.

By 1930, automatic dough dividers had changed little in principle but were greatly improved in efficiency and capacity. Multiple dividing was developed whereby two, four, or six pieces of dough could be cut and scaled at once. A forced lubrication system with a mineral oil to keep the dough from sticking to machine parts was also devised. A further addition was a good-sized hopper to facilitate the handling of larger amounts of fermented dough.

Moulding machines were similarly perfected. The head rolls invented in the 1890's, and through which the dough pieces passed, did not change basically; their design, however, was improved such that closer pressure adjustments could be made. In addition, the speed of the machine was increased to meet the continuous flow of dough from the overhead proofer.

After 1900, flour handling equipment, like that for other baking processes, underwent considerable improvement. Within a decade, some larger bakeries had virtually eliminated the need for hand labor in flour handling by the addition of automatic conveyors. From a large receiving bin, a bucket-type elevator system conveyed the flour to a central storage bin. The flour then traveled by means of a screw-type conveyor into a smaller bin directly over the large mixing hopper. A hand-operated metal cut-off plate at the bottom of the bin prevented overfilling the hopper. At about the same time, flour blenders to combine various types of flour and automatic flour scales were introduced. By 1930, aside from minor improvements in conveyors, the basic design and construction of mechanical flour storage and handling remained unaltered.

Oven Developments

Despite their limitations, the peel ovens continued to give satisfactory baking results well into the 20th century. It was not until the 1920's, in fact, that the traditional peel oven began to lose its overwhelming dominance. The peel lent itself to most types of bakery operations, even in large-scale bakeries where, in batteries, it met the requirements of mass production. By 1920, it had been largely converted to gas, the cheapest of the fuels, and also incorporated double-deck construction. Several variants of the peel oven had also become quite popular by that time, including the draw-plate and rotary types as well as the rack oven, one in which dough was baked on removable metal shelves.

But the trends of oven use in the large-scale plants were foreshadowed by the development of the traveling oven. About 1910, as a result of joint effort by a Canadian baker, D. Harrison, and his engineer associate, W. D. Roberts, the first practical traveling oven appeared. This "traveling hearth" or tunnel oven had a baking plate fifty feet long and six feet wide. Of brick construction, it was a massive piece of equipment requiring an area of more than 1,000 square feet. Like most ovens at that time, it was fired with gas and heated indirectly through flues built around the baking chamber. Bread and other baked goods were loaded at one end and unloaded at the other. This oven was ideal for large-scale baking operations, for it could perform the work of several peel ovens and do it on a continuous rather than a batch basis.

In another ten years, a second mobile oven made its appearance. This was a tray-type traveler built and put into operation by F. H. Haller of the Haller Bakeries, Pittsburgh, Pennsylvania. In this original model, the trays moved in an up-and-down direction over an endless chain. Later models were designed which incorporated a back-and-forth tray movement as well. Like the tunnel oven, the traveling tray oven was capable of doing the work of three or four peel ovens, but it required no more space than a single peel oven. This was a vital consideration in most medium-sized bakeries where space was at a premium.

While all mechanical ovens—tunnel, traveling tray, and reel—were better adapted for large bakeries than the peel, their widespread use had to await a number of major improvements in construction and engineering. Foremost among these were steel construction, electricity for motor power, and precision instruments for temperature control. The substitution of fabricated steel ovens for those built of refractory materials such as brick was especially important. The great heat storing properties of heavy materials made temperature regulation very inflexible. Steel, on the other hand, permitted rapid adjustment of the heating mechanism to the temperature requirements of the particular products being baked. Moreover, there was no time lost in heating and cooling ovens, a necessary procedure with peel ovens.

During the 'twenties, the mechanical ovens gained a strong foothold among bakers, although a great number of small bakeshops continued to use the peel oven. In 1923, the first year figures on ovens were made available, peels accounted for over 93 per cent of the 25,582 ovens in the industry, while draw-plate, reel, rotary, and traveling ovens made up the balance. Six years later, peels numbered little more than 50 per cent of 28,262 ovens in use. Three mechanical ovens—reel, traveling hearth, and traveling tray—showed the greatest gains.[3] While not the most numerous ovens in operation, it was clear by 1930 that they were essential to large-scale operations.

Slicing, Wrapping, and Cooling Equipment

The mechanization of bakery production did not end at the baking stage. It embraced the cooling, slicing, and wrapping of bread, all of which were extremely important to a successful bakery operation.

Wrapped bread was essential for two reasons. First, its use as an advertising medium could not be overlooked. Second, consumer concern about sanitation demanded it. But until 1911, bread was either wrapped by hand with paper and string or merely put into paper sacks. At that time, the first wrapping

---

[3] *U. S. Census of Manufactures, 1929.*

machine in the industry appeared. Unlike the modern machines, it merely applied a wax seal to the ends of a paper wrapper, eliminating the need for string. But within three years, the forerunner of the modern wrapping machine was put into operation. Using fully waxed paper, it automatically folded the paper around the loaf and sealed the wrapper by means of a heating plate. These early machines were crude affairs, hard to operate, and subject to frequent breakdowns, but they were far more satisfactory and economical than hand wrapping. By 1930, with improved engineering and design, specifically better heat controls and variable speeds, automatic wrapping was in full use except in the retail bakeshops.

Slicing machines were a later development. The first slicer was invented in 1917, but it was destroyed, plans and all, in a fire before it was generally made available. It was not until 1928 that another machine was invented which did an efficient job.

The mechanized problem of the slicing machine was a difficult one, for the slices had to be held together until they moved to the automatic wrapper. Many devices were tried including rubber bands, string, and wire pins. These were finally abandoned in favor of a collapsible cardboard bread tray, patented earlier by a St. Louis baker, G. C. Papendick. With Papendick's device, the loaf was fitted into a tray and held firmly while being sliced, and the entire unit, slices and tray, was then wrapped. Even then, many bakers hesitated to add such equipment to their plant until they were sure the housewife was willing to pay the cost of having her bread sliced.

Bread cooling equipment was found only in the largest and most modern plants. As late as 1930 cooling was largely carried out by stacking the bread on whatever was near at hand, on benches, tables, or bread racks. The first mechanical bread cooler, introduced in 1922, consisted of a simple conveyor, traveling over large reel-type end drums, which carried the loaves to an unloading chute and then to a sorting table. Two greatly improved mechanical bread coolers were available by 1929 to the industry. One, a tunnel-type or counter-flow cooler, was invented by W. W. Reece. It carried the bread on a conveyor belt through a tunnel, in which fans blew cool, washed air against the flow of bread. The moving air absorbed the heat from the hot loaves and was expelled at the tunnel's entrance. The other was a vacuum-type bread cooler which conveyed bread through a tunnel where the loaves were tempered with washed air of controlled temperature and humidity. From the tunnel, the bread entered a vacuum chamber where the desired temperatures were obtained by means of a vacuum pump.

The Mechanization of Bread Making

By 1930, marked progress in bread baking had been made toward an integrated production system. Equipment and machines were available for each of the operations in the baking process with little to remind the observer of the traditional artisan methods. Especially important was the use of conveyors to provide mechanical handling between most machine operations. Hand loading and unloading were unnecessary from the receipt of flour to the mixing machine, from the divider to the rounder, intermediate proofer, and moulder, and from the bread cooler to the slicer and wrapper. In a few plants wrapped loaves were automatically carried to the loading dock. Only the fermentation process defied machine handling, for it was a drawn-out chemical process which required limited sized batches of dough. Nevertheless, it was effectively synchronized with the entire production system .

In keeping with the progress in mechanization, factory bakeries by 1930 had taken on a modern assembly line appearance. The elimination of the maze of overhead shafts and pulleys occurred about the time of World War I with the widespread installation of direct motor drives for all bakery machines. Electricity accounted for nearly 100 per cent of all power used in bakeries in 1930 as against a mere 11 per cent at the turn of the century. And like most factories of the time, a horizontal movement of goods largely replaced the old gravity feed system.

These advances in the development of an integrated and mechanized production flow were paralleled by scientific control over the baking process. Once prepared and baked by almost exclusive reliance upon experience and intuition, bread was increasingly produced under exact chemical and engineering conditions. Interest and knowledge concerning the chemistry of baking spread rapidly not only among bakers, but among ingredient suppliers and machinery manufacturers. Formula testing and analysis of ingredients became commonplace. For all types of baking operations, exact standards were developed for temperature, humidity, timing, and weight conditions. The development of precision measuring instruments made possible the application of the growing body of scientific knowledge that emerged. Illustrative of the progress being made was the founding, in 1919 by the American Bakers Association, of a scientific and educational center for the industry, the American Institute of Baking. While basically a baking school, the Institute's program developed a wide range of activities from analysis of production processes to sanitation and nutrition research. Any baker could make us of the school's services to help him determine not only what baking conditions and ingredients were best for his particular operation, but why poor results were obtained and what could be done to correct them.

The major results of the progress in bread-baking technology between 1900 and 1930 were twofold. First, as engineers rather than craftsmen, bakers were able to produce consistently a high quality, uniform loaf of bread. The degree of control exacted over formulas, ingredients and production processes were now far beyond the skills of the housewife to match. Second, bakery mechanization and quality-control brought about an enormous increase in productive capacity. The largest bakeries, which in 1900 turned out 15,000 loaves of bread daily, by 1930 produced more than 100,000 loaves each day. On an hourly basis, capacity often surpassed 2,000 loaves. Yearly sales ran above $2 million compared to a high of $200,000 in 1900. Although not representative of the entire industry, these comparisons illustrate the extent to which large-scale production had been carried.

Advances in Variety Goods Technology

Under the impact of increasing demand, the production of cakes, pies, doughnuts, and yeast-raised sweet goods became highly mechanized between 1900 and 1930. Flour handling and baking equipment developed for bread baking were easily converted to the production of variety products. Mixing, however, required several modifications. For one thing, smaller vertical mixers were required instead of the huge horizontal bread kneading machines. Then too, special mixing machines had to be devised for cake doughs that were chemically leavened with baking powder, or for doughs which required a creaming or rubbing action to obtain sufficient aeration. Similarly, for mixing pie and sweet doughs, a new machine, called the Artofex mixer, was introduced to simulate hand kneading.

Dividing machines and proofing equipment similar to those used in bread making were also applicable to the production of pies and yeast-raised sweet goods. And although wrapping presented a few more difficulties than bread wrapping, machines for this purpose had also been put into operation by 1930.

Machinery for more specialized operations in variety goods production proceeded apace. Cake, cookie, and cup-cake depositors which placed the mixed batter into pans were devised about 1910. Machinery to sheet out pie dough and place it in pie tins appeared about the same time. The first fully automatic doughnut-making machine came on the market in 1921. A host of other equipment—cookers for pie and sweet goods fillings, cruller apparatuses, special scales and depositors, and icers—also made their appearance. By 1930, mechanization and machine handling had progressed to the point where factory-type operations had become a reality in variety-goods production.

Specialization in cake, pie, and doughnut production developed accordingly, so that many bakers were able to turn out a wide variety of products—cakes, pies, and other sweet goods—in addition to bread products. They had, in effect, three or four separate production units sharing certain facilities in common.

The Scope of Machine Baking

In contrast to 1900, machine methods, in whole or in part, had been extended throughout the entire industry by 1930. Their use in the large plants is obvious. Even the small-scale retail bakeshops utilized the newer automatic equipment, notably ovens and mixers. The completely handicraft operation was a thing of the past. The rest of the industry exhibited varying degrees of mechanization depending upon size and types of products produced.

Although there were still wide ranges in size among bakeries, greater mechanization meant generally increased output per plant throughout the industry. (See Table 1) There was hardly a bakery which had not increased its sales level as shown by the fact that compared to 1900 fewer bakeries were in the lower size categories by 1930. The small scale retailers, for example, enjoyed sales which averaged several times those attained thirty years earlier. The larger bakeries got still larger. In 1900, they accounted for 25 per cent of industry output. In 1930, those with annual sales over $100,000 boasted a two-thirds share of the industry total. Moreover, this greater output was achieved with a less than proportionate increase in the number of employees. In 1900, output per employee amounted to $2,050; thirty years later it had climbed to over $6,800. Even after allowing for price changes, efficiency had risen by more than 80 per cent.

TABLE 1

SIZE DISTRIBUTION OF BAKERIES BY VALUE OF PRODUCTS
PRODUCED, 1929 *

Dollar Value of Product	No. of Bakeries	Per Cent	Value of Products ($000's)	Per Cent	No. of Wage Earners	Per Cent
$5,000 to 20,000	10,458	50.3	$ 111,722	7.3	19,896	9.9
20,000 to 100,000	8,165	39.3	351,133	23.0	49,525	24.6
100,000 to 1,000,000	1,935	9.3	559,774	36.7	75,660	37.7
Over 1,000,000	227	1.1	503,482	33.0	55,760	27.8
TOTALS	20,785	100.0	$1,526,111	100.0	200,841	100.0

* *U. S. Census of Manufactures,* 1929. Includes 375 biscuit and cracker bakeries. Bakeries with less than $5,000 annual sales are not covered by the Census Bureau.

CHAPTER 9

MASS DISTRIBUTION

THE TREMENDOUS INCREASE in the production of commercial bakery products between 1900 and 1930 was in large part made possible by the revolutionary effects of an increased demand for bakers' goods and the technological changes in baking methods. It was also brought about, in part, by an equally important revolution in the distributive structure of the industry as the industrial baker sought wider markets in which to sell his increased output.

Up to World War I, his efforts were largely confined to expanding bread sales through grocery store outlets. At this point, small scale distribution through innumerable retail bakeshops still provided the bulk of industry output. House-to-house and institutional sales were of relatively minor importance. Most baking was still done in the home and mechanized production was limited, for the most part, to turning out bread.

By 1930, however, the industry, so long characterized by small markets and limited distribution, had experienced a radical alteration of its distributive structure. With the increased demand for commercially baked foods and the widespread adoption of "factory" methods of production, industrial bakers who distributed over areas extending to more than 150 miles from their plants, had become the major sellers in the industry. Selling not only bread but a limited line of variety goods, they marketed their products in all of the nation's more than 300,000 retail grocery outlets. Institutional sales and the home delivery market also became a part of the new order as the industrial bakers took advantage of their marketing opportunities. The growth of multi-unit retailing provided mass distribution for large scale plants in still another form. Finally, as the nation's major chain store organizations established their own bakeries after World War I, an entirely new segment of distribution was added to the industry.

Wholesaling

From 1900 through 1930 wholesaling not only dominated industrial bakery distribution but became the leading single type of marketing operation generally. From less than 25 per cent of total sales in 1900, wholesale-to-grocery delivery grew until it accounted for more than 50 per cent three decades later.[1] In part, this growth reflected the increase in the number of wholesale bakers, for once the ground for mass distribution was broken, more and more bakers began selling through grocery stores. Of greater importance, however, was an expansion in the scale of individual operations. Wholesale bakeries, already the largest single plants in the industry, grew even larger. New modes of transportation, improved baking techniques and experience with mass marketing, constituted powerful incentives.

In 1900, the typical wholesaler operated from two to ten routes, with the majority probably falling nearer the lower end of the range. The average route grossed less than $150 per week ($7,800 per year), and a firm was considered large if its annual sales exceeded $30,000. Data on plant size a quarter of a century later provide a striking contrast. In 1926, a survey by the Federal Trade Commission of some 300 plants, most of them operated by multi-plant wholesalers, the largest

---

[1] *Census of Distribution, 1929.*

Early Overhead Proofer, 1910

An Early Prefabricated Proof Box 1097

High Speed Mixing Machine of the 1920's

Typical Draw-Plate and Brick Peel Ovens of the 1920's

Slicing Machine of the Early 1930's

An Early Traveling Oven

An Early Traveling-Tray Oven, 1921

The Electric Truck, 1910

The Motor Truck, 1911

establishments in the country, revealed that such plants maintained an average of twenty-nine routes, with weekly sales per
route slightly exceeding $500.[2] These figures imply average
annual sales of $750,000, as compared to the $80,000 that a
large ten-route plant could earn in 1900. Price changes over the
twenty-five-year period, of course, exaggerate the growth if
based on dollar-volume sales, but the increase in plant size,
when measured by physical output, is only slightly less impressive. The larger plants of 1926 produced over five times
more than those twenty-five years before.[3]

Census data, exhibited in Table 1, present a more compre-
hensive picture of the size of wholesale plants in 1929.

TABLE 1
SIZE DISTRIBUTION OF BAKERS SELLING AT WHOLESALE TO GROCERS, 1929 *

Sales Size Category	Value of Sales (000)	Per Cent of Sales	Per Cent of Total Sales Sold Wholesale to Grocers	Number of Plants	
				Total	Selling Exclus.
Over $500,000	$293,098	48.6	62.2	290	158
$100,000–$500,000	190,232	31.5	60.6	1,029	596
$50,000–$100,000	54,750	9.1	41.2	1,058	349
Less than $50,000	65,249	10.8	24.3	4,041	1,077
TOTAL	$603,329	100.0		6,418	2,180

* Source: *U. S. Census of Distribution, 1929*, pp. 26-27.

Clearly, the larger firms dominated the field of wholesale
distribution. Less than 5 per cent of the firms accounted for
almost one-half of the total sales volume; less than 20 per cent

---

[2] Federal Trade Commission. *Competition and Profits in Bread and Flour.* Senate
Document No. 98, 70th Congress, 1st Session (1928), p. 29.

[3] At the turn of the century, the average route man delivered 3,500 loaves per
week. Hence a ten-route wholesaler produced 35,000 loaves weekly. In 1926, bread
sold for 8¢ per loaf, wholesale, so $500 weekly sales implied that each route man
supplied 6,250 loaves. For a twenty-four-route plant, weekly output averaged 181,250
loaves. This, of course, assumes that variety goods can be reduced to some type of
"loaf-equivalent."

accounted for over 80 per cent of total sales. The output of the largest bakeries, the "bread factories" as they were called, sometimes reached $50,000 per week. Although the smaller plants had outputs of less than $1,000 per week, they nonetheless produced almost as much as a medium-sized plant in 1900.

Much of the increased plant-size and output between 1900 and 1930 was made possible by wholesalers who progressively expanded their market areas. Although the expansion was carried on in several directions simultaneously, it can best be regarded as twofold movement. On the one hand, the radius of effective distribution for all wholesalers increased within the market areas surrounding their plants; on the other, they began to invade suburbs, outlying country, and even neighboring cities.

As early as 1899, a few bakers had pioneered the use of motor trucks, but the average wholesaler at that time relied on horse-and-wagon delivery. His effective route area was thus limited to the ten- or fifteen-mile radius a horse could traverse in one day.[4] The horse-drawn wagon amply served the market areas of the early wholesalers until their output required a broader market penetration. Then, large bakers began to experiment with automotive delivery. By 1910 both gasoline- and electrically-powered vehicles were no longer a novelty and were beginning to be used generally in the industry. Within a decade, however, the superiority of the gasoline truck had been demonstrated. By 1923, the first year for which census data are available, it had a substantial edge on all other means of transportation. By 1929, as shown in Table 2, it accounted for almost 80 per cent of all bakery delivery vehicles.

Reasons why the truck dominated are obvious. It was cheaper than horse-drawn delivery despite a higher original outlay. As early as 1910 "one baker reported that his single

---

4 Personal communication, Mr. Harold LeMar.

TABLE 2

VEHICLE OPERATION [a]

Year	Gasoline Motor Vehicle	Electric Motor Vehicle[b]	Wagon[b]
1923	23,331	2,921	12,293
1925	28,879	3,870	8,991
1929	42,524	3,983	6,715

[a] *Census of Manufactures, 1929.*
[b] By 1939 the electric truck and the horse-drawn wagon had all but disappeared in the industry.

gas truck did the work of three horses and saved him $265 a year." [5] Other estimates made about the same time put truck costs at two cents per stop, against six cents for the horse and wagon.[6]

Nor could horse-drawn vehicles match the truck's wider area of service and the new business it brought in. City routes, previously limited to but a few miles, were progressively extended; by 1930, they averaged twenty-five miles per day, and many of them were serviced more than once daily.[7] This route growth was especially significant. In 1930, for instance, city routes, representing approximately 75 per cent of total route business, accounted for over one-third of total industry sales.[8]

But expansion within urban centers was not the only advantage of the truck. As they became more efficient, wholesalers welcomed them for longer-distance hauling as a way to escape pressures of city competition. Actually this possibility proved somewhat illusory, for when one baker moved into outlying areas, others quickly followed. But the combined effect, from the distributive point of view, was to carry wholesale products progressively farther from the city. In 1919,

[5] *Bakers' Helper Magazine*, April 12, 1952, p. 70.
[6] *Ibid.*, April 17, 1937, p. 819.
[7] Federal Trade Commission, *op. cit.*, p. 29
[8] *Ibid.*, p. 29.

wholesalers dispatched their trucks to grocers only in the immediate environs of the urban markets, a distance of perhaps twenty-five miles. Within ten years, the distance covered by a single country route averaged sixty-eight miles per day, and in the more sparsely populated areas, trucks traveled as much as 159 miles daily.[9] Increasing route distances, along with greater purchasing power among the rural population, spurred an impressive rate of growth in out-of-town sales. From next to nothing in 1919, country deliveries were accounting for approximately 12 per cent of total industry sales a decade later.[10]

Distribution over a country route, however, was limited to the amount that the average truck could carry. For large scale distribution to distant markets some wholesalers during the early 'twenties resorted to depot, or branch operations, supplied by trailer trucks. These depots, located in outlying areas, had their own delivery trucks which, in turn, serviced the grocery stores in their areas.

The few wholesalers who could afford the investment in branch operation were mostly larger bakers. Fewer than 300 bakers in 1929 delivered through depots; less than fifty sold exclusively in this manner. The dollar value of depot sales in 1929 amounted to a little more than 2 per cent of total sales of the industry; of this amount, almost three-fourths was made by the bakers operating plants which produced over $500,000 annually.[11]

While branch operations were restricted to very large firms, smaller bakers obtained wider distribution through still another type of arrangement. As early as 1915, wholesalers had sold through independent distributors called "bobtailers," wagon jobbers who owned their own trucks. These "bobtailers" bought their goods at a discount and sold them

---

9 Federal Trade Commission, *op. cit.*, p. 29.

10 In 1929, grocery stores accounted for 50 per cent of industry sales. Country route business (sold principally to grocery stores) comprised 25 per cent of total route sales.

11 *Census of Distribution,* 1929, pp. 26-27.

to grocery stores, simply taking the place of the bakers' route driver salesmen. Some sold directly to consumers' homes.[12] By 1930, bobtail operations accounted for over 7 per cent of total industry sales.[13]

Bobtailers provided many wholesalers with a system of low-cost, wide-scale distribution. While the baker sold at a discount, he avoided the investment necessary for trucks and equipment. Generally, wholesalers employed bobtailers in markets where they did not have their own delivery routes, and they often used these jobbers to gain a share of a competitor's sales. Some 30 per cent of all bobtail operations represented the business of wholesalers who had no route delivery system of their own.[14]

House-to-House Distribution

While some bakers began specializing in house-to-house distribution as early as 1910, it remained relatively insignificant until the mid-'twenties, when product lines extended beyond bread and rolls. "Factory" production of variety baked goods, then, set the stage for rapid expansion of home delivery. By 1925, over 3,000 bakeries engaged in this type of distribution; over half of them dealt in it exclusively. An almost equal number (1,300) operated retail shops as well, reflecting the fact that many retailers had changed their scope of operations.

There were, however, finite limits to the economies of plant scale in the production of variety goods. Some producers had annual sales of over $500,000, certainly comparable even to the large wholesalers, but house-to-house bakers, in general, operated smaller-sized plants.

Home delivery operators also had to forego many economies of distribution because the route man served individuals rather than grocery stores. He made more stops per route, but

---

[12] Graf, *op. cit.*, p. 200.
[13] *Census of Distribution*, 1929, p. 26.
[14] *Ibid.*

not enough to offset the smaller sales volume per stop. As a result, the average house-to-house route in 1926 ran about $250 per week, compared to the $500 for wholesale routes.[15]

Because home delivery was primarily suited to densely populated areas, house-to-house bakers employed country routes less extensively than did wholesalers. Only an insignificant number were large enough to warrant branch operations. In house-to-house distribution, the average city route salesman in 1926 traveled some eighteen miles per day, while country route men averaged twenty-nine miles.[16] In fact, the shorter distances delayed the widespread use of motor trucks on home delivery routes. While horse-drawn wagons were insignificant in other branches of the industry, they accounted for approximately 70 per cent of all home delivery vehicles even as late as 1926.[17] Old Dobbin had learned to move down the block without guidance, while the driver visited his customers on both sides of the street. Old Dobbin's cooperation shortened both the distance the driver had to walk to get goods from the wagon and the time consumed in starting and stopping.

Selling to Institutions

Institutional trade offered commercial bakeries a somewhat more specialized market than that of grocery stores or house-to-house delivery. The conventional loaf of bread made up a large part of institutional demand, but these buyers also bought considerable amounts of steamed rolls and other hard-crusted hearth products. As bakers began to produce them in larger quantities, pies, cakes, and sweet goods were added to deliveries to institutional buyers.

Arrangements with institutional customers sometimes provided for no return of stales, in contrast to agreements with

---

15 U. S. Bureau of Census, *Biennial Census of Manufacture, 1925. Bread and Other Bakery Products.* (Washington: Government Printing Office, 1927), p. 51.
16 *Ibid.,* p. 36.
17 *Ibid.,* p. 38.

the grocer outlets. This reduction in service, plus the large individual orders, often permitted the baker to cut his delivered price.

At the beginning of this century, the institutional market was generally serviced by the grocery store wholesaler. No more than a handful of bakers delivered exclusively to hotels and restaurants. Salesmen of the wholesaler called on these outlets in much the same manner as they called on the grocers. So long as the demand remained small, such servicing was adequate.

But as the institutional demand expanded, and while the regular wholesalers continued to be the most important sellers in this market, more bakers undertook an exclusive institutional business. Frequently they concentrated on one line, such as pies or cakes.

The institutional demand, initially limited to hotels and restaurants, soon extended to hospitals, military and naval installations and other public institutions. Such sales, because of their size and, on occasion legal specifications as well, were usually awarded by contract. The baker submitted a bid which provided for daily delivery of specified quantities of several types of bakery products over a certain period of time. On occasion, bakers who did not sell regularly to institutions would bid for contracts if their need for greater volume was a pressing objective.

By 1930, as shown in Table 3, institutional sales totaled almost 37 million. While amounting to only slightly more than 3 per cent of industry output, the institutional market was, nevertheless, a significant one compared to its negligible value three decades earlier. Unlike other segments in the industry, it derived its significance from the fact that it provided additional outlets to bakers who sold primarily through other channels. As shown in the table, less than 7 per cent of the bakers serving the institutional market did so exclusively. The great majority were large scale wholesalers selling to grocery stores. House-to-house distributors and a few retailers also made use of marginal institutional sales. For many, this market may well have meant the difference between success or failure.

TABLE 3

SIZE DISTRIBUTION OF BAKERS SELLING AT WHOLESALE
TO INSTITUTIONS *

Sales Size Category	Value of Sales (000)	Per Cent of Sales	Number of Plants Total	Number of Plants Selling Exclus.
Over $500,000	$15,108	41.0	53	4
$100,000–$500,000	9,281	25.2	151	28
$50,000–$100,000	5,694	15.4	178	30
Less than $50,000	6,798	18.4	685	108
TOTAL	$36,881	100.0	1,067	170

* *U. S. Census Distribution, 1929, pp. 26-27.*

The Expansion of Multi-Unit Retailing

The developments in the mass distribution of commercial bakery products were not confined to wholesaling and delivering direct to the home. Many retailers also joined in this trend through the establishment of multi-unit retail outlets.

The basis for the growth of multi-unit retailing was the desire on the part of certain retailers to gain some of the economies of large-scale production and still remain in the traditional retail business. As in the growth of house-to-house distribution, the development of factory methods of production for variety baked goods provided retail bakers with the opportunity to expand their operations. Thus a number of them opened or otherwise acquired several retail sales stores and enlarged their main baking plant. They performed the baking operations in one larger bakery and delivered the products each morning to the branch sales stores. From all outward appearances these bakers were just like the single-unit retailers; they produced the same types of products and sold from each outlet in exactly the same manner. Yet, they had become a definite part of the industrial baking group by engaging in large-scale production and distribution.

From an insignificant share in 1900, multi-unit retailing expanded until by 1930 it accounted for between 5 and 6 per cent of total industry sales. While not a spectacular increase when compared to the sharp expansion in the industry generally, it did much to offset the relative decline in the importance of the traditional retailers, whose share of total distribution fell from some 75 per cent of industry output in 1900 to roughly 20 per cent in 1930.

The Emergence of Chain Store Baking

Aside from the rise of the wholesale-to-grocery store segment of the baking industry, the entry of the chain stores into the field of baking was probably the most important distributive change during the thirty-year period ending in 1930. By that time, the chains had captured 5 to 6 per cent of total industry sales compared to no recorded sales in 1900.

The first entry by a chain store into the baking industry came in 1901. In that year, B. H. Kroger, founder of the Kroger grocery chain, formed the Kroger Grocery and Baking Company. He began operations with two double-deck draw-plate ovens and fourteen bakers to supply a portion of his forty-two retail outlets.[18] This was an isolated case, however, and there is no evidence that it was repeated by any other chain store organization prior to World War I. The real era of chain store baking began in the years following the War and reached its peak during the 'twenties.

By this time, grocery chains occupied an important role in the retailing of all food products in the United States. By 1929, they accounted for one-third of all food store sales.[19] The decade of the 'twenties was indeed the chain store era

---

[18] "The Organizing Era, 1897–1904," *Bakers' Helper Magazine*, April 17, 1937, p. 761.

[19] E. A. Duddy and D. A. Revzan, *Marketing, An Institutional Approach*, Second Edition (New York: McGraw-Hill Book Co., Inc., 1953), p. 202.

not only in terms of the share of retailing done but also in terms of the pressures put on the manufacturers who supplied the chains. In one field after another, the large volume of business enjoyed by chains enabled them to secure attractive trade discounts from most of their suppliers. When such discounts were not forthcoming, the chain stores often established their own manufacturing and processing facilities.

Bakers did not long escape the pressure of the chain organizations for price concessions. While the bulk of the bakers' business went to independent food stores, the chain store market was especially attractive because of the large individual orders involved. In some instances, wholesalers acquiesced to the pressure and gave secret discounts in order to keep their chain store customers. As the demand for discounts by the chains became more widespread, however, the wholesale bakers faced a growing dilemma. As one writer noted, "The . . . industry had nearly always followed a uniform price for customers of all sizes. The chain stores began to question this and reasoned that they were entitled to special benefits. Their sales per store were considerably higher than the average grocer . . . and their purchases in the aggregate were tremendous. So they demanded discounts and more discounts." [20] In general, however, the reaction of the wholesale bakers was to refuse to make price concessions to the chain store buyers. As a result, the chains, especially the larger ones, responded by setting up their own facilities for producing bread and a limited amount of variety goods for distribution in their own stores. By 1930, the Kroger Company was operating twelve bakeries and producing cakes, pies, and crackers in addition to bread products. The Great Atlantic and Pacific Tea Company, the largest food chain in the nation, owned thirty-five bakeries in 1930, as compared to two ten years earlier.[21] Other chains, both national and regional,

---

[20] Graf, *op. cit.*, p. 198.

[21] Federal Trade Commission, *Chain Stores: Chain Store Manufacturing* (Washington: United States Government Printing Office, 1933), p. 14.

followed suit. In most instances, they preferred to build rather than purchase existing plants, and their establishments generally utilized the most modern equipment. As a group, the chains had the largest plants in the baking industry.

In terms of costs, the chains gained certain distinct advantages, both in manufacturing and in distribution. By concentrating on straight bread-type products and a limited line of sweet goods, they took full advantage of the newest machine methods of production. They were able to operate their plants close to optimum capacity because the needs of their stores could be estimated with considerable accuracy. The percentage of stale returns was below that of the average wholesale baker, and, by favorable display, they could push the sale of their own brands over competing lines.

But the greatest single source of savings to chains came in the distribution end. Where wholesale bakers employed driver salesmen working on a commission basis, the chains simply used regular truck drivers, who delivered bakery products along with other foods to the individual branch stores. According to a Federal Trade Commission study covering the years 1923 through 1925, the saving of this system over the traditional route method came to about $1.012 per hundred pounds of baker bread.[22] In 1927, the typical wholesale baker in Chicago paid $50 for a bread salesman while the chain store baker paid from $37.50 to $41.00 for truck driver services.[23] Moreover, "the man whom the chain store hires for $41.00 probably delivers five tons of bread a day as against a thousand or fifteen hundred pounds a day for the $50 man." [24]

The cost savings on bread were passed on to consumers by the chains in the form of lower prices ranging from one to three cents per loaf below the prices charged on regular bakers' brands. In a basic convenience goods such as bread, purchased several times each week, lower prices were defi-

---

[22] Federal Trade Commission, *op. cit.,* p. 317.

[23] Minutes of the General Managers' Conference, 1927, The W. W. Long Co., p. 191.

[24] *Ibid.,* p. 192.

nitely attractive to the housewife. Some chains went so far as to refuse to handle any bread other than their own. In most cases, however, they had to yield to the pressures of their customers who preferred a free choice in the matter. Still others frequently used their own bread as a loss leader in order to attract additional customers into their stores. While not a prolonged practice, it did much to cause people to buy chain store bread.

The apparent success of large chains soon brought repercussions among smaller chains and the so-called voluntary chains such as I.G.A. (Independent Grocers Alliance), Clover Farms, and others. They demanded a price from the wholesale bakers sufficiently low to permit them to meet the competition of the larger chains. Some threatened to build their own bakeries. Others insisted on a private label contract. Under this arrangement the wholesale baker contracted to bake products under a distributor's private label at a discount sufficient to permit smaller and voluntary chains to sell at prices competitive with the large chains who owned their own bakeries. Many bakers acceded to these demands thus accelerating the era of private brands.

The competition of chain store baking was felt primarily by the wholesale bakers selling to grocery stores. In one market where a chain store built its own bakery, a large wholesaler lost $15,000 in weekly sales.[25] Retailers and house-to-house operators, being in different segments of the industry, had little direct competition from the chains.

Yet the chain stores did not dominate the industry as so many bakers feared. Far from it, the chains produced less than 10 per cent of industry output. There were several reasons for this. Primary among them was the fact that entry into the baking business required a substantial capital investment. Only the large chain stores could afford the venture. Secondly, the great majority of consumers preferred the

---

[25] Graf, *op. cit.,* p. 198.

brands to which they had become accustomed. Some expressed the belief that chain-store bread, being cheap bread, was not as good as the regular brands. Wholesale bakers took advantage of this belief in their advertising. Thus, even in the chains' own stores, the major brands were the leading bread sellers. Finally, the rapid decline in home baking and the over-all increase in demand for commercial products provided the baking industry with a continued expansion sufficient to offset the inroads of the chains.

Summary

Stimulated by expanding demand and improved technology, the distributive system of the baking industry underwent a revolution between 1900 and 1930. At the beginning of the century, about 90 per cent of the nation's bakeries were single-unit shops. Together with a handful of multi-unit retailers, they accounted for three-quarters of the industry's sales. The remaining 25 per cent was distributed by a small number of industrial bakers who sold primarily to grocery stores. Thirty years later, this pattern had been almost completely reversed. The large scale industrial bakeries dominated the industry, with less than 20 per cent of sales coming from the single shop retailers.

The relative significance in 1929 of the various marketing channels in the distribution of commercially produced bakery products is shown below. (Cf. Table 4.) The importance of the grocery store market in the total is clearly revealed. So too is the decline of the single-unit retail stores, although their exact status cannot be accurately measured.

Within the various distributive segments, a wide variety of bakery operations had emerged. While the wholesalers delivering to grocery stores contained most of the largest bakery operators, they also included many small operators. On the other hand, many bakers marketing through other channels rivaled the largest grocery wholesalers in size. Diversity in product mix also characterized the bakers in the same chan-

TABLE 4

RELATIVE PERCENTAGES OF SALES IN THE BAKING INDUSTRY, BY DISTRIBUTIVE CHANNELS

ACCORDING TO SIZE OF TOTAL PLANT SALES, 1929 *

Sales Size Category	To Grocery Stores	To Institutions	Percentages of Total Sales				Total
			Through Multi-Unit Retail Stores and Chain Stores	At House-to-House and through Single-Unit Retail Stores	To Bob-tailers	Through Depot Operations	
All Plants' Sales	50.8%	3.1%	11.1%	25.2%	7.4%	2.4%	100.0%
Over $500,000	62.2	3.2	13.1	11.1	6.1	4.3	100.0
$100,000–$500,000	60.6	3.0	11.0	13.8	10.2	1.4	100.0
$50,000–$100,000	41.2	4.3	9.3	35.3	9.1	0.8	100.0
Under $50,000	24.3	2.5	8.6	58.1	5.5	1.0	100.0

* U. S. Bureau of the Census, *Census of Distribution: 1930*, Vol. II, *Distribution of Sales of Manufacturing Plants* (Washington: Government Printing Office, 1932), pp. 26-27. The sales categories were derived from differently worded census categories.

nel of distribution. Wholesalers especially illustrated the range of variation. Most were bread producers, but many had added a limited variety of sweet goods to round out their line. A few had become specialists, concentrating on variety products, especially cakes and pies. Even the institutional and the house-to-house bakers showed evidence of choice in product-mix. The multi-unit retailers, although producing the widest variety of goods, were generally more similar as a group.

Nor were the channels of distribution mutually exclusive. Most bakers concentrated on only one method of distribution, but of the 16,016 bakeries reported in the curves of distribution of 1929, roughly 6,500 delivered through several channels.[26] It was not unusual to find bakers who marketed their products through half a dozen different distributive channels, including private label operations for chain stores.

The structure of distribution in 1930 was therefore an extremely varied one, not much different from the present-day arrangement. By size of operation, types of products produced, and methods of reaching the final consumer, the industry presented a sharp contrast to the picture seen at the turn of the century. It was no longer characterized as primarily a retail trade; it was characterized by the large-scale production and mass distribution of industrial baking plants.

---

[26] *Census of Distributions,* 1929, p. 26.

CHAPTER 10

CONSOLIDATIONS AND MERGERS:
THE GROWTH OF MULTI-PLANT FIRMS

ONE OF the most colorful chapters in the entire history of the American baking industry was the merger movement that flourished between 1900 and the late 1920s. This movement had two phases, one, a series of local consolidations that were particularly important from about 1907 to 1920, and the second, the multi-market mergers that were especially prominent between 1910 and 1926.

Prior to 1900 there were few instances of the growth of baking firms through amalgamation or purchase. The family-owned, single-plant establishments grew principally by natural means, internal expansion. The largest of these were, of course, those which had made the change from retail operations to wholesaling through grocery stores. The extra capital required was ordinarily met by the resources of the individual firm.

Many of these early family businesses were the nuclei of companies that are well-known in the industry today. The Ward Baking Company, founded in Pittsburgh in 1849, became a component part of the vast Ward enterprises which were to emerge during the 'twenties. Others who trace their origins back to the latter 19th century include Cushman of New York, Campbell and Nafziger of Kansas City, Kolb and

Friehofer of Philadelphia, Schulze and Livingston of Chicago, Taggart of Indiana, Corby of Washington, D. C., Wagner of Detroit, and Stroehmann of West Virgina.[1] Most of these firms grew initially by normal expansion within their respective market areas. Because of their established reputations and financial strength they were among the leaders in the first phase of the merger movement which took place within local markets.

Local mergers were largely responses to expanding demand and to improvements in technology and transportation that had increased both plant size and market areas for individual bakers. Plants previously isolated were now brought into direct competition at the grocery store level. In the battle to establish and maintain individual market shares, competition was fierce and unbridled. Bakers found themselves engaged in a series of price wars which benefitted no one. They realized the need for effective means to control output and the high costs of distributive competition.

During the 1920s especially, stock promoters played a part in the formation of local mergers. Hardheaded, independent bakers who had nursed bakeries into thriving businesses were ripe prospects for a skillful promoter. Baking trade journals of the day publicized his talents. He skillfully brought together the leaders of opposing companies—men not likely to be frightened into mergers by the threat of competition—by holding out the prospects of bigger earnings and greater power under the proposition he had to offer.

The American Baking Company, formed in 1907, was one of the earliest examples of local mergers. Stock promoters had a hand in the negotiations. Seven firms—each had its own plant—came into the new company. The basic aim of its founders was simply to reduce competition and eliminate unfair trade practices that had raised havoc in the St. Louis market. Still another idea was involved in the merger; the idea of

---

[1] Carl L. Alsberg, *Combination in the American Bread-Baking Industry* (California: Stanford University, January, 1926), p. 9.

integration, of forming an efficient unit out of a number of fragments. Two plants were immediately shut down and, by 1924, three more had closed leaving two to carry on operations.[2]

The Shults Bread Company in southern New York State followed a similar course. Organized in 1910, the Shults Company brought together twelve wholesale bread bakeries. Six were located in Brooklyn, three in Manhattan, two in Hoboken, and one in Mt. Vernon. Only one had a capacity of over 1,000 barrels of flour (roughly 275,000 pounds of bread) a year, but the competition resulting from their overlapping distributive areas had gotten out of hand.[3] Merger apparently provided a simple solution, for the company fared well from its very beginning.

Local market mergers became frequent over the next ten or twelve years. The Flour State Baking Company of St. Paul, Minnesota, for example, was incorporated in 1916 to consolidate the St. Paul Bread Company and the Sanitary Bread Company of Minneapolis. The former had been founded in 1897 and the latter in 1903. The Manor Grocers Baking Company, organized about 1921, similarly combined a number of Cincinnati bakeries. In 1922, the California Baking Company, the Holsum Baking Company, the ABC Baking Company, and the Golden State Baking Company were formed. Other consolidations purely local in nature were the City Baking Company of Baltimore; the United Baking Company of Cleveland; the Washington Bakers of Seattle, Washington; and the Golden Chief-Remar Baking Company of Oakland and Berkeley, California.

While local mergers reduced the number of sellers in any market, any marked advantage enjoyed by the merged bakeries was usually short lived. For a short time they may have had the upper hand, but entry into the whoesale market remained relatively easy—especially for established retail bake-

---

[2] *Ibid.*, p. 11.
[3] *Ibid.*, Appendix, p. 132.

shops. With a rapidly growing market and frequent improvements in technology, the merged bakeries still had to face the fact that new competitors could challenge their market position.

Multi-Market Combinations

In an era of mergers, the next step—that of multi-market combinations—was a natural one for the baking industry for a number of reasons.

In the first place, the promised advantages of local market mergers, as noted earlier, had not lived up to the bright hopes of its apostles. The local mergers, for instance, proved a dubious cure for price wars and cutthroat competition. But, confident that the principle was sound, bakers began their march for bigger and better combinations, embracing a number of markets on a regional basis. The prevailing mood was that intensive competition was largely a local affair and was unlikely to affect all of the markets at the same time.

Along with this search for stability, there was a very general desire, on the part of the bakers, for greater financial strength. They needed more funds than they could supply on their own, for new machinery, new plants, and new employees. Under multi-market mergers, they could get the capital required by pooling the funds of constituent companies. Furthermore, under such mergers, it would prove easier to negotiate with banks for short-term loans for working capital and to deal with investment houses for long-run capital needs.

Multi-market mergers had other attractions of an internal character. They were pools of talent as well as of capital, making for up-to-date and efficient management. Inefficient plants could be shut down and existing plants improved. The production and distribution methods that had proved especially effective in one or more of the plants under control of the merged organization could be utilized. Larger organizations could also realize savings in their purchase of supplies, either through the size of orders or through a better bargaining position *vis-a-vis* the sellers.

Finally, as the multi-market mergers came to include bakeries operating over a wide geographic area, there was the attraction of economies to be gained through national advertising.

One aspect of the drive to expand by merger deserves special mention. That is, physical plant was not the main concern in the search for companies to bring into a proposed merger. Rather it was the search for going bakery routes that was the principal objective. It was thought more important to have a good distribution base in a market, where the fight for the grocer's shelf space and the housewife's recognition had already been waged, than to have an efficient manufacturing operation. Production problems could be more easily handled than distribution problems on which the economic feasibility of a large scale wholesale bakery operation depended.

The General Baking Company, incorporated in 1911, was one of the notable pioneers in multi-market mergers. A consolidation of some twenty bread companies with plants in seventeen different cities, this company embraced a wide area. Its main concentration was along the east coast around Boston, but it extended also to New Orleans and St. Louis. Most of these companies were not competitors. They included the most efficient and soundly managed companies in their respective localities. Their owners acquired substantial interests in the new concern and with few exceptions remained as managers of their respective plants.[4]

In the vanguard were other pioneers. To cite a few and the dates of their appearance: The New England Baking Company incorporated in Massachusetts in 1915; the Massachusetts Baking Company incorporated in 1917; the Tri-State Baking Company formed in New York in 1919; and the Grennan Baking Company organized in Detroit in 1924.[5] Like the

----

4 *Ibid.*, p. 138.
5 *Ibid.*, Appendix, pp. 133-140.

General Baking Company, these firms acquired bakeries in separate markets on a more or less regional basis, attempting in part to achieve the economies of the large-scale firm.

Early in the 'twenties, the multi-market merger entered a new phase marked by the emergence of the national giants of the industry. This phase was a logical outgrowth of the earlier regional combinations and was in keeping with the multiplication of company mergers in American industry, in which the holding company had become a popular device. In the accompanying speculative mania, promoters of the new giants had little difficulty in acquiring ample capital for the towering corporate structures they designed. In this period, America's four largest bakeries today—the Continental Baking Corporation, the Ward Baking Company, the Purity Bakeries Corporation, and the General Baking Company—had their origins; and the keynote they struck resounded throughout the industry.

Of these four organizations, three were the creation of William B. Ward, without doubt the most colorful and influential individual in the great multi-market promotions of the 'twenties. Ward was the great-grandson and namesake of a baker who first started in business in 1849. His father organized a bakery in Pittsburgh in 1878, and in 1912 young Ward moved to Buffalo to found a baking business of his own. Through his family, he knew personally most of the important bakery executives of the day. But beyond his knowledge of the baking industry, he had the instincts of a financial promoter and a keen appreciation of the organizational difficulties besetting many of the local and regional firms.[6]

Ward had three trump cards in the scheme that he used to promote his plans: money, promotional ability, and sound bakery management plans.

Ward had two sources of funds. One, the result of private financial backing from persons unknown, always seemed at

---

[6] John H. Dahn and Frederick Roselius have been very helpful to the author in piecing together the story of Ward's career.

hand when he needed cash to close purchases. Perhaps more important was Ward's ability, through astute publicity, to develop a wide market for his stock. This meant that he had access to large amounts of capital and as long as the public subscribed for his stocks, his ability to acquire new firms would remain intact.[7]

Ward's second trump card was a thorough understanding of the strength and weaknesses of both the bakery firms he sought to acquire and their owners. By the 1920s many of these firms were headed by second generation management, many of whom were not as keenly interested in the bakery business as the founders had been. Often the management picture had been clouded by previous mergers such that no one person had absolute control. Ward offered them the chance to solve gracefully the organizational problems that grew out of rapid and sometimes poorly planned mergers.

Tactically, Ward was extremely flexible, varying his approach as circumstance directed. He did not hesitate to bring pressure on individuals who were reluctant to sell. In one instance, after an offer had been rejected by a local baker, Ward's lieutenants went into the community and made surveys of several available plant sites. Later Ward himself visited the community, spoke to a service club group, and donated a small sum to local charity. It appeared that a new Ward bakery was about to rise in the town. To no one's surprise, the reluctant seller came to Ward, two weeks later, offering to sell.[8]

In his buying campaigns, Ward normally offered the baker a sum to cover the value of his tangible assets less outstanding liabilities, plus a sum for goodwill. The total sum usually amounted to between five and ten times the average annual profit of the plant over several previous years. The amount paid by Ward for goodwill depended on the bargaining power

---

[7] It is reported that the senior Fleischmann was one of Ward's private financial backers.

[8] John H. Dahn, one of Ward's close associates in purchasing several firms, recounted the circumstances of this purchase.

of the baker but Ward set an upper limit. That limit was keyed to the market potential of the bakery if its methods were improved to the maximum. Thus a plant not employing the most progressive methods would command a higher price relative to current earning rates than one that had reached its full technical and administrative potential.

These selling tactics were obviously dependent upon the third factor in Ward's success, his ability to improve upon the bakeries he purchased. But at this task, Ward, or rather the men with whom he surrounded himself, was extremely able. Better wrapping and package design, the introduction of a wider line of cake products, more efficient route control, and a concentrated advertising program were but a part of these improvements. Many newly acquired bakeries quickly showed improved earnings under Ward control.

Ward's first major promotion came in 1922, with the formation of the United Bakeries Corporation. Organized as a holding company, United Bakeries controlled the seven operating plants of the Ward and Ward Baking Company of Buffalo, New York—Ward's original venture into the industry; three plants of the Ward Brothers Baking Company in Rochester—another of Ward's early operations; and nine plants of the Campbell Baking Company of Kansas City. Exchanges of stock were effected between United and the three firms, but control remained in the hands of William B. Ward. In less than two years, Ward added eighteen more bakeries and by the end of 1924, United Bakeries controlled more than forty bakeries in thirty different cities. Some of these additions were brought into the holding company through stock exchange plans; others were purchased outright, usually at a price that was more than satisfactory to the sellers.

Late in 1923, Ward organized a second holding company, the Ward Baking Corporation, to take over the operations of the seventeen plants of the Ward Baking Company of New York which had been owned and operated by his uncle, George S. Ward. The younger Ward became president of the new company, having resigned in November of 1923 as a director and president of the United Bakeries. However, there can be little doubt that he retained control of United, for one of his close associates, George B. Smith, succeeded him as president of that organization.

While Ward and his associates were organizing the United and Ward companies, another large combination was in the making. Although in no way connected with the Ward group, the organization of the Purity Bakeries Corporation followed a somewhat similar pattern. Incorporated as a holding company in December, 1924, it acquired the Tri-State Baking Company and the Purity Baking Company as its nucleus. The Tri-State Baking Company was one of the early multi-market mergers, having been incorporated in 1919 with the combination of plants in several cities. By the time Tri-State was acquired by Purity Bakeries, it had itself been expanded to include six or more plants in half a dozen cities. The Purity Baking Company was an outgrowth of the former Flour State Baking Company of St. Paul, organized in 1916 as a local combination. The Flour State Baking Company had subsequently acquired the Purity Bread Company of Duluth and another bakery in Minneapolis. It had also taken over several plants in Cincinnati, Columbus, and Hamilton, Ohio, as well as another in Indianapolis.

In April of 1925 the Purity Bakeries Corporation also acquired the Nafziger Baking Company, an old firm which in 1921 had been incorporated to bring together several interests of the Nafziger group in the Kansas City-St. Louis area. Purity also acquired additional plants in Illinois, Iowa, Oklahoma, Texas, and Michigan. Among these was its acquisition in May, 1925, of the Grennan Bakeries of Detroit which had been organized in 1919 to combine several cake bakeries in Detroit, Chicago, Cleveland, and St. Paul. By the end of 1925, Purity was operating thirty-three bakeries in twenty-four cities in twelve states. It served an estimated 45,000 retail grocery stores from approximately 1,000 delivery routes, and employed some 1,200 salesmen.[9]

Big as was the Purity operation, however, it did not begin to compare with the grandiose plans Ward and his associates began to unfold at about the same time.

For in late 1924, Ward organized the Continental Baking Corporation of Maryland, with an authorized capitalization of $200 million. Incorporated as a holding company, the Continental was chartered to enter not only baking operations in all its branches, but also flour milling and other lines of food manufacture. Probably to allay any suspicion of violation of anti-trust legislation, Ward held no office with the new concern. A 21 per cent ownership of voting stock, however, gave him a controlling interest.

One of the first moves of the new holding company was the acquisition of the United Bakeries Corporation. Next, the corporation launched a vigorous program of acquiring bakeries throughout the country. In rapid succession, it bought the Wagner Baking Company of Detroit (1 plant) and the Livingston Baking Company in Chicago (3 plants). In January, 1925, Continental added the Standard Bakeries Corporation (8 plants), and four months later, the United Retail Bakeries, Inc. The latter firm had been organized in February by Ward to gain control of four house-to-house bakeries, one in Detroit, one in Buffalo, and two in Cleveland.[10]

The American Bakery Company of St. Louis was added to the Ward empire in May. This firm itself was the result of the first local merger in the industry. Other firms were rapidly acquired, some of which were themselves the results of combinations; others had been family firms that had grown to considerable size. Primary among these were the Consumer Baking Company of New Jersey (2 plants), the Taggart Baking Company of Indiana (2 plants), and the Massachusetts Baking

---

[9] Federal Trade Commission, *Bakery Combines and Profits*, Senate Document No. 212, 69th Congress, 2nd Session (Washington: United States Government Printing Office, 1927), p. 5.

[10] *Ibid.*, p. 245.

Company (8 plants). By 1926, Continental controlled ninety-one plants in the United States and nine in Canada, and operated in more than seventy-three cities located in twenty-eight states and the District of Columbia.[11] It was the largest corporation in the baking industry. The transactions that brought this about are charted below.

Ward was, in a sense, just beginning. With Continental fully under way by May, 1925, he waited only until October before forming the General Baking Corporation of Maryland, in cooperation with Paul Helms. Their purpose was to take over one of the pioneer multi-market firms, the General Baking Company, which they did. Thus, immediately following its incorporation, the General Baking Corporation had thirty-three bakeries located in twenty-five cities. Within another month, General took over the Smith-Great Western Company, a holding company operating nine bakeries in seven cities. This company had been organized early in 1923 to combine the Consumers Bread Company of Kansas City, the Tulsa Bread Company, the Smith Baking Company, the Enid Bread Company, and the Cripe Baking Company. By 1926, General Baking's holdings had swelled to forty-two bakeries in thirty-two cities.[12]

In retrospect, it seems obvious that Ward's promotion of the three largest companies in the industry was but a prelude to an even more ambitious program. For on January 30, 1926, the Ward Food Products Corporation was chartered in Maryland as a super holding company. Its announced purpose was to bring Continental, Ward, and General under its banner, covering in all approximately 20 per cent of the commercial production of bread in the United States.

But Ward was not to have his way.

On February 8, the government abruptly blocked the way, by bringing an anti-trust suit against Ward and his whole

---

[11] *Ibid.*, pp. 260-261.
[12] *Ibid.*, p. 242.

CHART 1
FORMATION OF CONTINENTAL BAKING CORPORATION[a]

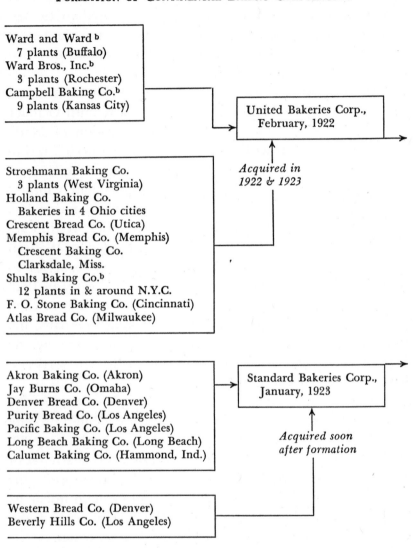

Ward and Ward [b]
  7 plants (Buffalo)
Ward Bros., Inc.[b]
  3 plants (Rochester)
Campbell Baking Co.[b]
  9 plants (Kansas City)

United Bakeries Corp.,
February, 1922

Acquired in
1922 & 1923

Stroehmann Baking Co.
  3 plants (West Virginia)
Holland Baking Co.
  Bakeries in 4 Ohio cities
Crescent Bread Co. (Utica)
Memphis Bread Co. (Memphis)
  Crescent Baking Co.
  Clarksdale, Miss.
Shults Baking Co.[b]
  12 plants in & around N.Y.C.
F. O. Stone Baking Co. (Cincinnati)
Atlas Bread Co. (Milwaukee)

Akron Baking Co. (Akron)
Jay Burns Co. (Omaha)
Denver Bread Co. (Denver)
Purity Bread Co. (Los Angeles)
Pacific Baking Co. (Los Angeles)
Long Beach Baking Co. (Long Beach)
Calumet Baking Co. (Hammond, Ind.)

Standard Bakeries Corp.,
January, 1923

Acquired soon
after formation

Western Bread Co. (Denver)
Beverly Hills Co. (Los Angeles)

---

[a] Carl Alsberg, *Combination in the American Bread-Baking Industry,* Miscellaneous Publication No. 3, Food Research Institute (California: Stanford University, 1926), Appendix.
  Federal Trade Commission, *Competition and Profits in Bread and Flour,* 70th Congress, 1st Session, Senate Document No. 98 (Washington: Government Printing Office, 1928), pp. 228-272.
[b] Previous consolidation.

CHART 1 *(Continued)*
FORMATION OF CONTINENTAL BAKING CORPORATION

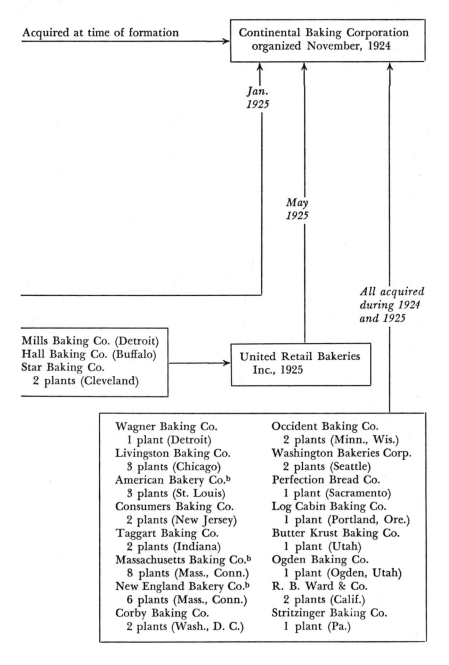

Acquired at time of formation

Continental Baking Corporation
organized November, 1924

*Jan.
1925*

*May
1925*

*All acquired
during 1924
and 1925*

Mills Baking Co. (Detroit)
Hall Baking Co. (Buffalo)
Star Baking Co.
  2 plants (Cleveland)

United Retail Bakeries
Inc., 1925

Wagner Baking Co.
  1 plant (Detroit)
Livingston Baking Co.
  3 plants (Chicago)
American Bakery Co.[b]
  3 plants (St. Louis)
Consumers Baking Co.
  2 plants (New Jersey)
Taggart Baking Co.
  2 plants (Indiana)
Massachusetts Baking Co.[b]
  8 plants (Mass., Conn.)
New England Bakery Co.[b]
  6 plants (Mass., Conn.)
Corby Baking Co.
  2 plants (Wash., D. C.)

Occident Baking Co.
  2 plants (Minn., Wis.)
Washington Bakeries Corp.
  2 plants (Seattle)
Perfection Bread Co.
  1 plant (Sacramento)
Log Cabin Baking Co.
  1 plant (Portland, Ore.)
Butter Krust Baking Co.
  1 plant (Utah)
Ogden Baking Co.
  1 plant (Ogden, Utah)
R. B. Ward & Co.
  2 plants (Calif.)
Stritzinger Baking Co.
  1 plant (Pa.)

empire.[13] The government petition charged that, in violation
of the Sherman Anti-Trust Act, the defendants were "engaged in a combination and conspiracy in undue and unrea-
sonable restraint of trade and commerce." [14] It also charged
that, in violation of the Clayton Act, the "defendants had acquired, are acquiring and propose in the immediate future to
acquire the whole or substantial part of the stocks of corpo-
tions in the baking and related industries for the purpose of
lessening and eliminating competition between these corporate defendants." [15] The petition was the customary one ask-
ing the court for a perpetual enjoinment free from any act by
the defendants that would result in common corporate
control.

After negotiations between the Department of Justice, the
Federal Trade Commission and the defendants, a consent decree was entered into on April 3, 1926, under which Ward,
Paul H. Helms, and George G. Barber, and the corporations
involved were ". . . perpetually restrained and enjoined from
any act that would bring the several defendants under common control or that would restrain or monopolize interstate
trade in the future."

The corporate defendants were also enjoined

. . . from acquiring the whole or any part of the share capital
of any of the other baking corporations engaged in interstate
commerce where the effect of such acquisition may be to
substantially lessen competition in such commerce between
the corporation whose stock is so acquired and the defendant
corporation or tend to create a monopoly.

The individual defendants were not to acquire, receive,
hold, vote, or act as the owners of any of the voting shares
of the capital stock of more than one of the defendant corpo-

[13] A petition was filed against the Ward Food Products Corporation, the Ward
Baking Corporation, Ward Baking Company, the General Baking Corporation, the
General Baking Company, Continental Baking Corporation, United Bakeries Corporation, and various individuals interested in these organizations.
[14] Federal Trade Commission, *op. cit.,* p. 271.
[15] *Ibid.*

rations and its subsidiaries or to acquire any of the physical assets of more than one of these corporations. The consent decree also provided that the Ward Products Corporation should relinquish its charter.[16]

The decree put an effective stop to any further attempts to form a super holding company in the baking industry. It also marked the end of the career of William B. Ward, who died shortly after the court order.

The extent to which the multi-market and national organizations realized the economies of operation visualized at the outset of their formation cannot be accurately measured. It is clear that a number of the companies organized on a regional or inter-regional basis had difficulty for some time in coordinating the activities of the middle management group, composed largely of former owners. While this problem may have been less crucial for the top management of the large concerns organized after 1922, such managements, particularly the "Ward" group, found themselves saddled with unwieldy financial structures.

This situation may be illustrated by an impasse reached in the affairs of Continental. At the time of its formation it was tremendously overcapitalized. Its assets were carried on the books at greatly inflated values and were barely sufficient to cover the par value of the preferred stock. As a result, the holders of both classes of common stock were left with no equity in the company whatsoever. As late as 1937, even after assets had been whittled down by some $18,000,000, the company still carried on its books an item of $10,295,999.64 for "goodwill and patents." Moreover, an $8.00 cumulative dividend on preferred stock seriously restricted the payment of dividends to the common stockholders. In fact, although Continental's annual profit never fell below a depression low of $1,902,000 in 1935, profits were never large enough until 1943 to pay off the dividend on the preferred stock and have

---

16 *Ibid.,* pp. 272-273.

anything left over for the common stockholders. It was not until 1945 that the oppressive $8.00 cumulative preferred stock was completely eliminated.[17]

The Ward Baking Corporation and the General Baking Corporation faced similar difficulties. General, in fact, was overcapitalized to such an extent that the consent decree itself directed the firm to reduce its stock.

Despite these difficulties, the fact that the multi-market firms became a permanent part of the industry structure is sufficient evidence of their ability to establish and maintain their competitive position. But the survival of the independent bakers also makes it equally clear that economies accruing to the multi-market firms did not give them a decisive competitive advantage.

It should not be supposed, however, that the independents maintained their competitive position during this period without a struggle. In addition to the challenge of multi-market concerns, they were also under pressure from the chain stores that began during the 1920s to bake and distribute their own products on an increasing scale. Their survival was, to a considerable extent, a tribute to their adaptability to changing competitive conditions. The big firms undoubtedly enjoyed some advantages in respect to finances and management. But the growth of baking service organizations, such as the W. E. Long Company of Chicago, gave the individual operator access to services such as the laboratory analysis of ingredients, package design, and attractive brand names, management and engineering advice, and accounting and comparative cost data.

In addition to improving his methods of production and distribution, the alert independent baker learned that he could operate successfully within his local market by catering to its particular needs. In contrast to the manager of a branch plant, he was in a position to adapt more quickly to changing market conditions. Outside the metropolitan areas

---

[17] Lou Kennedy, "Continental, the Wonder Bakery," *Bakers' Helper*, Chicago, November 26, 1949 (reprinted).

the independent baker often appealed effectively to local pride. He was quite likely to belong to the chamber of commerce and to be active in civic affairs. He usually received financial support from the local banks and might, and did, claim that his business kept "money from going outside the community."

At the same time, experience showed practically no differentials in the manufacturing and distribution costs of multi-market firms and independent companies. The only information available on the comparative operations of the independent and the multi-market bakeries is contained in a study by the Federal Trade Commission in 1924. While the findings of this study, summarized in Table 1, are in terms of averages

TABLE 1

REALIZATIONS, COSTS, AND PROFITS PER POUND OF BREAD FOR EXCLUSIVELY WHOLESALE PLANTS OF SINGLE AND MULTIPLE PLANT COMPANIES, 1922–1925 *

(Cents per pound)

Item	Plants of single-plant companies up to 30,000,000 pounds	Plants of multiple-plant companies up to 30,000,000 pounds
Flour	2.292	2.272
Other ingredients	.958	.893
Total ingredients	3.250	3.165
Manufacturing	1.605	1.698
Selling and delivery	1.547	1.581
General and administrative	.392	.205
Total cost	6.794	6.649
Profit	.572	.729
Sales realization	7.366	7.378
Total cost to doors of plant	4.855	4.863
Total cost less ingredients	3.544	3.484
Plant years	163	447
Average production per plant	7,121,712	10,006,368

* Federal Trade Commission, *Competition and Profits in Bread and Flour*, 70th Congress, 1st Session, Senate Document No. 92, U. S. Government Printing Office, Washington, 1928, p. 308.

and do not indicate the range between the most and the least efficient firms in each category, they may be accepted as reasonably typical.

The data in Table 1 show that the multi-market plants had lower ingredient costs, probably due to the central purchasing program of the parent company. Local plants, on the other hand, at least partially offset this advantage with their lower manufacturing, selling, and delivery expenses. Multi-market plants gained their greatest advantage from lower general and administrative expenses. Spread over many facilities, these expenses amounted to less than one-half of those for the single-plant companies. Total costs reflected this advantage as did profits where the multi-market plants showed an edge amounting to .164 cents per pound. As noted by the Federal Trade Commission, however, the total cost and profit differences may be somewhat misleading because of the withdrawal of profits by local operators in the form of higher executive salaries which abnormally swelled their general and administrative expenses. Making adjustments for their ballooned administrative outlays, single-plant companies would not be expected to show spectacular cost reductions when brought under the control of large firms.

Summary

Mergers and the subsequent development of multi-market firms were a part of the evolving structure of the baking industry. They were perhaps more spectacular than other structural changes that marked this period of baking history, but like the emergence of industrial baking itself, they constituted one type of response to the changed conditions faced by the industry. That they came at a time when mergers were general throughout the nation is certainly not surprising. That they were carried to an extreme by one man—W. B. Ward—there can be no doubt. But, it is extremely doubtful that without him they might never have occurred. They can be considered an economic result of the natural attempt to off-set the uncertainties of local market structures.

The effect of the mergers was a different matter. Like the entry of chain-store bakers, the emergence of multi-market firms created an atmosphere of confusion among other industry members who were worried that these giants would eliminate any and all competitors. But by 1930, when the air had cleared, it was found that their impact had not been as great as had been feared. Their advantages over the independents were not so great as to prevent parallel existence in each local market. This local nature of baking prevented any effective concentration by the larger firms; even on a national basis, the four largest firms in the industry had less than 20 per cent of total bakery sales.

CHAPTER 11

THE EXPERIENCE OF INDUSTRIAL COMPETITION

THE IMPACT of the many changes in the baking industry between 1900 and 1930 was nowhere more strongly realized than in the market place. Reflecting the industry's expanded demand, the widespread application of machine baking and modern methods of distribution, and the growth of multi-plant firms, competition among bakers became more complex than when the industry was dominated by a series of retail bakers selling over the counter. The problems of inter-plant competition at the distributive level brought about a new way of life for the baking industry; the lessons learned did not come easily.

The retail bakeshops that sold the great bulk of commercially baked products at the turn of the century had little direct contact with their competitors. Operating in market areas which, except at the periphery, did not overlap those of other shops, they sold to customers who were largely attracted by the convenience of location. No doubt they could and did strengthen customer loyalty by personal contact, by catering to particular tastes, and by establishing a reputation for quality.

If any sellers in 1900 were in a position to perceive the dim outline of the changes in competitive relationships which were to emerge during the succeeding ten to twenty years, it was that handful of bakers already engaged in wholesale or house-to-house distribution. For in the grocery store or at their doorstep, consumers now had at least the beginnings of a choice among the products of several bakeries. Bakers distributing to these markets became increasingly conscious of the problem of advancing or maintaining their share of total market sales. Save for their house-to-house salesmen, these bakers lost personal contact with their customers and were confronted with a need to develop other means of gaining consumer preference.

As more and more of the industry's product shifted from the retail bakeshops into other channels of distribution, the commercial bakers experimented with new tools of competition. Over the succeeding two decades, experience of industry members had run the gamut from price cuts to give-away programs, and they had become familiar with the relative advantages of different methods of stimulating or maintaining sales. But this sophistication came only after a series of market upheavals. The typical pattern began with relatively stable market relations, followed by intensive competition as a new form of distribution made its appearance or as new firms entered a market area. Relative stability again re-emerged with the establishment of a new pattern of market shares. The expectation, however, that a new cycle could start at any time new entrants came into particular market areas or began to distribute through different marketing channels, soon became an integral part of the competitive mental framework of bakery management.

As already noted, one of the first reactions of wholesale bakers to competition in local markets was to cut prices in the expectation that lower unit prices would be more than offset by an expanded volume of sales. This strategy was also used by multi-market firms in the invasion of other market areas. Members of both groups soon experienced the devastating effects of this type of competition as rivals countered the initial price cuts.

While price wars continued to play a role in industry competition over its later history, bakers soon sought other means of acquiring or increasing sales. Certain of these methods were little more than substitutes for straight price cutting, e.g., "hidden" price concessions. Others were designed to attract consumers by differentiation of product quality, convenience, and service. Typically, bakers under strong competitive pressure could utilize both price and non-price methods in their struggle with competitors, the precise pattern depending upon a particular set of circumstances.

The first significant use of non-price methods of competition began about the turn of the century. It was the morning of the comic-strip age when the tremendous trivia of the *Yellow Kid,* the *Katzenjammer Kids, Little Jimmy* and the like had caught the public's fancy. It remained only for wide-awake advertising men to combine the eye-catcher—the cartoon hero—and a brand name. In 1904, the "Butter-Nut Boy" appeared, the creation of Paul and William Schulze. As a promotion device, the "Butter-Nut Boy" brand proved to be a success almost over night.[1]

In a few short years, the idea spread rapidly within the bread industry. It became big business, in a way, when bakery advertising bureaus began licensing or franchising popular heroes of the comic strips to eager bakers. Many of the best known brand names date from this period; for example, *Bamby, Tip Top, Holsum, Teddy Bear, Mary Jane,* and *Buster Brown.* Of all their creators, W. E. Long, father of *Buster Brown,* was the master. For his clients, Long hired midgets and bulldogs, fitted out as *Buster* and *Tige,* and paraded them down Main Streets. Sixty-five bakeries, so Long claimed, were using the *Buster Brown* label by 1907.[2]

Spurred by such advertising, competition in the baking

---

[1] Sperry, "65 Years of Baking Advertising," *op. cit.,* XCVII (April 12, 1952), p. 152.

[2] A court decision later ruled that brand names could not be sold in the manner described, but this was after the franchising practice had disappeared. E. J. Sperry, *Bread Brands* (Chicago: E. J. Sperry—Industrial Publications, 1949), p. 34.

industry found vigorous expression over the next decade or so. The use of prizes, premiums, and give-aways became widespread, and contests were designed to appeal to children and adults. One popular series of contests awarded winners Shetland ponies "complete with a book on how to take care of them." [3] To increase sales, some bakers offered the housewife valuable merchandise in exchange for a sufficient number of bread wrappers. As premiums, others offered coupons redeemable in cash. Still others inserted pictures of reigning baseball stars or movie greats within the bread wrappers.

Bakery sales promotion, like similar selling campaigns in other fields, did not ignore retail distributors. Gifts to grocers, or any device that might induce the grocer to promote a brand were especially widespread. Petty emoluments were common—cigars, cigarettes, and free passes to athletic events. In a more ostentatious attempt to win grocers' favors, glass cases to house bread on sale were commonly provided by bakers. When wrapping became general, bread racks were used for the same purpose of display.

One aspect of the mounting struggle for increased market sales soon came to be cause for real alarm. This was the great increase in both the volume and the proportion of stale returns which had to be absorbed by the bakeries. The excessive loading of groceries with bread in an effort to promote sales, although initially considered by wholesalers as a temporary measure, quickly crystallized into a permanent practice. As a result, stale returns, instead of amounting to no more than a normal 1 per cent of sales, rose to levels which seemed fantastic. At first, stale bread losses of 6 to 10 per cent of production became common even among efficient operators. In periods of more intense competition, losses running as high as 25-30 per cent frequently occurred. In November, 1917, the United States Food Administration estimated that loss from return of stale bread amounted to "upwards of 600,000

---

[3] Sperry, "65 Years of Bakery Advertising," *op. cit.*, XCVII (April 12, 1952), p. 328.

barrels" of flour a year, equivalent to about 2.7 million bushels of wheat.[4]

As in the case of direct price competition, bakers found their competitors rapidly reacting to other forms of sales promotion. Operating in markets where the number of sellers was relatively small, most industrial bakers were affected by the successful programs introduced by rivals. Unless a response in kind was quickly resorted to, the risks of permanent deterioration of market positions appeared overwhelming. Advertising campaigns, prize contests, more generous arrangements for the return of stales, and similar tactics of rivals were all matched by devices that promised to be at least equally effective. The employment of these new-found tools of competition had results less happy than the restoration of balance among members in a given market. Their use, in an intensive manner, frequently resulted in the havoc that was associated with straight price wars.

The potential instability of competitive relations in the baking industry was especially evident during the 1920s. As the motor truck extended market areas, invasion of new markets became common. So too were the results, as home-town bakers found themselves locked in aggressive struggles with invading wholesalers.

The institutional markets also proved particularly susceptible to the outbreak of competitive warfare. Because many wholesalers considered sales through this channel as marginal business, they were prepared to grant substantial price concessions to secure additional orders. After a realignment had been reached among suppliers, the sharpness of competition would subside, but for only so long as another major supplier did not enter the field.

Probably the most vigorous competitive campaigns during the 1920s came with the emergence of large holding companies and the rise of chain-store baking.

---

[4] "The Stale Bread Problem," *Wheat Studies of the Food Research Institute* (Stanford University, Calif.: Stanford Univ. Press, 1936), XII, p. 221.

The multi-market firms had to do a larger and larger volume of business to achieve economies of scale to spread their management outlays, and to keep earnings up to meet the financial obligations of increased investment. The acquisition of existing firms by these giants seemingly had done nothing to allay the compulsion for expanded market shares. Their entry into an area was usually followed by the whole gamut of competitive practices evolved over the preceding decades. One especially effective device to increase routes and sales was to pirate driver-salesmen—and their customers—from rivals.[5]

In 1922, South Bend witnessed the competitive warfare employed by multi-market firms. That year, the Ward Baking Company acquired the South Bend Baking Company and was also trying to take over a local competitor, the Busse Baking Company. When F. W. Busse refused to sell, Ward set about to force Busse out of business. A price war followed, sending bread prices tumbling by an average of 33 per cent. In addition, the Ward firm offered, with its bread, free coupons ranging in value from two to five cents. Despite the conciliatory efforts of other local bakers, the battle continued until December when Busse finally capitulated. On December 17, 1922, the original price levels were restored.[6]

As early as 1922, the American Bakers Association attempted to curb the use of destructive competitive practices. It asked its members to comply with a code of competitive ethics which was little more than a general pledge to abstain from unfair trade practices except as compelled by competitive conditions. Within a few short weeks of its adoption, the code was discarded because of a price war in Kansas City, Missouri, in which the association's president, W. Campbell, was in-

---

[5] In one case where a multi-market baker hired his competitor's route man, the competitor suffered a 70 per cent loss of business on that particular route. Federal Trade Commission, *Competition and Profits in Bread and Flour*, Senate Document No. 98, 70th Congress, 1st Session (Washington: U. S. Government Printing Office, 1928), p. 76.

[6] Federal Trade Commission, *op. cit.*, p. 186.

volved. It had been claimed that his company brought on this conflict on the heels of its purchase by Ward and Ward, Inc., a subsidiary of the United Bakeries Corporation. The ill feelings which ensued terminated both the code and Mr. Campbell's incumbency.[7]

Aggressive competitive tactics occurred in market after market wherever multi-market firms sought to expand sales volume. Not until the wave of mergers had been halted in the late 1920s did many of the markets once again enjoy more stabilized competitive relationships. To be sure, price wars and other forms of intensive competition reappeared on occasion, for there continued a constant jockeying for market position which frequently got out of hand. But after the consent decree of 1926, the multi-market firms, especially those formerly associated with Ward, were in no position to continue the use of destructive trade practices. Indeed they were so beset with problems of reorganization and operation that little time was available for aggressive activity. Moreover, the F.T.C. and the Anti-Trust Division of the Department of Justice, was according more than usual attention to the industry.

That the tides of competition in the 1920s ran as high as they did for the local baker was due also, in no small part, to the stress and strain of the competition offered by the chain store bakeries. As noted before, the endless friction between the baker and the chain store had resulted in the entry of the latter into the baking field itself. By the mid-twenties, that entry had become a challenge of no mean size. For good reason: the newcomer was upsetting marketing arrangements because his lower operating costs permitted him to lower retail prices.

In markets affected, general confusion reigned. Among bakers, there was a furious debate. Some held that the chain store bakery was merely a temporary phenomenon. Others

---

[7] *Ibid.*, p. 80.

held that it was a permanent fixture. In either case, the local bakers did everything in their power to compete with the newcomer. They fought back by price cutting and advertising. With respect to price cutting, the advantage clearly lay with the chain stores, who met each price change and initiated several of their own, always keeping a spread between their prices and those of the wholesalers. On the other hand, the local baker had the advantage of a well-known established brand as well as the appeal of a local businessman. They played the theme that chain-store bread was cheap bread, not comparable to their own.

The chains retaliated with some new competitive tactics of their own in markets where competition waxed hottest. Some refused to allow the wholesaler to place his bread in their outlets. Where the wholesaler continued to sell, the chain-store manager effectively discriminated against him in respect to display and rack space. Chains were often accused of keeping large amounts of wholesalers' brands concealed until the chain brand had been sold. It was also claimed that the chains often offered bread as a loss leader (i.e., at prices below cost), as a patronage promotion. Such practice was probably less frequent than the wholesalers charged.

Chain-store competition was not diminished when wholesalers undertook the manufacture of bread-stuffs under the private brands of voluntary chain organizations. Such arrangements had the same price effects as when chain stores did their own baking. Wholesalers who supplied the voluntary chains were sharply criticized not only by the independent grocers, but also by other wholesalers who accused them of abject surrender to the chains. Frequently, bakers who baked under private label for the voluntary chains were in a weak market position and had seized this opportunity to survive. In some cases, wholesalers also supplied chain-store organizations in markets other than their own. Bakers in the invaded markets often retaliated in kind, with the mutual interpenetration ending in strong competitive battles.

By 1930, the initial shock of chain-store competition had run its course. Wholesalers realized that it was not temporary, and they accepted the fact, albeit reluctantly, that they could not match low chain prices. Still, it appeared that most consumers preferred non-chain-store baked goods, for the chains had only 5 per cent of the entire baking industry sales. This fact, together with the realization that the financial power of chain stores was so much stronger, brought an end to widespread hostilities. There was a general realignment of positions in each market and competition tended to resume a less aggressive relationship. Price wars continued, but they were restricted affairs caused by local conditions rather than part of a broader wholesaler-chain-store struggle.

Between 1900 and 1930 the nation's bakers faced a competitive situation that provided one of the most dynamic periods in the industry's history. The changes in the structure of the industry were boldly reflected in new patterns of competition, patterns that contrasted vividly with the almost helter-skelter activity of former days, and which were no freer of the incessant and shifting forces of industry change. But experience soon demonstrated that application of powerful weapons usually elicited either violent responses in kind, or different responses from unanticipated quarters. Greater familiarity with the ground rules of competition in enlarged, dynamic markets generated a mounting caution in the promiscuous use of price competition that might throw markets into prolonged periods of warfare. With that growing caution, bakers increasingly sought to channel their competitive resources into advertising, sales promotion, and services that would bring an evolution rather than a disruptive revolution of market balances. If the 'twenties did not remove the potential instability of competitive relations, they did make most participants in baking markets more aware of the sources of instability and the need to condition their competitive responses accordingly.

CHAPTER 12

THE GROWTH AND STRUCTURAL PATTERN
OF THE BAKING INDUSTRY: A SUMMARY

MEASURED BY any yardstick, the growth of the American baking industry during the first three decades of the twentieth century was impressive. By 1930 it could be numbered among America's major industries. The principal dimensions of the industry's expansion are shown in Table 1.

With respect to output, dollar volume increased more than nine times totaling over $1.25 billion in 1930. Because of a general upward movement in prices, physical volume experienced a smaller increase, amounting to about five and one-half fold. Yet the rate of growth of physical output continued to be impressively large; volume more than doubled during the first decade and increased at rates of 70 and 50 per cent, respectively, during the next two decades. Moreover, the absolute increases in volume each decade were greater than that for the entire fifty-year period preceding 1900.

The average number of wage earners increased approximately three times between 1900 and 1930. Like the figures on the increased output in the industry, these also represent a large absolute growth. In the decade 1920 to 1930 the total number of wage earners added to the industry exceeded the total number employed in 1900. As was true of United States industry generally, the rise in total employment was accom-

TABLE 1

GROWTH OF THE BAKING INDUSTRY: A FEW KEY MEASURES,
CENSUS YEARS, 1899–1929 [a]

Year	Number of Estab.	Value of Product ($000)	Index of $ Value	Index of Physical Volume[b]	Average No. of Wage Earners	Index of Employment
1899	14,917	$175,369	35.6	42.4	60,192	48.5
1904	18,226	269,583	54.8	63.1	81,278	65.6
1909	23,926	396,865	82.3	88.1	100,216	80.8
1914	25,963	491,893	100.0	100.0	124,052	100.0
1914	25,797	402,409	100.0	100.0	99,016	100.0
1919	24,919	947,876	235.5	148.4	107,251	108.3
1921[c]	20,024	902,463	224.3	142.8	117,026	118.2
1923	18,572	911,118	226.4	162.1	127,496	128.8
1925	17,490	1,023,668	254.4	172.4	128,034	129.3
1927	17,909	1,145,710	284.7	195.0	139,013	140.4
1929	20,410	1,251,621	311.0	222.6	166,970	168.6

[a] While the Census of Manufactures did not report separate data for the perishable bakery products industry until 1914, the indices in Table 1 have been computed on two bases; one up to 1914 includes the biscuit and cracker industry, the other from 1914 to 1924 applies only to the bread-baking branch of the industry. By this method, the indices can be used throughout the entire thirty-year period. The growth of the bread branch of the industry is thus only slightly underestimated since the biscuit and cracker industry accounted for 28 per cent of total baking industry sales in 1900 and 19 per cent in 1914.

[b] Computed from 1899 to 1914 by dividing index of value of product by indices for Washington, D.C., Cincinnati, Ohio, and New York City of unweighted wholesale bread price "per loaf before baking." Source: U.S. Department of Labor, Bureau of Labor Statistics, *Wholesale Prices, 1890 to 1923*, Bureau of Labor Statistics Bulletin No. 357, p. 74.

Computed from 1914 to 1929 by dividing index of value of product by the average retail price index of white bread. Source: Bureau of Labor Statistics, *Average Retail Price per Pound of White Bread, 1913–1949*.

Price indices on other bakery products were not available; the assumption is made that these indices would generally follow that of bread.

[c] Data from 1921 through 1929 represent establishments with an annual value of products of $5,000 or more.

panied by a significant increase in worker productivity (80 per cent), a reflection of the growing use of mechanical production techniques.

While Census data indicate that there was an increase in the number of bakery establishments between 1900 and 1930 equal to about 37 per cent, such information does not give a precise picture of the full significance of that growth. First, use of the absolute number conceals the larger average size of bakeries as of 1930. Second, the data after 1919 include only those firms with minimum annual sales of $5,000.

As in the preceding fifty-year period, the overall expansion of the baking industry more than kept pace with the growth of manufactures generally. (See Table 2.) From eighteenth position, measured in dollar volume in 1900, baking rose to twelfth place by 1929. And by that date, it was thirteenth in value added by manufacture and in average number of wage earners and first in number of establishments.[1]

In 1929, baking accounted for about 2 per cent of the nation's manufacturing industry in terms of value added and number of employees. This represented a healthy increase over the approximately 1.74 per cent and 1.34 per cent in these categories thirty years earlier. Biscuit and cracker bakers, of course, are included in these data. The unevenness of the expension reflects differing price levels as between baked goods and other manufactured products.

Among all food industries, baking exhibited an even greater relative growth. Moving from less than 7 per cent of the value of output of all food processors at the turn of the century to more than 10 per cent by 1930, the nation's bakers were in several respects the leading food manufacturers in the country. They ranked first in total wage earners employed, number of establishments, and value added by manufacture. By dollar volume, only the meat packing industry occupied

---

[1] Bakery establishments, however, included the single-unit retail shops whose great number made the total number of bakeries out of proportion with all manufacturing plants.

TABLE 2

GROWTH OF THE BAKING INDUSTRY AS A PER CENT OF ALL
MANUFACTURING INDUSTRIES, CENSUS YEARS 1899–1929[a]

Census	% of No. of Establish- ments	% of $ Value of Product	% of Value Added by Manufacture	% of Average No. of Wage Earners
1899[b]	7.29	1.59	1.74	1.34
1904[b]	8.54	1.89	1.89	1.57
1909[b]	9.03	1.99	1.95	1.60
1914	9.61	1.73	1.83	1.50
1919	11.85	1.58	1.42	1.27
1921[c]	10.43	2.12	2.24	1.81
1923	9.67	1.57	1.73	1.56
1925	9.51	1.68	1.80	1.63
1927	9.54	1.90	2.13	1.77
1929	9.88	1.84	2.03	1.99

[a] Statistics on all manufacturing industries gathered from the *Historical Statistics of the United States, 1789–1945*. A supplement to the *Statistical Abstract of the United States;* Series J, 1-12. *Manufactures—General Statistics for all Manufacturing Industries: 1849 to 1939*, p. 179. These figures on manufactures in general have been adjusted by the deduction of certain minor data.

[b] Includes biscuit and cracker bakeries.

[c] Excludes establishments having products valued at less than $5,000 as in subsequent years.

a position superior to baking. Bakers had thus surpassed their principal supplier, the flour milling industry, their products being valued at one-fifth more than those of flour mills.[2]

The growth of the baking industry was primarily a reflection of the increased demand for commercial bakery products, the mechanization of bakery production, and the expansion of mass distribution, all of which have been examined in preceding chapters. By 1930, with commercial bakery output equal to 60 per cent of total bread products, bakers could claim for the first time that they produced more than housewives. Despite the overall decline in the per capita consumption of bread occasioned by a change in Americans' food habits, the rapid decline in home baking and a continued rise in

[2] *U. S. Census of Manufactures*, 1929.

population were more than sufficient to produce a tremendously increased demand for commercially baked bread. In addition, by 1930 bakers were producing a significant amount of all variety-baked goods (some 20 to 25 per cent of total consumption). Variety baked goods provided about one-third of total value of commercial bakery production.[3]

Stemming from the increased demand for commercial bakery products, and in turn contributing to it, were the changes in technology and in distribution. By the end of the period the craft tradition of baking had virtually disappeared as machine production proved itself capable of turning out a uniform, tasty, quality product. Bread-making machines were introduced and improved to such point that, in the largest plants at least, production had become a continuous flow, assembly-line type of operation. Even the baking of variety goods had, to a considerable extent, been converted to machine production techniques. For all bakers the application of machinery to baking increased the optimum size of plant operations and put pressure on them to enlarge the volume of sales.

Concurrent with its expansion were the basic structural changes which encompassed almost every aspect of the baking industry. Moreover, the pattern that had emerged by 1930 was to remain virtually unchanged over the succeeding quarter century of the industry's history.

The introduction of the motor truck was a prime factor in extending the geographic limits of the markets which could be effectively served by individual bakeries. This expansion, plus the general growth in demand for bakery products, encouraged industrial bakers to enter and develop new channels of distribution. While grocery stores continued to be the most important customers, sales to institutions and through house-to-house delivery were, by 1930, especially important additions to the business of wholesale bakers.

---

3 *Ibid.*

The most striking structural change was the development and expansion of a relatively few, large-scale, industrial bakeries. Table 3, showing the sales-size distribution of baking establishments, is in sharp contrast to the situation existing at the turn of the century, when less than one-tenth of the bakeries accounted for approximately 25 per cent of total industry output. As of 1930, 12 per cent of the nation's bakeries were producing two-thirds of total dollar volume.

Without exception, these large-scale bakeries were operated by the industrial bakers, who had become dominant in the industry. According to the Census, industrial bakers as a group produced almost 80 per cent of industry's output in 1929. The remainder was accounted for by individual retail bakeshops, still by far the most numerous in the industry, whose share some thirty years before had amounted to 75 per cent.

TABLE 3

SIZE DISTRIBUTION OF BAKERIES BY TOTAL DISTRIBUTED SALES,
CENSUS YEAR, 1929[a]

Sales Size Category	Value of Sales (000)	Per Cent of Sales	Number of Plants	Per Cent of Number
Over $500,000	$ 470,845	39.7	419	2.6
$100,000–$500,000	314,129	26.5	1,512	9.4
$50,000–$100,000	133,009	11.2	1,947	12.2
Less than $50,000	269,007	22.7	12,138	75.8
Totals[b]	$1,186,990	100.1	16,016	100.0

[a] U. S. Census of Distribution, 1930, Vol. II, Distribution of Sales of Manufacturing Plants, p. 26.
[b] The totals for dollar value of sales and number of plants differ from the figures given in the Census of Manufactures because 4,394 bakeries with aggregate sales of $64,631,000 failed to report their total distributed sales by class of customer for the Census of Distribution.

A brief review will indicate the growing complexity of the operations of the industrial bakers. In 1900 they were single-plant firms delivering almost exclusively to grocer outlets in a given, closely circumscribed, market area. Thirty years later the multi-market firms had taken a place alongside the single-plant operators. Depending upon the principal type of distribution employed, industrial bakers fell into various categories. While members of each segment might engage in several types of distribution simultaneously, they were nevertheless classified as grocery store wholesalers, house-to-house bakers, institutional sellers, chain store bakers, or multi-unit retailers, depending on the main market character of sales. Within these groups, the grocery store wholesalers were the most important, accounting for over one-half of total industry sales as compared to the approximate 25 per cent for the others.

It was within this structure and the competitive relations it imposed, that the bakers were to work out the grim problems brought on by the major economic depression that lay ahead.

PART

FOUR

BAKING THROUGH DEPRESSION
AND WAR

1930–1950

DEPRESSION AND RECOVERY, 1930–1940

PROBABLY FEW MEMBERS of the baking industry in 1929 considered that the 1930s would be anything other than a decade of a continuous rise in the long-term upward trend of commercial baking. Within a year, however, bakers began to awaken from the complacent assumption, built up from the previous experience of baking with periods of economic slump, that the baking industry was practically "depression proof." By 1933, there was no longer any doubt; baking, too, was caught in the downward spiral that reversed the prosperity of the 'twenties.

The four short years between 1929 and 1933 witnessed a general economic collapse for the nation as a whole, a collapse more severe than ever before experienced. National income fell by more than 50 per cent; the dollar volume of manufactures experienced a 55 per cent drop, as did the nation's payrolls. Unemployment rose from 429,000 in 1929 to an estimated 15,000,000 early in 1933, representing 25 per cent of the total available labor force. Total corporate net profits fell from $10 billion to net losses of $2 billion, a reduction totaling 119 per cent.[1] The depression was indeed a period of crisis for almost all groups in the economy.

Some groups, of course, were hit harder than others. The

---

[1] Historical Statistics of the United States, *op. cit.*, pp. 12 and 65.

durable goods manufacturers and farmers probably suffered the most. The latter experienced a 60 per cent decline in income as farm prices plunged by more than 50 per cent from their 1929 level; literally thousands were wiped out or otherwise left their farms. In the durable goods field demand diminished toward the vanishing point with consequent cuts in employment, payrolls, production and earnings. The value of output of the iron and steel industry, for example, declined almost 70 per cent.

The nation's food processors fared slightly better, although only in a relative sense. Employment declined approximately 16 per cent while payrolls fell about 33 per cent. The dollar volume of sales in 1933 was 43 per cent below its 1929 peak. But physical volume showed only a slight decline. This was because food products, being primarily necessities of everyday life, were not as sensitive to the effects of the business cycle. Per capita food consumption decreased from 1,576 pounds in 1929 to 1,499 pounds in 1933, a decline of less than 5 per cent.[2] There were few changes in the relative trends of various individual foods making up the total.

For the baking industry, the onset of the depression saw the long upward trend of demand wobble and then turn downward. (Cf. Table 1.) By 1931, dollar sales of bakery products had fallen 21.7 per cent from their 1929 level; by 1933, the decline totaled almost 39 per cent. The $770,000,-000 sales recorded by the industry in 1933 was the lowest since before World War I. As sales dropped, bakery product prices were lowered in the hope that physical volume could be retained. Between 1929 and 1933 bread prices fell from a high of 8.8 to a low of 6.5 cents per pound, a reduction totaling 26 per cent. The prices of sweet goods, although not available for this period, can be assumed to have fallen as much or more. Nevertheless, physical volume fell about 25 per cent, the lowest it had been in over ten years. As a result, there was a reduction in employment and a general lowering of

---

[2] Consumption of Food in the United States, 1909–1952, *op. cit.*, p. 144.

TABLE 1

THE BAKING INDUSTRY, CENSUS YEARS,
1929–1933[a]

Census Year	Number of Establishments	Value of Product ($000)	Index of $ Value of Product	Index of Physical Volume[b]
1929	20,410	$1,251,621	100.0	100.0
1931	17,718	979,904	78.3	89.5
1933	14,830	770,332	61.5	76.3

[a] *U. S. Census of Manufactures.* Establishments with an annual volume of products of less than $5,000 not included.

[b] Based on computations using Bureau of Labor Statistics, Retail Price of White Bread. While prices on other bakery products were not available, it was assumed that these would generally follow the price of bread.

wages. Employment fell off to 88 per cent of the 1929 peak. Payrolls dropped to 66 per cent of their 1929 level; this meant that those workers who did retain their jobs had to accept lower wages.[3]

What had happened was that people were eating less baked goods generally, and in particular less commercially baked foods. On the one hand, it might be expected that in a period of depression and falling personal income, people would cut their consumption of the most expensive baked foods such as cakes, pies and other sweet goods. But in light of the fact that increasing income was an important factor in the long-run decline of per capita bread consumption, it is somewhat surprising that such a trend continued between 1929 and 1933 for bread products. It might, in fact, have been expected that with lower incomes people would increase their consumption of cheaper foods such as bread by substituting them for the more expensive meats, fruits, vegetables and dairy products. The pressures were definitely in this direction, for people were forced by necessity to alter their eating habits. But it was not so much a change in the types of food consumed as a

[3] *U. S. Census of Manufactures, 1933.*

more frugal utilization. In other words, with lower incomes, there was much less wastage of bread and other foods as compared to the period before 1930. This was, of course, reflected as a decline not only in bread consumption but in the consumption of almost all foods.

The reduced output of the baking industry between 1929 and 1933 was also due to a return to home baking. Income pressures were such that the minor cost differences between homemade baked goods and bakers' products became significant for many people. For the first time in the history of the baking industry in America the long-run decline in home baking was reversed. There was a shift back to home baking of approximately 4 per cent.[4] It took a major economic depression to bring it about.

The effect of both the reduced consumption and the return to home baking was more strongly felt in the production of sweet goods than of bread products. From 1929 to 1933 the commercial production of bread and rolls declined about 16 per cent compared to an approximate 50 per cent drop in sweet goods output.[5] These figures were reflected in changes in the relative proportions of bakery products turned out by the baking industry. (Cf. Table 2.) While total dollar sales declined in all categories, the relative decrease in variety baked goods was far greater than that of bread. Bread, rolls and yeast-raised sweet goods together rose from about two-thirds to three-fourths of dollar output, while other products suffered a relative decline.[6]

In terms of industry structure this meant that the variety goods bakers—wholesale cake and pie bakers, the multi-unit retailers, the small-scale bakeshop operators and, to a limited extent, the house-to-house bakers—suffered relatively more than did the bread bakers. The hardest hit were the single-

---

[4] R. W. and U. B. Stone, "The Baking Industry Under N. R. A.," *The Journal of Business of the University of Chicago*, VI (April, 1936), p. 6.

[5] *Ibid.*

[6] Within this category there can be little doubt that yeast-raised sweet goods experienced a greater percentage decline than bread and rolls.

TABLE 2

PRODUCT BREAKDOWN OF THE BAKING INDUSTRY, CENSUS YEARS, 1929-1933 *

Product Class	Millions of Dollars			% of Total Value		
	1929	1931	1933	1929	1931	1933
Bread	} $849.8	} $668.4	} $577.2	} 67.9%	} 68.3%	} 75.0%
Rolls						
Yeast-Raised Sweet Goods						
Cakes, Pastry & Doughnuts	299.1	241.0	144.9	23.9	24.5	18.7
Pies	83.9	62.2	40.7	6.7	6.4	5.3
Biscuit and Crackers	5.0	3.0	4.8	0.4	0.3	0.6
Miscellaneous Products	13.8	5.3	2.7	1.1	0.5	0.4
Total	$1,251.6	$979.9	$770.3	100.0%	100.0%	100.0%

* U. S. Census of Manufactures. Since all firms did not report detailed product breakdowns, the original data were adjusted on the assumption that the non-reporting firms had the same average product mix as those reporting such product divisions. The percentages to total value of product for the industry accounted for by reporting firms were as follows: 1929, 89.5%; 1931, 88.6%; 1933, 91.4%.

unit retailers who depended so strongly on the sales of luxury baked stuffs. Literally hundreds of them were forced to close their doors by 1933. Altogether the census reported 5,580 fewer bakeries in 1933 than in 1929, a reduction of over 27 per cent. Some of these establishments remained in business but were not reported by the census because their annual sales fell below $5,000; most, however, were small bakeshops and can be presumed to have gone out of business. Even the larger bakeries, including those producing primarily bread products, found it difficult to show any profit at all. Of the 15,000 bakeries which survived, more than 50 per cent operated at a loss.[7]

While the core of industry problems lay with the general fall in demand, much of the red ink on bakers' books was due to price reductions. The lowering of prices probably had very little effect in stemming the fall of demand, but its effect in bakery markets and on bakers generally was, to say the least, disruptive. For as one firm cut prices, others followed suit, sometimes matching, sometimes exceeding the original reduction. And with the demand for baked foods continuing to decline, balances were upset in market after market by cutthroat competitive tactics. By 1933, as market wars became commonplace, overt price shading, hidden rebates, the excessive use of stale returns and shadow concessions of all sorts were everywhere extant.

Every attempt possible was made to relieve the situation. Wage cuts were successively applied; hours of work for employees stretched out; and per-unit productivity increased. Equipment replacement was greatly reduced and bargaining with suppliers over price and conditions of sale intensified. As a matter of fact, supply conditions were such that the cost of materials fell by a greater relative amount than did bread prices; flour prices were reduced some 35 per cent between 1929 and 1933 and the total cost of materials fell by almost 41 per cent. Nevertheless, profits continued to fall and members

[7] Stone and Stone, *op. cit.,* p. 9.

of the baking industry lost what little faith they had in the "self-generating forces of business recovery." [8] After four years of cut-throat competition, of falling volume, prices and profits, bakers considered themselves to be part of a sick industry. "The opinion was widespread that the period of expansion of commercial baking was definitely ended and that in consequence future competition would be more severe than in the past." [9]

Under the Blue Eagle

In many ways, therefore, the industry had good reason to cheer the jumble of hastily improvised emergency measures of the New Deal. Of specific importance to the baking industry, as it was to most industries, was the National Industrial Recovery Act administered by the National Recovery Administration. The Act had as its purpose both recovery and reform, but there is little doubt that bakers in general viewed it simply as a means of ending the years of lean profits and ruinous competition. For this they looked to the N. R. A. code of fair competition. Significantly, it was announced that the enforcement of anti-trust laws would be suspended for the duration of N. R. A., although the Act itself prohibited monopolies and monopolistic practices.[10]

By mid-1933, before the blanket N. R. A. code was established, it had become apparent that the baking business was voluntarily to write its own codes and was to be virtually self-governed. Like most other industries subject to N. R. A., the baking industry was spurred to early action. Incentive was supplied not only by the urgent need to restore market stability, but also by the belief that an early code presented to the government might gain for the baking industry more favorable provisions. Between May and June, 1933, the various bakery trade associations worked feverishly, each intent

---

[8] *Ibid.*, p. xi.
[9] *Ibid.*, p. 9.
[10] S. H. Morison and H. S. Commager, *The Growth of the American Republic*, Vol. II (New York: Oxford University Press, 1942), p. 601.

on writing into the final code provisions favorable to their particular interests. The very diversity of interests, stemming from differences in size of operations, market area and character and product line, called forth as many as 125 active trade associations at one time.[11]

Agreement would probably have been impossible had not leadership been assumed by the American Bakers' Association. The ABA was certainly the most important of the industry trade associations both in size and prestige. Although accounting for only one-fifth of the nation's baking establishments, the members of the ABA were the titans of the industry—the large industrial bakers whose output made up 60 per cent of the industry's product. ABA thus set the tone for the entire trade as well as effectively compromising intra-industry differences.

In August, 1933, the Association called the nation's bakers together for the purpose of devising a workable code. Over 600 delegates met in Chicago where all but two states—Arizona and Nevada—were represented. The range of interests is indicated by the divisions into which the conference divided itself: multi-state wholesale, local wholesale, wholesale cake, wholesale pie, specialty dark bread, specialty white bread, house-to-house, multi-unit retail and retail. Chain stores later became a separate division.[12]

For three days the bakers aired practically every grievance known to their industry. The local wholesale section, the most powerful group at Chicago, alone discussed some twenty-six topics, ranging from "discounts" and "sales below cost" to "extremely long pans" and transparent wrapping of bread.[13]

By the end of the third day bakers had reached substantial accord as to definitions and code administration. With respect to labor policy, they gave only token support to the famous Section 7(a) of the National Industrial Recovery Act provid-

---

[11] Stone and Stone, *op. cit.,* p. 12.

[12] Philip Talbott, *History of the Code of Fair Competition for the Baking Industry* (unpublished MS.), p. 2.

[13] Stone and Stone, *op. cit.,* p. 35.

ing for mandatory collective bargaining and to the President's Re-employment Agreement calling for a forty-hour week maximum. Union representatives were, in fact, excluded from the conference and bitterly opposed the bakers' proposals: 48 hours per week for office workers; 45 and 54 hours for mechanized and handicraft shop employees; 6 days per week for outside salesmen.[14] No provisions were made for collective bargaining or for unions generally, since only the handicraft and specialty shops were unionized to any great extent.

Bakers were clearly more concerned with the problem of competitive practices. Yet they had to be content with a statement of general policy because of the pressure of time and conflicting interests. For example, the battle over consignment selling and its resultant excessive use of stale returns was a heated affair. Large multi-state wholesalers had used this competitive tool too often and too well when invading new territory to voluntarily surrender it now. They found an ally in the wholesale pie and cake bakers, in whose depressed markets the problem of stales was particularly pressing. On the other hand, small wholesalers—particularly in rural areas—knew that the elimination of stale returns would help insulate their markets against the pressures of larger competitors. Retail bakers also opposed the stale return privilege. After a long debate, the Chicago conference voted 357 to 55 against consignment selling, but the issue was by no means settled.

With apparent agreement, bakers also voted to condemn selling below cost, gifts of bakery goods to promote trade, reductions in prices when baked goods were used in "combination sales" with other items, and all other forms of discounts, premiums and loans to customers. On the positive side, all firms were to file price lists open "to all persons having a legitimate interest in the matter, including particularly customers, prospective customers, competitors, the

14 *Ibid.*, p. 25.

press and the government." Lest such prices be below cost, industry members were also required to file cost data, based on cost-accounting systems that allocated "a fair proportion" of overhead "to each class of product."

The job of writing and presenting the baking industry code at a public government hearing in January, 1934, fell to the code committee of the National Bakers' Council, a 16-man body formed at the Chicago conference. Originally designated as the central coordinating committee of the Chicago meeting, the Council ultimately became the administrator of the code. It was fairly representative of all segments of the industry and sustained only minor personnel changes over time. Retail bakers had the largest single representation of any group on the Council, with five men from the single-unit and one from the multi-unit retail segment. Local wholesalers, as such, had only three representatives; multi-state wholesalers only two. Each of the other segments sent one man to the Council.[15]

The Council had no easy task in preparing the code, for from the close of the Chicago conference on, it was besieged by "suggestions" from various industry groups. By the time of the January hearing, certain of the Chicago recommendations relating to trade practice had been modified or eliminated in an attempt at compromise. Labor proposals were also changed, generally reducing the work-week recommendations. At the hearing itself, the entire code was debated in detail, and again the trade practices and labor provisions came under the fire of dissenting groups. The bakery workers' union was allowed to submit views, but it was largely ignored. It was apparent by the end of the hearing that the Council had to find a less explosive atmosphere if a solution was to be worked out.

After three months of working with bakers and labor and government representatives, the Council submitted a final code-draft for government approval. Minor changes brought

---

15 *Ibid.*, p. 16. Chain stores were not originally in the Council.

further delays. It was not until May 28, 1934, that the baking industry code became law.

In general, the final code followed the pattern set up in the Chicago conference. Discounts, rebates, prizes, premiums, advertising allowances and loans to customers were prohibited as was the use of combination sales. Filing of prices and price changes was still required, but instead of being open to the press, customers, competitors and the government, price lists were henceforth to be "generally published and available." [16] This seemingly minor change undoubtedly made price shading easier. The prohibitions against selling below cost were retained, but industry members were allowed to meet competitors' price cuts, even at less than cost, provided they notified the local code authority within twenty-four hours. In emergency areas where destructive price-cutting arose, the code authority was empowered to determine "the lowest reasonable cost" and, with N. R. A. approval, set prices accordingly. [17]

The major compromise was on the much disputed issue of consignment sales. Industry opinion was distinctly divided, being strongly in favor of the practice in areas with many large wholesalers, strongly opposed in areas where wholesalers were relatively weak. The Council had recommended leaving the matter to be settled at the discretion of industry members at the state or regional levels. This seemed the most reasonable solution to the threatening impasse, and it was included in the final version of the code.

The labor provisions of the code marked another retreat from the original industry recommendations. Mechanized shop workers and office workers were limited to forty hours per week, and driver salesmen and all handicraft shop employees, to a maximum of forty-eight hours. [18] The wage provisions were complex, but the forty-cent-per-hour minimum

---

[16] National Recovery Administration, *Code of Fair Competition for the Baking Industry* (Washington: U. S. Government Printing Office, 1934), p. 17.

[17] Talbott, *op. cit.,* p. 18.

[18] Stone and Stone, *op. cit.,* p. 26.

rate established in all industry codes raised wages from 52 per cent to 84 per cent over previously existing minima.[19] The Bakery and Confectionery Workers' Union (A. F. L.) was extremely disappointed with the code which it labeled a "sell-out." It fell considerably short of the hours and wages the union considered necessary for adequate re-employment. Nor did it appear to offer a strong bargaining position for unionizing the large bakeries.

The difficulty of administration and enforcement of the code quickly became apparent. Although the National Bakers' Council was to be the code authority for the industry, local code groups were organized on a state basis; a few regional units were also established. The Council largely regarded itself as an advisory and coordinating body and attempted to delegate a great deal of local responsibility. But the local staffs, usually small and frequently incompetent, were unable to reach quick decisions and referred most problems back to the National Code Authority. This group was soon overburdened with detail, making enforcement extremely difficult. The National Code Authority eventually retreated to a policy of moral suasion and only resorted to direct intervention in regions where local authorities demonstrated incapability in handling problems.

A prime problem throughout the code administration was that concerning the market area. Within each local code authority, the immediate market area was supposed to be the basic unit of control. A high degree of confusion, however, resulted from the inability to define precisely a market area. In May, 1934, the National Bakers' Council defined it as, ". . . an area in which competitive conditions for the baking industry are quite uniform; . . ."[20] For administrative purposes this definition was useless.

To these problems was added the matter of finances, which

---

[19] The code allowed a five-cent per hour lower minimum wage in certain southern states in recognition of the differential existing prior to the code. N. R. A., Code of Fair Competition, *op. cit.,* p. 5.

[20] Stone and Stone, *op. cit.,* p. 57.

in the end crippled the administration of the entire code. The Council called for a budget of $900,000 to finance the operations of itself and the regional offices. Revenue was to have been provided by industry members, based on a percentage of sales. Collections were difficult, however, and less than one-half of the amount due was ever received. At the time N. R. A. was declared unconstitutional, in May, 1935, only two or three regional offices at most were solvent; National Code Authority ended as a deficit operation.

Compliance by the baking industry with provisions of the code, especially those relating to trade practices, was spotty. Despite the fact that open price-filing was required and that gifts and premiums were specifically prohibited, competitive wars continued to erupt in market after market. It was difficult, of course, to avoid such situations. Demand continued weak, and bakers struggled to retain a reasonable share of the market, some cynically, others from an honest conviction of the impossibility of holding their share without resorting to aggressive tactics. Once any baker initiated competitive violations, others felt compelled to follow suit in self-defense. In some cases, loopholes in the code were cleverly exploited. Several bakers gave premiums and prizes indiscriminately, and not, as was prohibited, as a direct consequence of purchase of their bread. Certain bakers circumvented the ban against discounts by providing grocers with a stock dividend based on their bread purchases, usually in the amount of one cent per loaf. In such cases competitors were quick to retaliate, and in so doing they were not concerned with legalities.

A common complaint, and one conducive to serious market wars, was the tendency of certain bakers to sell below cost. It was particularly directed against chain-store bakers, against wholesalers who provided private-label bread for voluntary chains, and against other chain retailers who did not do their own baking. No evidence was supplied in support of these charges beyond the simple contention of complainants that

"no one could sell bread at that price and make a profit." [21]
While chain stores were not above using bread as loss leaders,
the complaints against them were primarily the emotional
reactions of bakers, unable to match the low chain prices.

Altogether, over 5,500 complaints charging violation of
trade practices were filed.[22] Undoubtedly, thousands more
were never recorded because of a growing conviction by
bakers that effective enforcement was impossible. The National Code Authority and its local offices simply could not
handle the problem. This was owing to the complex me-
chanics of administration and enforcement. Only 50 per cent
of all wholesale bakers ever complied with the required filing
of open prices, and of this number only about three-fourths
kept price lists current.[23] N. R. A. itself was not blameless,
for it seemed "meticulously legalistic and almost entirely
negative in character." [24] Moreover, each complaint was handled as a special case, which proved a time-consuming task dis-
couraging to industry members. Markets were restored to a
semblance of order only after lengthy investigation and drawn-
out compromises. In general, bakers in most areas were left
to work out solutions to their problems with but minimum
assistance from the Authority.

With respect to the labor provisions, the Authority assumed
relatively little responsibility for enforcement. In many cases,
however, enforcement or threats of enforcement of the labor
provisions were effectively used to enforce the provisions on
trade practice. Through its agencies, the Authority received
a total of 3,834 labor complaints,[25] but these were primarily
concerned with wage and hour provisions and little else.

The N. R. A. experiment came to an abrupt end in mid-
1935 when the Supreme Court declared it unconstitutional
in the famous Schecter case. It is difficult to judge the effects

21 National Recovery Administration, *op. cit.*, p. 42.
22 *Ibid.*, p. 36.
23 *Ibid.*, p. 34.
24 Stone and Stone, *op. cit.*, p. 77.
25 *Ibid.*, p. 69.

of N. R. A. upon the baking industry in isolation from what
might have occurred had uncontrolled marketing tactics continued. In general, however, destructive trade practices
seemed greatly reduced during the life of the code as compared to pre-code days. Particularly was this true of gifts,
prizes and premiums, as well as the use of discounts, rebates
and allowances in their myriad forms. Competing bakers became aware of the instigators of such tactics, and their very
prohibition by the code made possible the effective use of
negotiation and pressure tactics. In other words, in the environment of N. R. A., bakers were able to cooperate in a
manner which in other times would be *prima facie* evidence
of collusion. The major ingredient of success, however, was
the conviction increasingly held among bakers that the practices were bad business for all. Furthermore, open price wars
were reduced in number and frequency. They presented such
open violation of the code that a strongly determined effort
was made to keep them localized and of short duration.

Although left to the discretion of local groups and not
specifically banned in the code, a reduction of the stale returns associated with consignment selling was achieved. The
larger wholesalers, especially, made a concerted drive to
eliminate this practice, for it was a costly one. A survey of
twenty-three regional code offices found that, generally, stale
returns were less during and immediately after the code than
before, and that the problem of stales imposed relatively few
hardships.[26]

The code's labor provisions with respect to hours and wages
were generally realized, albeit grudgingly. While not up to
union demands, they represented substantial improvement
over pre-code conditions, as indicated in a survey reported by
the National Bakers' Council. Among the large mechanized
bakeries, over 85 per cent of those surveyed were operating
forty hours or less per week in September, 1934, as compared
to less than 7 per cent eighteen months earlier; the propor-

---

[26] National Recovery Administration, *op. cit.*, p. 113.

tion working forty-four hours or less was 13 per cent in
March, 1933, and 92 per cent in September, 1934.[27] The
change in weekly working hours was less apparent in the case
of the handicraft shops, but even here a reduction had been
achieved. While the code permitted work weeks of fifty and
forty-eight hours in such shops, 97 per cent of the bakers
surveyed were reported in September, 1934, as having their
employees work fifty-two hours or less.[28] Similarly, there were
increases both in employment and payrolls under N. R. A.
By September, 1934, approximately 10,000 workers had been
re-employed while payrolls had gone up approximately 21 per
cent over mid-1933. While there was little or no change in
real income for the whole economy, it would appear that
N. R. A. was at least partially responsible for the improvement in employment and payrolls that took place by the end
of 1935.

On other matters, organized labor did not fare as well as
union leaders hoped. The promises of collective bargaining,
held out by all industry codes, were not realized; employer
hostility continued strong, and the unions were weakened
because collection of dues from workers with low incomes
was difficult. Organization drives by the Bakery and Confectionery Workers' International Union failed among the mechanized bakeries. Union membership did rise from 16,000
to almost 20,000 between 1932 and 1935, but remained somewhat below the 1929 level and well under the 1921 peak.[29]

The overall changes in the industry clearly indicated a
slowly rising trend in prices from the 1933 low. The price of
white bread rose from 7.1 cents per pound in 1933 to 8.3 cents
in 1935, an increase of 17 per cent. It was still below the 1929
price of 8.8 cents, but it represented a more stable market
situation. More important, perhaps, were the changes in vol-

---

[27] Stone and Stone, *op. cit.*, p. 84.

[28] *Ibid.*

[29] A. L. Taggart, III, *Collective Bargaining in the Bread-Baking Industry of
Middle Western United States* (unpublished senior thesis, Princeton University,
1948), p. 60.

ume of production and number of bakery establishments. By the end of 1935, dollar volume had risen above the $1 billion level, and represented about 84 per cent of the 1929 peak. Physical volume showed a greater increase, totaling almost 90 per cent of the 1929 output. The increase in dollar volume substantially explains the addition of over 4,000 bakeries between 1933 and 1935. The increase as reported by the Census was primarily due to the fact that many bakeries, previously excluded, were now counted because their sales rose above $5,000 per annum.

Although figures are not available, it appears that the pre-depression trend of a decline in home baking was again taking hold as employment and income began to rise. The bakers themselves had contributed to this trend by producing a softer, larger-volume loaf during the depression years. Called the "honk" loaf because housewives squeezed it to test its freshness, it gave consumers more for their money and was difficult to bake at home.

The efforts of the N. R. A. notwithstanding, the industry structure at the end of 1935 still showed the effects of the depression. The relative shares of industry segments were quite different from those of 1929. The small-scale retail bakeshops, hit hardest by the depression, had not regained their lost volume, accounting, together with the house-to-house bakers in 1935, for some 23 per cent of total industry output compared to more than 25 per cent in 1929.[30] Moreover, it is probable that the house-to-house operators, who were able to get good driver salesmen rather cheaply, increased their share relative to the small-scale retailers. Similarly, institutional sales and sales through bobtailers failed to return to their 1929 levels. In 1935 these two channels of distribution accounted for 6.5 per cent of total sales compared to 10.5 per cent 6 years earlier.

On the other hand, the wholesalers selling to grocery stores

---

[30] Census of Business, Volume V, *Distribution of Manufacturers' Sales, 1939* (Washington: U. S. Government Printing Office, 1942), p. 22.

enjoyed a slight increase in their relative share of the market, from 50.8 per cent in 1929 to 52 per cent in 1935. It seems apparent that their concentration on bread-type products enabled them to hold their own despite an absolute loss of volume during the depression. The chain store bakeries, however, experienced the greatest increase as a result of the depression, despite the efforts of the baking industry under N. R. A. to curb their activities. By 1935, together with multi-unit retailers, they accounted for 16 per cent of total industry sales as compared to 11 per cent in 1929. Of this amount the chains probably had in excess of 10 per cent, or even more, in light of the fact that the multi-unit retailers experienced a decline during the depression. Some have estimated the chains' share to be 14 per cent. While their relative strength can only be guessed at, it seems fairly clear that the low price policy of the chains increased their share of baking during the 1933 period of low national income.

Understandably, technological advances were few during the depression. According to reports of sales by equipment manufacturers, however, the mechanical equipment of the baking industry was not fully maintained, much less increased.[31] Had the labor provisions of the code appreciably changed the labor costs of production, tendencies to increase the use of mechanical equipment would have resulted. There was, of course, a strong incentive for bakery operators to give more attention to production control and costs, but on the whole it was more a matter of getting maximum efficiency from installed equipment rather than acquiring new machinery.

In general, bakers reflected the typical attitude of the business community toward N. R. A.'s demise. Many of the codes had been little more than pious pronouncements while others, like the bakers', which had some merit, proved unenforceable or unworkable. By 1935 bakers were almost unanimous in their antipathy to government intervention. Bureaucratic re-

[31] *Ibid.*, p. 98.

quirements, failure to prosecute violators and the general atmosphere of government control strongly influenced this view. What positive achievements there were, such as raising output and employment, were conceived of as having occurred almost in spite of N. R. A. In effect, the Supreme Court had merely administered the *coup de grâce* to an already defunct bird; the peak of the crisis was past.

Recovery Continues

The years following 1935 were years of cautious optimism not only for the baking industry but for the nation as a whole. Except for a short-lived recession in 1937–38, the nation's economy surged back in absolute terms to the high levels of activity characterized by the late 'twenties. The effects of the great depression were still near at hand, but everywhere could be found the evidence of a revived economy. Heightened private investment, coupled with government spending, relief and employment programs, resulted in more jobs and a greater national income. By 1939 employment totaled forty-five million compared to forty-eight million in 1929; national income rose to $72.5 billion, in real terms only 2 per cent below 1929. Disposable personal income had risen from $45 billion to $70 billion between 1933 and 1939, which when allowances were made for price changes, more than equaled the previous high recorded in 1929.[32] And consumers, who used their higher income to restore former standards of living, were buying as many goods and services as they had in the late 'twenties.

The baking industry benefited from the general recovery. Total output increased by more than 18 per cent between 1935 and 1939. (Cf. Table 3.) In terms of dollar sales, it was still slightly below the 1929 high, but in terms of physical output production was more than 30 per cent higher than it had been in 1933 and almost 8 per cent above its 1929 value. Employment in the industry reached a record 201,533, up

---

[32] Historical Statistics of the United States, *op. cit.*, pp. 12, 13, 65 and 236.

TABLE 3

THE BAKING INDUSTRY, CENSUS YEARS,
1935–1939[a]

Census Year	Number of Establishments	Value of Product ($000)	Index of $ Value of Product[b]	Index of Physical Volume[c]
1935	19,068	$1,052,464	84.1	89.2
1937	17,193	1,217,865	97.3	99.6
1939	18,399	1,211,024	96.8	107.8

[a] *U. S. Census of Manufactures.* Establishments with an annual volume of products of less than $5,000 not included.

[b] 1929 equals 100.

[c] 1929 equals 100. Based on computations using Bureau of Labor Statistics, Retail Price of White Bread. While prices on other bakery products were not available, it was assumed that these would generally follow the price of bread.

some 7 per cent over 1935. And with bakery product prices having risen some 11 per cent since the worst depression year, the industry had reason to believe that it had once again resumed its long-term trend of a rising demand.

In the past the trend had been primarily a function of two factors. First, the increase in the number and density of population had created a growing demand for both home-made and commercially baked foods. Second, rising disposable incomes had enabled the housewife to pay for the leisure that commercially baked products offered. Following 1935, the first set of factors did not work completely in favor of the industry. Population increased 2.6 per cent between 1933 and 1939, but the long-term downward trend of per capita wheat-flour consumption, evident since the turn of the century, continued at approximately the same rate as did population growth. It fell 3 per cent despite a 4 per cent increase in total per capita food consumption which restored the 1929 level.[33] Thus, had the proportions between commercial and home baking remained the same, the industry would have neither gained nor lost volume.

[33] Consumption of Food in the United States, *op. cit.*, p. 144.

The saving factor in the situation, however, was the increased consumption of commercially baked foods. With rising disposable income, and with an increasing availability of bakers' products through the expansion of market areas as well as a continued farm-to-city population movement, former consumption patterns reasserted themselves and housewives began again to buy rather than bake. By 1939 bakers were producing about two-thirds of all bread consumed compared to approximately 60 per cent in 1929. Even more important from a relative point of view were the inroads made in the sweet goods field. At the end of the decade of the 'thirties the nation's bakers boasted an estimated 30 per cent of all variety-baked-foods consumption compared to 25 per cent ten years earlier.[34] Such a gain was all the more significant because consumers were, at the same time, increasing their per capita consumption of such goods. Thus, not only did the demand for commercially baked foods increase at the expense of home baking as it had prior to the depression, but it generally reverted to its pre-depression pattern.

These changes in the demand for baked foods following the depression were reflected in the industry's product-mix. (Cf. Table 4.) Though still the keystone of industry sales, bread gradually became less important as a percentage of the total market. It fell from perhaps more than 60 per cent in 1935 to about 55 per cent in 1939; during 1933 its value had been as high as 65 per cent. Cakes, pastry, doughnuts and pies, on the other hand, rose to more than 30 per cent of industry sales by 1939. With the addition of yeast-raised sweet goods they accounted for approximately 35 per cent, the highest in industry history.

There were further evidences of expansion within the industry. On the distribution side, the number of delivery vehicles rose to more than 66,000, some 13,000 greater than in

---

[34] Bureau of Labor Statistics, U. S. Employment Service, *Job Descriptions for the Bakery Products Industry, June 1939* (Washington: Government Printing Office, 1941), p. 6.

TABLE 4
Product Breakdown of the Baking Industry, Census Years, 1935–1939 *

Product Class	Millions of Dollars			% of Total Value		
	1935	1937	1939	1935	1937	1939
Bread	} $751.9	$711.2	$671.3	} 71.5%	58.4%	55.4%
Rolls		} 130.3	} 141.2		} 10.7	} 11.5
Yeast-Raised Sweet Goods						
Cakes, Pastry & Doughnuts	227.5	278.1	289.9	21.4	22.7	24.1
Pies	56.9	75.9	76.7	5.5	6.5	6.4
Biscuit and Crackers	9.3	16.0	20.3	0.9	1.3	1.6
Miscellaneous Products	7.0	6.3	11.6	0.7	0.4	1.0
Total	$1,052.9	$1,217.8	$1,211.0	100.0%	100.0%	100.0%

* U. S. Census of Manufactures. Since all firms did not report detailed product breakdowns, the original data were adjusted on the assumption that the non-reporting firms had the same average product mix as those reporting such product divisions. The percentages to total value of product for the industry accounted for by reporting firms were as follows: 1935, 93.7%; 1937, 94.4%; 1939, 97.9%.

1929. The horse-drawn wagon and electric truck, which had accounted for one-fifth of all vehicles in 1929, had for all practical purposes disappeared by 1939. Moreover, the motor truck of that year was a greatly improved vehicle, larger and capable of longer hauls. For the baking industry it made possible both a more intensive coverage of city routes and an extension of country routes. Trailer trucks, for example, became more commonly used for depot or branch operations, especially by the larger wholesale and house-to-house bakeries.

Larger-scale distribution was also facilitated by the gradual increase in the number of grocery stores—both independent and chain—taking on the supermarket form of operation. Originally started by independent grocers to combat the rise of chain stores, supermarkets rose from approximately 400 in 1934 to almost 5,000 in 1939.[35] Their larger size made possible more bakery sales per stop for wholesalers. Moreover, the self-service characteristics of supermarkets and their corresponding mass displays of merchandise helped immeasurably to facilitate consumer acceptance of variety baked foods in the grocery store. They did much to make these products, like bread, items of impulse purchase on the housewife's shopping trip. The supermarket, in some cases, also created separate bakery departments in their stores and leased them to local multi-unit bakeries. The bakers involved staffed the department, and aside from paying a fixed fee for the privilege of leasing, ran it as if it were another retail bakery outlet in their chain of stores. To them it was additional sales revenue; to the supermarket operators it was another device for attracting customers. In a few instances supermarket operators began to do their own baking much as the chain stores had in the 'twenties on a larger scale.

On the production side between 1935 and 1939 the trends toward increased mechanization and larger size were again reestablished. Reporting only on establishments whose output amounted to 78 per cent of industry sales, the Census in 1939

---

35 Duddy and Revzan, *op. cit.,* p. 221.

recorded expenditures for plant and equipment of more than
$35 million.[36] Of this amount 69 per cent was allocated for
new machinery and operating equipment. From flour and
other bulk-handling equipment to slicing and wrapping machines, and from bread baking to the baking of variety goods,
there was increased emphasis on newly designed machines of
greater capacity. Slicing machines, for example, which had
been introduced in the late 'twenties, were by 1939 commonplace throughout the industry; moreover, the need for collapsible bread trays to hold the sliced bread as it was being
sliced was eliminated with the development of an automatic
slicer wrapper. Increased mechanization was especially no-
ticeable with respect to oven use. The number of standard
peel ovens in the industry between 1929 and 1939 decreased
by almost 1,500 while the total number of ovens rose by
1,300; peel ovens in 1939 totaled less than 52 per cent of the
almost 30,000 ovens in use. Mechanical ovens, on the other
hand, showed an amazing increase. The number of traveling-
tray ovens increased from 565 to 1,699; traveling-hearth ovens,
from 410 to 664; and reel ovens, from 1,430 to 3,169. Significant to these changes, of course, was the increased capacity of
the mechanical ovens as compared to the peel types. Together with greater capacity in other areas of production, they
did much to increase the average size of bakeries from $61,300
in 1929 to $65,800 in 1939, an increase after price level cor-
rections of more than 11 per cent.

Between 1935 and 1939 there occurred a significant change
in the industry's relations with organized labor. Under the
favorable political conditions, the principal unions in the
baking industry—the Bakery and Confectionery Workers',
and the International Brotherhood of Teamsters—greatly increased their membership and on a broadened scale engaged
in collective bargaining with bakery operators. In fact, the resultant change in the labor relation pattern provided what

---

[36] *Census of Manufactures, 1939.*

many considered the major structural change experienced by the industry in the entire decade of the 'thirties.

The unions, curiously, accepted the Supreme Court's invalidation of N. R. A. with relief. The right of workers to organize and bargain collectively, as guaranteed by Section 7(a) of the code, had proven less conducive to union growth and strength than had been expected. Government continued its support of organized labor, however, by enacting, shortly after the demise of N. R. A., the National Labor Relations Act, and by vesting its enforcement in the successor to the old National Labor Board of N. R. A. The rulings and orders of the reconstituted National Labor Relations Board following 1935 generally freed labor organizations from the unfriendly environment of earlier years and encouraged organization campaigns. Business, in many instances, refused to obey N. L. R. B. orders and found support in rulings of the lower courts. In April, 1937, however, the Supreme Court sustained the constitutionality of the Act.

In the baking industry, both before and after the Court's action in 1937, the Bakery Workers and the Teamsters invaded successive market segments, picking up thousands of recruits in drives which rebuilt long-dormant locals and created new ones. The organization drive of the Bakery Workers' Union started with an invasion of the mass production plants. The early opposition by bakery managements failed to check the drive. By the end of 1936 union membership had about doubled, rising to almost 30,000 from the depression low of 16,000.[37] Strengthened by its early victories, the union sought contracts with the powerful chain stores and the established leaders in the industry, the larger baking corporations. Success once more crowned union efforts as closed shop agreements in city after city were signed with such firms as Continental, Ward, General, A & P and Kroger. By the close of

---

[37] Taggart, *op. cit.*, p. 60.

1937, membership exceeded 56,000,[38] and within three more years the union claimed over 80,000.[39]

Despite the obvious administration sympathy for the stronger organized labor movement, the success of the union would not have been possible without a basic organizational change. The traditional craft structure of the union, while adequate for organizing the small bakeshops, was totally inadequate for organizing industrial bakeries using mechanized factory methods of production. This meant that the union had to alter its policy and mode of operation and take into its fold all levels of unskilled and semi-skilled bakery workers. While adaptation to the revised structure was not accomplished without creating serious problems and conflicts among union leaders, the union lost its craft character much as had the bakers themselves over twenty years before.

The impact of such changed relationships with organized labor on the industry was mirrored in the pattern of collective bargaining that emerged. Due to the local nature of production and distribution, contract negotiation and union organization took place at the local level. To the disadvantage of many bakery operators, both the Bakery Workers and the Teamsters skillfully varied their application of bargaining techniques from market to market. Upon occasion negotiation with a single employer in a weak bargaining position resulted in a contract whose provisions formed a base whereby other bakers were outflanked. At other times, negotiations were conducted with several bakers simultaneously, or even with all bakers in a given market, depending upon the relative degree of bargaining strength such firms possessed. These tactics, in many markets, proved to be well beyond the skill levels of management bargaining; in such cases the unions acquired decidedly favorable contracts. Not until the 'forties did bakers counter union tactics on a broad basis by collective

---

38 *Ibid.*, p. 61.
39 *Ibid.* No information is available on the organization of bakery driver-salesmen by the Teamsters Union, but it can be assumed that a similar success was achieved.

cooperation in local markets for the conduct of contract negotiations.

Largely as a result of organized labor's activities, a much greater share of the bakers' sales dollar was allocated to payroll. In 1939 salaries and wages paid to all employees totaled almost 28 per cent of the total dollar value of products sold.[40] This represented a significant increase over the 1935 level of less than 25 per cent, or the 22 per cent for 1929. The wage and salary costs of baking, therefore, had increased faster than had the prices of baked goods. Thus the industry which, during the 1920s, had experienced no increase in the relative amount of its labor bill found itself operating under conditions of rising labor costs.

While the many changes in the baking industry by the end of the 'thirties indicated that the disastrous effects of the depression had been overcome, all segments of the industry did not benefit equally. The larger bakeries and those producing machine-made products garnered most of the industry's increased business. As a proportion of total industry output, sales direct to grocers—primarily handled by the large-scale wholesale bakers—were about 52 per cent; although relatively unchanged since 1935, they were at an all-time high in terms of both dollar value and physical volume. Sales to bobtailers and through depot operations, served by the larger wholesale and house-to-house bakers, totaled 9 per cent in 1939 compared to 7 per cent four years earlier. Institutional sales of 2 per cent, again serviced by the larger operators, were up a very slight one-half of 1 per cent. But the largest relative gains were recorded by those bakeries, other than single-unit retailers, selling through their own retail outlets. These were primarily the chain store and multi-unit retail bakeries and, to some extent, the baking business of supermarket operators who had their own baking facilities. In 1939 they accounted for 22 per cent of total sales compared to 16 per cent in 1935. The small-scale bakeshops, on the other hand, lost volume be-

---

[40] *U. S. Census of Manufactures, 1939.*

tween 1935 and 1939. Together with the house-to-house operators they dropped from 23 per cent to 15 per cent of total
sales. There seems little doubt that the bulk of this decline
was suffered by the single-unit retailers.

These changes in the relative importance of industry segments are explainable primarily in terms of consumers' shopping habits with respect to baked foods. In the main, people
were buying an increasing amount of such goods in grocery
stores, chains as well as independents. And included in these
products were variety baked foods in addition to bread, for
housewives were generally becoming used to buying the
standardized, mass-produced sweet goods instead of depending on the fancier handmade goods. Therefore, while it might
otherwise have been expected that the increased sales of variety goods would have helped the small-scale bakeshops, the
larger wholesalers and chain-store bakers were able to garner
much of this business in addition to their already increased
bread sales. Having begun the production of sweet goods in
the early 'twenties, they were easily able to use their technological inheritance to turn out such goods "en masse." Moreover, the multi-unit retailers also benefited because where
people did not prefer to buy their variety baked foods in the
grocery store, they seemed to buy them from the larger bakery chain retailers. It must be pointed out, however, that
some small-scale retailers thus affected by such changes were
not completely unprepared. Many began supplementing their
traditional business with wholesale sales to grocery stores or
bobtailers, primarily specialty-type breads and small cakes
and pies.[41] A few carried this business to the point of becoming wholesalers rather than retailers, just as had so many
about the turn of the century. But in general, the small-scale
retailers failed to keep the pace of recovery achieved by their
larger competitors.

---

[41] Such sales were not recorded by the Census as retail sales which means that
the 15 per cent figure credited to single-unit retailers and house-to-house operators
represents an understatement of their share of the market.

CHAPTER 14

THE WAR AND ITS AFTERMATH, 1940–1950

IN CONTRAST TO THE 1930s which brought to the baking industry loss of volume and generally depressed conditions, the decade of the 'forties proved to be a period of unparalleled expansion and prosperity. The key to the boom was, of course, the war and the high level of spending and business activity it created. While there were no war contracts for the baking industry—other, perhaps, than the supplying of baked foods to domestic military bases—the war nevertheless brought forth a greatly increased demand through its effects on home baking. Not only did the war bring increased incomes with which to buy baked foods but it offered countless jobs to women who might otherwise have done their own baking. Like the early 1930s, the war period was one of government control and regulation for the baking industry, but because of the favorable demand conditions that prevailed, it was a period entirely different from the frustrating days of the N.R.A. The return to normal market conditions following the end of the war fortunately brought a continuation of the high level of demand that had emerged in the years before. Those consumers who during the war had come to depend upon the commercial baker continued afterwards to purchase rather than to bake their bread and other baked foods.

The Pre-War Years

Throughout 1940 and 1941 the war which had started in Europe and which finally involved the United States had a marked effect on the American economy. By the end of 1941 national income totaled 104 billion dollars, representing a 43 per cent increase over 1931, and was the highest figure ever attained; personal income was similarly at an all-time high and significantly increased over 1939. The index of production of all manufactures rose from 109 in 1939 to 168 in 1941, an increase of more than 54 per cent. Unemployment, still a major source of concern a scant two years earlier, had by the end of 1941 declined to 2.7 million, a drop of some 70 per cent. In terms of consumers' consumption expenditures there was a 22 per cent rise between 1939 and 1941.[1] Even after allowing for change in the value of the dollar—a very mild drop of 5 per cent—these figures indicate clearly that America was approaching, and rapidly, a state of full employment with a corresponding high level of spending.

Most of the nation's enhanced economic activity, of course, was centered in the heavy industries such as iron and steel and machinery which were an integral part of the obvious preparation for war and for aid to the allied nations. The value of output of all durable manufactures, for example, almost doubled between 1939 and 1941. Other industries benefited as well, although not to the same degree. The output of all non-durable manufactures increased approximately 30 per cent during this period. The food industry group, while not as sensitive to the business cycle as the heavy industries, experienced an 18 per cent increase. The baking industry started out more slowly. At the end of 1940, productivity was up a modest 3 per cent over 1939. Within another year output totaled over 8 per cent more than the 1939 level.

Clearly the baking industry was not leading the rise in business activity but was rather following slowly in its wake.

---

[1] Historical Statistics of the United States, *op. cit.,* pp. 12, 65, and 180.

This had long been characteristic of commercial baking and was therefore to be expected. Commercial baking was still an industry which depended for its growth upon enhanced economic activity in other industries to create the necessary favorable environment for expansion. Thus the industry at the end of 1941 was just beginning to receive the benefit of an emerging war economy. Of specific importance to baking were increased consumer incomes and a rising number of women gainfully employed. These benefits, as in the past, primarily took the form of a continued decline in home baking. Increased incomes obviously exerted pressure on housewives to buy rather than to bake their bread and other baked foods. Similarly, increased female employment, from approximately eleven million in 1939 to more than thirteen million at the end of 1941, strongly contributed to a decline in home baking.[2] Such a decline was in turn responsible for the increased demand for commercial bakery products between 1939 and 1941. No figures are available which directly support this contention, but it seems a common sense conclusion. It is true that population increases contributed somewhat to the higher baking industry output, but since the rise in population between 1939 and 1941 was less than 2 per cent, its effect was small indeed. Nor is there evidence to indicate that people were eating more baked foods than formerly. The per capita consumption of flour, in fact, remained fairly constant over the two-year period. It may have been true that, following the trend set in the 'twenties and again in the late 'thirties, consumers were increasing slightly their consumption of baked foods other than bread, but again it seems unlikely that this could have been significant over such a short time period. A decline in home baking appears to be the major explanation for the industry's increased output.

The trend away from home-baked foods was perhaps enhanced by one other factor in addition to increased consumer

---

[2] *Ibid.*, p. 63.

income and the employment of more women. This was the production of enriched bread begun early in 1941. While not extremely significant until during and after World War II, enriched bread has since become of such importance to the baking industry and to consumers that its introduction deserves careful consideration.

Actually, enrichment gathered its initial momentum during the 'thirties and was first specifically related to baking in 1939 when the Council on Foods and Nutrition of the American Medical Association approved the restoration of vitamins and iron to bread and white flour.[3] Such a pronouncement had been made possible in part by the development of production methods for making synthetic vitamins and minerals in commercial quantities and at costs which were not prohibitive. In connection with this pronouncement, the United States Food and Drug Administration opened hearings in September of 1940 pursuant to a determination of federal standards for enriched white flour. Shortly thereafter, in late November, the Food and Nutrition Board of the National Research Council organized the nutritional status of the American people; flour and bread enrichment was considered a prime implement for the program then in the planning stage.

Throughout this period bakers and millers strongly supported the proposed enrichment program. Being acutely aware of the vitamin and mineral deficiencies of their products, these food processors, through their national organizations—the American Bakers Association, the American Institute of Baking, the Associated Retail Bakers of America, and the Millers' National Federation—met with nutritionists,

---

[3] R. M. Wilder and R. R. Williams, "Enrichment of Flour and Bread, A History of the Movement," *National Research Council*, Bulletin No. 110, November, 1944, p. 2. The Council preferred restoration rather than fortification of bread and white flour. By restoration was meant the addition of a sufficient amount of vitamins and minerals to restore a given food product to the same vitamin and mineral content as that contained in any natural or unprocessed food of its class. Fortification, on the other hand, meant the addition of more vitamins and minerals than originally contained in a food's natural state.

medical men, and all government agencies involved to help further the cause of enrichment. By January of 1941, despite the fact that official standards for enriched flour were yet to be made final by the Food and Drug Administration, tentative standards were accepted by the flour milling industry based on the generalizations already determined. By that time, also, hearings were pending relating to enriched bread; and to allow progress to be made by bakers in turning out an enriched product, tentative bread standards were proposed by the Food and Nutrition Board of the National Research Council. These standards shown below were accepted by the baking industry in May, 1941, at the time of the National Nutrition Conference for Defense held in Washington.

RECOMMENDATIONS FOR ENRICHED BREAD [4]

(As Proposed January, 1941)

Per Pound of Bread	Minimum mg.	Maximum mg.
Thiamine	1.0	2.0
Niacin or Niacinamide	4.0	8.0
Iron	4.0	16.0
Riboflavin (optional)	0.8	1.6
Calcium (optional)	300	200

[4] "Enrichment of Flour and Bread," *op. cit.*, p. 21. Riboflavin was to remain optional only until a larger commercial supply could be made available. It was also decided that bakers would have an option with respect to methods of bread enrichment. They could purchase enriched flour which would automatically satisfy enriched bread requirements, or they could add enrichment wafers at the bakery or use any other method so long as the final product contained the nutritional qualities agreed upon and did not contain any harmful ingredients.

Having established temporary standards, the Food and Drug Administration opened hearings in July of 1941 in an attempt to work out all the details necessary to final enrichment standards for bread and flour. There were many questions yet to be answered and much testimony to be taken before official standards could be outlined. In the meantime, any food enrichment with respect to bread and flour was to be entirely voluntary on the part of bakers and millers. There were no requirements that these food processors had to enrich their products but if, however, they chose to enrich, they were compelled to follow the temporary standards already agreed upon. Unfortunately, the coming of the war postponed all hearings indefinitely before official standards could be proscribed.

Throughout all of 1941, therefore, the entire enrichment program had no permanent official status. How did bakers and millers react? Obviously, enrichment was not a costless operation and there was some hesitancy on the part of bakers and millers as to how consumers would respond to the new products. In the case of flour it was relatively easy for the miller to add his enrichment costs to the price of a bag of flour since these costs amounted to a few cents a bag. Still, the public had to be educated to believe enrichment was worth the small extra price. The baker selling enriched bread could not pass on to the consumer the fractional costs of enrichment. He had to advance his price a penny a loaf or not at all; since he chose the latter alternative, he could only hope to get his additional costs back by expanding his sales. This made many bakers hesitate about beginning a large-scale enrichment program until nutritionists, government, and other supporters of enriched foods had properly prepared the public as to the values of enriched foods. But despite the fact that little educational work of this sort was done throughout 1941, the voluntary enrichment of white bread and flour in that year reached a level of about 30 to 35 per cent of the entire output of these products.[5]

The extent of the contribution of enriched bread to the increased output of the baking industry prior to America's entry into World War II is not known. Clearly many people were uninformed concerning the advantages of enrichment. Without extensive government and nutritionist support, it was difficult for them to judge just what the term "enriched bread" meant; to some it may have been considered as merely

---

[5] *Ibid.*, p. 45.

another form of advertising. A small part of the population, however, undoubtedly was aware of the increased nutritional values of enriched bread—aware of the fact that bread need no longer be subject to attacks claiming vitamin and mineral deficiencies. As a result, some housewives may have given up home baking in order to purchase enriched bakers' bread. They could have bought enriched flour and continued to bake at home, but the extra cost of such flour may have induced them to buy enriched bread which sold for no more than did ordinary bread. In general, therefore, the enrichment of bread by the end of 1941 had made some small contribution to the increased output of the baking industry through its effects on home baking and on the general reputation of commercial bakers. While unimportant perhaps compared to the effects of increased income and the rising employment of women, it nevertheless represented the initial step of a movement later to become extremely significant in promoting industry sales.

The Baking Industry in Wartime

The coming of the war found the baking industry with a slightly increased output, having benefited indirectly from the nation's expanded economic activity. How would the war affect baking? What could be expected to happen in such an industry—one not directly related to the war effort, but yet one producing a daily necessity and using materials and equipment likely to be in short supply? Would the industry enjoy a boom period and erase the memory of the recent depression? Would government regulation prove to be too controlling? These questions and many more were being asked by baking industry people as America began an all-out mobilization under a war economy.

Baking industry leaders were quick to realize the wartime necessity for cooperation between government representatives and industry groups. Such a relationship was essential to a fuller understanding on the part of the government of the problems faced by the industry. It was also essential to the effective compliance with the emergency measures soon to be put into effect. As a result, many industry members, too numerous to mention, left their industry positions to take up duties with one or more government agencies. Others served on various advisory committees designed to serve as liaisons between government and industry. The jobs performed by these men cannot be overstressed. Many of the provisions of the wartime regulations affecting the industry could not have been written without their express help.

One of the immediate effects of the war which involved the baking industry was the General Maximum Price Regulation issued by the Office of Price Administration in April, 1942. This regulation, to take effect in early May, rolled the nation's prices back to their March levels. OPA had been created a year earlier as part of a broad program to exert control over the war economy; more specifically, it was to stabilize selling prices which were creeping upward under the inflationary pressures of increased production and employment. It was inevitable that the baking industry would be subject to price control. The OPA was well aware of the importance of bread as a cost-of-living indicator and that other food processors might use increases in bakery prices to argue for similar price relief. In fact, bread was deemed such a basic food item that as early as June, 1941, before being given legal authority to act, OPA Administrator, Leon Henderson, had requested the baking industry to refrain from advancing bread prices without first consulting his office.[6] In general, prices did hold fast for a period of about three months. At the end of that time, again acting on a basis of moral suasion, OPA granted bakers an increase of from one-half to one cent per loaf to give relief from rising costs. By the time of the General Maximum Price Regulation, this increase had been incorporated into bakers' prices.

---

[6] Edward C. Collins, *History of the Bakery Section, Cereal Feeds and Agricultural Branch, Food Price Division, Office of Price Administration, December 1941–December 1946.* Unpublished ms., p. 5.

The history of bakery product prices during the war was one of tight control. Following the freeze period of March, 1942, bread prices, as shown in Table 1, remained relatively

TABLE 1

NATIONAL AVERAGE—RETAIL PRICE PER POUND OF BREAD *

Year	White	Whole Wheat	Rye
1940	8.0	9.0	9.4
1941	8.1	9.0	9.2
1942	8.7	9.5	9.7
March 1942	8.7	9.5	9.6 Freeze Period
1943	8.9	9.8	10.0
1944	8.8	9.7	9.9
1945	8.8	9.7	9.9

* Source: U. S. Bureau of Labor Statistics.

constant throughout the entire period of the war. Sweet goods prices, on the other hand, were not considered as basic as bread prices and were allowed to rise some 12 to 20 per cent over this period owing to increases in the prices of ingredients and packaging. In fact, OPA grouped sweet goods under a special pricing formula in February, 1943, that permitted bakers to recalculate maximum prices semi-annually so as to reflect these increased costs. In general, however, aside from price adjustments necessitated by special hardship cases, bakery product prices held firm under OPA, and price control undoubtedly kept bakers' prices from rising as much as they otherwise would have.

Along with price control, the baking industry, like most other industries, was confronted with a host of additional government regulations. Almost all of these were embodied in War Food Order No. 1 (originally known as Food Distribution Order No. 1) issued in January of 1943 by the War Food Administration. This was by far the most important wartime regulation affecting the baking industry. Its provisions, slightly altered and modified throughout the war years, were of great help to bakers despite the regulatory and administrative problems involved. Basically, War Food Order No. 1 was part of the overall program of the War Food Administration to conserve critical foodstuffs; for the baking industry it had additional purposes, being aimed at simplifications and economies to facilitate price control at the then current levels. For one thing, it limited the number of varieties of bread that could be made. The limits were six machine-moulded and ten hand-moulded varieties, and three varieties of rolls, plus some other provisions on varieties for restaurants, house-to-house, and retail bakers. Twisting and cross-panning of loaves were also prohibited, as was the use of double wrappings. Moreover, bread wrappers could have only two colors, and the area covered by ink was cut to 20 per cent.

More significant, perhaps, were the provisions of War Food Order No. 1 which had an indirect bearing on competition. The order forbade all gifts of bread as well as the furnishing of equipment such as bread racks, screen doors, signs, and shelves to grocery store operators. The elimination of these competitive practices meant significant cost reductions for the entire industry. Of greatest importance, however, was the ban against consignment selling, the practice of taking back stale returns by the wholesale baker. This practice, long used as a competitive device in the industry, was considered by the government as inconsistent with the wartime goal of conserving food. In a study of 377 wholesale bakery plants made by the Federal Trade Commission in 1942, it was found that stale returns ranged from a low of 0.2 per cent of sales to a high of 33.11 per cent with an average of 5.84 per cent. Thus it was estimated that with the elimination of consignment selling, an additional annual saving of about 250,000,000 pounds of bread could be made.[7] Moreover, consignment sell-

---

[7] Federal Trade Commission, *Wholesale Baking Industry, Part I, Waste in the Distribution of Bread* (Washington: U. S. Government Printing Office, 1946), p. 6.

ing was actively fought by the smaller independent wholesale bakers who could not afford to use this competitive device to the same degree as could the larger multi-plant bakers. On these bases, and on the fact that the elimination of consignment selling would reduce bakers' costs and allow an increase in wheat and flour prices without an increase in bread prices, the government issued its ban against stale returns. Bakers thus achieved under government regulation what they had never been able to do by themselves.

War Food Order No. 1 also assisted the industry in still another way. It provided for the mandatory enrichment of all white bread and later, in March of 1943, all white rolls. In conjunction with this provision the use of shortening, milk solids, and sugar in bread formulas was fixed, but generally on the high side to facilitate the nutritional benefits of bread.[8] Actually, the enrichment order merely gave official recognition to what was almost a fact already. For by the end of 1942, 75 to 80 per cent of all white bread and white flour was being voluntarily enriched by the baking and milling industries.[9] By the time of War Food Order No. 1 the percentages were slightly higher. Moreover, in October of 1943, on the basis of hearings held from April through July, the Food and Drug Administration issued new standards for bread and flour which generally increased both the minimum and maximum enrichment requirements; riboflavin, now in adequate supply, was no longer optional, and Vitamin D was now required.[10]

---

[8] Walter N. Clissold, "Washington—Capital of the World," *Baking Industry Magazine*, April 12, 1952, p. 360.

[9] Wilder and Williams, *op. cit.*, p. 48.

[10] *Ibid.*, p. 22. The new bread standards were as follows:

Required	Minimum mg.	Maximum mg.
Thiamine	1.1	1.8
Riboflavin	0.7	1.6
Niacin	10.0	15.0
Iron	8.0	12.5
Optional		
Calcium	300	800
Vitamin D, U.S.P. units	150	750

Another wartime regulation which in a sense was of indirect aid to certain segments of the baking industry was Order No. 17 issued by the office of Defense Transportation in early 1943. Its purpose was to conserve gasoline and tires in all non-defense industries. Such industries were therefore ordered to reduce their truck mileage 25 per cent below the base period of 1942. For the wholesale bakers this meant each delivery vehicle was restricted to one trip daily, six days a week. House-to-house deliveries were limited to four per customer weekly.[11] This order helped bakers in that they could abstain from high-cost "fringe" business and still be relatively sure that the outer rim of their markets would be secure from invading competitors. It also eliminated the pressures of competition for more frequent deliveries, since all bakers were bound to the war-time order.

As did most non-defense industries, the baking industry found a general scarcity of metals throughout the war period which severely limited the equipment and machinery that could be purchased. There were a host of government regulations relating to such materials, and bakers were given various priorities ranging from AA-1 to AA-2X. The latter practically put baking ahead of all other industries not actually engaged in war or war-supporting production; but in the phrase coined at that time, they were "nothing but hunting licenses", for most bakery equipment firms were twelve months behind on deliveries.[12] Such conditions often resulted in production inefficiencies that might have been eliminated.

These then were the major regulations under which the baking industry operated throughout the entire war period. As to their effects on the industry, it seems rather clear that the major goals of the government were to keep bakery product prices, especially bread prices, from rising while at the same time trying to encourage a greater wheat and flour output for military use and for shipment to our allies. In large

---

[11] Collins, *op. cit.,* p. 11.
[12] Walter N. Clissold, *op. cit.,* p. 362.

they were successful, for between March, 1942, and the end of 1945, bread prices increased by only one-tenth of one cent per pound.[18] It is apparent, also, that War Food Order No. 1 and Defense Transportation Order No. 17 were of prime importance in keeping bakery prices at their pre-war level. Basically the purpose of these orders was to save bakers enough on the cost of bread production and distribution to enable them to carry an increase in flour prices and labor costs. This was to be done through limiting the varieties of bread that could be made, reducing wrapping expenditures, eliminating consignment selling and expensive gifts to grocers, and reducing route mileage. It is impossible to measure the costs of bakery operations for the industry as a whole during the war period, but some insights into the cost situation can be gained from a study of the larger wholesale bakeries made by the Federal Trade Commission. (Cf. Table 2.)

From Table 2 it can be seen that the government's goal of offsetting flour and labor cost increases with cost reductions in other areas was not fully realized. Wrapping costs were reduced, as were delivery vehicle expenses and administrative and general expenses, but not enough to prevent total costs from rising from 6.70 cents per pound to 7.55 cents, an increase of 12.7 per cent. Materials and labor cost increases were almost solely responsible for the recorded increase in total costs. Materials rose 2.85 cents per pound to 3.49 cents per pound, a rise of more than 22 per cent. Most of this increase resulted from higher flour costs due primarily to direct purchases of flour and wheat by the government for military purposes. It was also due in part to the government's policy of allowing the price of wheat to rise in order to encourage farmers to plant more wheat so that the United States could meet its growing food commitments both at home and abroad. Direct labor costs, including payment to production workers as well as route salesmen, rose by more than 15 per cent. It

---

[18] See Table 1.

TABLE 2

COST PER POUND OF BREAD AND ROLLS, 1942 AND 1945 *

	377 wholesale baking plants	283 wholesale baking plants
	Mar. 1942	Sept. 1945
Total pounds sold	365,924,100	299,107,725
	Cents per Pound	
Average sales realization Cost to produce and wrap:	7.07	7.76
Materials	2.85	3.49
Direct production labor	.74	.92
Indirect labor and overhead	.63	.68
Wrapping materials	.44	.41
Total cost to produce and wrap	4.66	5.50
Selling and delivery expense: Routemen's and supervisors' compensation	.85	.91
Delivery vehicle expense	.34	.32
Other selling expense	.47	.48
Total selling and delivery expense	1.66	1.71
Administrative and general expense	.38	.34
Total selling, administrative and general expense	2.04	2.05
Total cost to produce and sell	6.70	7.55
Net profit on sales	.37	.21

* Federal Trade Commission, Wholesale Baking Industry, Part II, Costs, Prices, and Profits (Washington: U. S. Government Printing Office, 1946), p. 39.

was virtually impossible to keep such costs from rising. Despite the efforts of OPA there was an 8 per cent rise in the cost of living between 1942 and 1945; moreover, there were strong economic pressures for pay raises because of alternative employment opportunities.

As Table 2 indicates, a large part of the net increases in cost was offset by higher sales realizations; these rose from 7.07 cents per pound to 7.76 cents per pound, an increase of 9.8 per cent. This change undoubtedly reflected some price increases granted by OPA because of hardship cases, but primarily it reflected the increased sales of higher price products.[14] Nevertheless, unit profit margins declined by 0.16 cents per pound, a reduction of some 45 per cent.[15]

Despite the apparent drop in profits on bread and rolls during the war years, it is doubtful that the baking industry was subjected to any genuine hardship. Certainly, in terms of volume the war years were prosperous ones for the nation's bakers. As shown in Table 3, bakery production achieved

TABLE 3

INCREASE IN BAKING INDUSTRY OUTPUT, 1941–1945 *

Year	Tonnage (1,000 pounds)	Percent of 1941 Output
1941	11,304,861	100.0
1942	12,422,809	109.9
1943	14,293,022	126.4
1944	15,724,414	139.1
1945	16,978,188	150.2

* Collins, *op. cit.*, p. 25. Data furnished by the American Bakers Association.

record levels, far exceeding the industry's best years in the past. By 1945 industry output was more than 50 per cent higher than it was in 1941; compared to 1939, it was 62.5 per cent higher. This meant an average increase of more than 12 per cent each year between 1941 and 1945. The baking industry was clearly enjoying its greatest output in history.

---

14 For example, a company in March of 1942, may have been selling a 24-ounce loaf of bread at a lower price per pound than it was selling a 16-ounce loaf. By September, 1945, it may have dropped the sale of the 24-ounce loaf in favor of the 16-ounce loaf at the higher price per pound.

15 Federal Trade Commission, *op. cit.*, p. 56. The same general results were shown by the Federal Trade Commission for a much smaller sample of house-to-house bakeries.

The reasons for the increased output are relatively clear. They stem primarily from an accelerated substitution of commercially baked goods for home baked goods during the hectic years of the war. Consumer disposable income in 1945 was up some 64 per cent over 1941, and there were relatively few goods on which to spend it. Increased wartime employment and overtime work meant more lunch boxes and bags, and these in turn meant a greater demand for sandwich-bread. More women found employment than ever before in our history; by 1945 female workers totaled over 18.5 million, an increase since 1941 of 43 per cent.[16] There was little time, let alone incentive, to bake at home. Instead, there was an increased demand for ready-prepared food products. Moreover, rationing of sugar and shortening, introduced in May of 1942, made it difficult for housewives to improvise substitutes and still turn out a tasty product. It was so much easier and more convenient for the housewife to buy bakers' bread and sweet goods than to make them herself. In addition, she knew that with bakers' bread and rolls, she was getting, at no extra cost, nutritionally improved products of proved reliability.

These economic pressures were too strong to be denied, and consumer acceptance of bakers' products reached an all-time high during the war. By 1945 an estimated 80 to 85 per cent of all bread consumed in the United States was commercially baked; a scant six years earlier bakers produced only two-thirds of total bread consumption. With respect to sweet goods no data are available, but the wartime conditions point to a significant increase in the bakers' 30 per cent share of such goods in 1939. It may have reached 35 per cent by the end of 1945.[17]

In addition to the obvious shift away from home baking, increased consumer consumption of food during the war contributed to rising baking industry output. Per capita food consumption totaled 1,674 pounds in 1945, the highest ever

---

[16] Historical Statistics of the United States, *op. cit.*, pp. 13 and 63.

[17] See Federal Trade Commission, *op. cit.*, p. 1.

recorded up to that time, representing an increase of 6 per cent since 1941. Over this same period, per capita civilian consumption of wheat flour reversed its long-run downward trend, rising from 153 pounds to 161 pounds.[18] And of this greater flour consumption, the nation's bakers were taking an increasing percentage, from an estimated 46 per cent in 1943 to approximately 62 per cent in 1945.[19] Thus the baking industry was increasing its productive share of baked goods consumption which in turn was increasing absolutely. It is impossible to measure separately the consumption figures on bread and other baked goods, but it is likely that they both increased over this four-year period.

The baking industry, therefore, found the war years pleasantly prosperous ones despite the rigors of price control and other regulations. Reduced profit margins on bread and rolls were offset by a greatly increased demand for these products. Moreover, the rising demand for variety baked goods added to the roseate picture. And on these products price control was not as stringent, bakers being allowed to pass on to the consumer most of the increases in ingredient and packaging costs. On balance, total profit rates for most bakery operations rose from their pre-war level. The Federal Trade Commission, in a study of 332 wholesale baking companies located in all sections of the country, reported increased profits for almost all bakeries surveyed. In 1941, the average rate of profits on sales totaled 4.38 per cent, rose to 6.38 and 7.63 per cent in 1942 and 1943, and dropped to 6.39 and 6.36 per cent in 1944 and 1945.[20] The largest baking companies generally reported the highest profit rates. The four largest baking companies—Continental Baking Company, Ward Baking Company, Purity Bakeries Corporation, and General Baking Company—almost doubled their 1941 earning rate in the peak

---

[18] Consumption of Food in the United States, 1909–1952, op. cit., p. 144.

[19] Wilder and Williams, op. cit., p. 32. Lloyd R. Wolf, "Baking—A Modern American Industry," General Managers Conference, 1947 (Chicago: The W. E. Long Company, 1947), p. 37.

[20] Federal Trade Commission, op. cit., p. 61.

year of 1943; they averaged 8.47 per cent in 1943 as compared to 4.54 per cent three years earlier. Yet in 1945 these large firms reported a smaller return than the average for the entire group. The smaller wholesalers were not without increased profit benefits. Even those with annual sales under $500,000 augmented their profit rate from 2.68 per cent in 1941 to 4.93 per cent in 1945. The medium-sized companies fared even better, and in 1945 reported profits totaling 6.93 per cent of sales.[21]

While there is little information available on the wartime positions of bakers other than wholesalers, it is unlikely that these firms endured financial hardship. Certainly, the larger house-to-house, institutional, and chain-store bakers must have fared as well as did the wholesalers. Even the smaller house-to-house operators, being more heavily engaged in variety goods production than were wholesalers, benefited from the advancing demand for such goods and had the afore-mentioned advantage of receiving semi-annual price increases on these products. In addition, they too benefited from the cost-reducing government regulations. Nor is there reason to doubt that the single and multi-unit retailers shared in the absolute increases of the war years. They offered the greatest product assortment to consumers at a time when people had the money to spend on fancier hand-made baked foods. More-over, they gained from the wartime elimination of consign-ment selling; they had long opposed this practice on the as-sumption that it hurt their own sales to have bread overloaded in the grocery store. Some of the very small retailers may have gone out of business during the war, but often as not it was a situation offering more attractive employment, as it was a case of difficulty in obtaining scarce ingredients or generally mak-ing a go of it. All in all, the entire industry prospered during the first half of the 'forties—perhaps to an extent it had neither foreseen nor experienced earlier.

---

[21] *Ibid.*

Baking Industry Progress in the Post-War Market

With the end of the war, pressures mounted to bring about an end to rationing and wartime government regulations. Shortage of consumption goods and a general lack of materials were still prevalent, but farmers, businessmen, and consumers generally were clamoring for a return to a free market. In the baking industry, there were similar pressures. In the Spring of 1946, partly as an attempt to give bakers relief from rising bread costs and partly to conserve wheat for export to stricken lands, the Office of Price Administration allowed bakers to reduce the weight of bread by 10 per cent. Because it was impracticable to reduce the price of bread by a fraction of one cent, weights were allowed to be trimmed without a corresponding change in price.[22] In effect, this allowance raised the price of bread by somewhat less than a penny per pound. Nevertheless, it is questionable whether bakers received any genuine benefit from the measure. Smaller pans were needed for the smaller loaves, and the still-enforced allocation of metals restricted the supply of pans to bakers. Moreover, several states which had weight laws limiting the size and weight of loaves of bread failed to permit bakers to change loaf weights. In June, however, more substantial action was taken which represented the first significant break in the "hold the line" order for the baking industry. At that time OPA allowed bakers an increase of one cent per dozen on rolls and one cent per pound on all bread except rye bread.[23] This action was taken to compensate bakers for a Department of Agriculture order, effective May 1, 1946, which reduced the domestic use of flour to 75 per cent of the quantity milled in the corresponding month of 1945 so as to relieve the world food crisis. Bakers had been indirectly affected through lower bread production and higher unit costs.

---

[22] Collins, *op. cit.*, p. 24.

[23] Federal Trade Commission, *op. cit.*, p. 86. Rye flour, not subject to price control, had increased by two cents per pound by April, 1946, and bakers had been consequently granted a compensating increase in the price of rye bread.

By the end of 1946 "the lid was off" when Congress brought an end to price control and most other wartime regulations either expired or were no longer enforced. By that time, also, the nation's prices had risen by as much as they had increased during the entire war period. From 1945 to 1946 the wholesale price index jumped 15 per cent; retail prices increased almost 10 per cent. Food prices, in the absence of controls, rose by 14 per cent. Bakery prices, which had been edging upward since the relief granted in April and June, moved still higher. Between March and September of 1946 the national average for white bread climbed from 8.9 cents per pound to 11.6 cents per pound, an increase of 30 per cent.[24] While increasing by much more than food prices generally, bread prices were merely catching up with those of other goods which had crept upward during the war. Moreover, bakers were no longer protected by government regulations which had tended to reduce certain costs of production and distribution. In addition, the absence of price controls on flour and other important ingredients brought further cost increases to bakers. Wholesale flour prices, after a modest 8 per cent increment during the war period, soared upward some 25 per cent between 1945 and 1946. The prices of lard, sugar, and milk, which had remained relatively stable during the preceding four years, advanced approximately 13 to 18 per cent.

For the most part, bakers were able to shift forward to consumers the higher costs they encountered. In this respect 1946 represented a continuation of the prosperous war years, for the demand factors that had worked to the industry's advantage during the war did not suddenly recede with the war's end. In fact, they were strengthened. Employment continued high and, despite rising prices, consumers, urged on by the increasing number of new goods that were coming onto the market, were spending more than ever before. Population in-

---

[24] Collins, *op. cit.*, p. 26.

creases further augmented the general demand. Especially important was the increased demand for convenience foods— quick-frozen foods and machine-made variety baked foods among others—reflecting the enhanced desire for leisure by housewives and the means of paying for it. Consumers apparently were not reverting to their pre-war shopping dietary habits. If they were changing them at all, it was to accelerate the trends already started. The nation's bakers found that the wartime habits of purchasing commercially baked foods continued strong. More specifically, there was a continued shift away from home baking. By the end of 1946 an estimated 85 per cent of all bread consumed was bought from commercial bakers; it is likely that the same upward trend existed for variety baked goods.[25] The fears of the industry as to a wholesale reversion after the war to home baking proved to be groundless. People had become rather completely accustomed to bakers' products. Moreover, because of the war, many young homemakers had had virtually no experience with home baking. The effect of the enrichment program which bakers voluntarily continued after the demise of War Food Order No. 1 was also important in aiding the increased demand, for consumers were far more conscious of nutrition needs than before the war. As a result, total industry output continued its upward wartime trend. Production of all bakery goods in 1946 was 15 per cent higher than in 1945.[26]

The year 1947 affords us our first detailed look at the baking industry since 1939. Based on Census of Manufactures' data, the industry status reflected the growing post-war market. It was a huge industry in every sense of the word. There were over 22,000 bakeries operating, employing almost 250,000 workers. Annual sales of all products totaled approximately three billion dollars compared to $1.2 billion less than ten years earlier. Physical volume was up some 70 per cent

---

25 Federal Trade Commission, *op. cit.*, p. 1.
26 Data furnished by the American Bakers Association.

over 1939 at approximately the same level estimated for 1946.[27]

Industry structure in 1947 reflected some of these changes experienced by the industry since the beginning of the war. (Cf. Table 4.) Although the Census categories are obviously

TABLE 4

NUMBER AND DOLLAR VOLUME OF BAKERIES
BY INDUSTRY SEGMENT, 1947[a]

Industry Segment	Number of Bakeries	Per Cent of Bakeries	Sales Volume ($000)	Per Cent of Sales
Bakeries Selling Primarily to Grocery Stores	3,455	15.3	$1,493,585	50.2
Chain Store Bakeries	90	0.4	150,174	5.0
Bakeries Selling Primarily to Hotels, Restaurants, and Institutions	1,564	7.0	271,383	9.1
Bakeries Selling Primarily at House-to-House	624	2.8	281,937	9.4
Retail Multi-Unit Bakeries	1,064	4.7	219,812	7.4
Retail Single-Unit Bakeries[b]	15,686	69.7	562,372	18.9
Totals	22,483	100.0	$2,979,263	100.0

[a] *U. S. Census of Manufactures, 1947.*
[b] *U. S. Census of Business, 1948.*

not mutually exclusive, the table gives a good indication of the relative importance of each industry segment. The industrial bakers, for example, accounted for over 81 per cent of total sales with but 30 per cent of the nation's bakeries. This per cent of total output was slightly less than their 1939 share. Within the industrial baking group itself, the bakers delivering primarily to grocery stores clearly remained the most important type of bakery operation in terms of sales volume.

---

[27] *U. S. Census of Manufactures, 1947.* These figures exclude the value of products of bakeries with sales of less than $5,000 annually.

They accounted for more than half of all industry sales.[28] The institutional, house-to-house, and multi-unit retail bakers had approximately equal shares of industry output, all having gained relatively since 1939. Surprisingly, the chain-store bakeries, despite their price differential advantage maintained since the 1920s, produced no more than 5 per cent of aggregate sales. This percentage tends to obscure the strength of the chains because it does not include the many private-label arrangements made by bakers with the chains nor the price discounts they were able to command. It does, however, indicate that throughout the war and immediate post-war periods, consumers generally preferred the brands of the traditional bakers despite the higher price involved. The single-unit retailers, differing so markedly from the larger industrial bakers, were not omitted from the general prosperity. They had increased their share of total sales from less than 15 per cent in 1939 to almost 19 per cent in 1947. While they were operating by far the smallest bakeries in the industry, they nevertheless obviously benefited from the increased demand for luxury bakestuffs that had developed since the 'thirties.

The shifting pattern of consumer preferences toward more variety in baked foods referred to above was one of the major industry changes that had become apparent by 1947. Basically it was a trend that had its beginning in the 'twenties, reversed itself during the depression years, and resumed again by 1939. By 1947 under the impetus of increased incomes and a continued desire for variety in the diet, this trend had progressed to the point where bread sales accounted for less than one-half of baking industry dollar volume. As shown in Table 5, bread sales were less than 47 per cent of total output; comparatively, in 1939 they had totaled 55 per cent. Variety goods, on the other hand, rose from less than 40 per cent in 1939 to 46.5 per cent eight years later. Bread and rolls continued to

---

[28] Total sales through grocery stores were undoubtedly higher than 50 per cent due to the fact that other bakery operators, including many of the single-unit retailers, also sold to grocers.

TABLE 5

PRODUCT BREAKDOWN OF THE BAKING INDUSTRY, 1947[a]

Product Class	Sales Volume (Millions of Dollars)	Per Cent of Total
Bread	$1,378.7	46.5
Rolls	206.6	7.0
Yeast-Raised Sweet Goods	305.5	10.2
Cakes, Pastry, Doughnuts	764.1	25.6
Pies	216.4	7.6
Biscuit and Crackers	45.2	1.5
Miscellaneous Products	51.7	1.6
Total	$2,979.3 [b]	100.0

[a] *U. S. Census of Manufactures, 1947* and *U. S. Census of Business, 1948.* Since all firms did not report detailed product breakdowns, the original data were adjusted on the assumption that the non-reporting firms had the same average product mix as those reporting such product divisions. The percentage to total value of product for the industry accounted for by reporting firms was 93.7 per cent.

[b] Includes an estimate of the 1948 production of the single-unit retail bakers separately reported in the U. S. Census of Business, 1948. The estimate is based on the assumption that these bakers had the same product mix as did the multi-unit retailers.

be the principal products of the industry and the chief source of revenue, but it was obvious that, barring another depression, they would continue to decline in relative importance.

The reactions of the various segments of the industry to the changing preferences of consumers were generally along the same line, yet each segment tended to have a different product-mix from each of the others. The chain-store bakers and those delivering to grocers were unique in that they were the only operators whose bread output totaled more than 50 per cent of sales. Nevertheless, they had significantly increased their volume of variety goods over precious levels until by 1947 such goods amounted to more than 34 per cent of their output. The house-to-house segment of the industry in 1947 produced an approximate equal proportion of bread and other baked goods; this also represented an increase in sweet goods production. To an even greater extent the institutional bakeries had turned to the sale of products other than bread. They differed from others, however, in that their customers preferred a different type of product. The retail operators, both multi-unit and single-unit, continued to concentrate on sweet goods much as they had done for several decades; here again, however, their emphasis within this group was unique, involving a greater amount of fancier handmade goods.

The years between 1947 and 1950 witnessed further evidence of progress and expansion in the baking industry along the lines established by 1947. Total output continued to rise, although at a slower rate than that established during the war years. And again, as in the past, the prime impetus came from a further gradual decline in home baking. By 1950 it was estimated that the nation's bakers were producing from 85 to 90 per cent of all bread consumed, a slight increase since 1947. The corresponding share of sweet goods consumption probably pushed close to 40 per cent. Despite the frequently heard preference for "grandma's old-fashioned baking", consumers apparently showed no indication of reverting back to home-made baked foods. This trend was all the more important to the baking industry after 1947, for by then the per capita consumption of wheat flour had once again resumed its secular decline, implying a reduction of total baked foods consumption. Between 1946 and 1950 consumption of flour fell from 154 pounds per capita to 133 pounds, a drop of almost 14 per cent.[29] Apparently the shift away from home baking was more than enough to compensate for whatever small reduction there was in baked foods consumption so that the baking industry's output continued to rise absolutely.

There were both old and relatively new reasons for the industry's continued success in limiting and capturing more of the home baking market. Among the former were the obvious ones based on a continuing high level of economic activity—

[29] Consumption of Food in the United States, 1909–1952, *op. cit.*, p. 123.

sufficient employment and consumer income, and a corresponding desire for more leisure and convenience in living. There were also one or two new product developments in the baking industry which served to promote an increased demand for commercial bakery products. One, the production of a firmer, harder bread product than the more popular loaf, was actually not a new development; such a product had long been produced by a few bakeries through the country, but by 1950 its production had apparently increased relative to all types of bread products. While most consumers continued to prefer the softer, fluffy loaf introduced during the 'thirties, the firmer type of bread may have appealed to many who might otherwise have preferred homemade bread. A more recent product development was the so-called Brown N' Serve process as applied to breads, rolls, and pastries. The process was introduced in 1949 by General Mills, Inc., after acquiring rights to the innovation from a Florida baker who had accidentally discovered it. Subsequently General Mills gave up its rights to the process, and it was gradually adopted by most bakers. Basically, the Brown N' Serve process involves the production of semi-finished products that are fully formed and prebaked except for crust browning. The purpose is to make available to the housewife bakery products of great keeping quality which she can finish baking in her own kitchen, thereby providing her with oven-hot baked goods. While it is still too early to judge the potential of the Brown N' Serve process, it has undoubtedly contributed to increased industry sales.

The progress made by bakers in the area of mechanized production also contributed to the increased consumer acceptance of commercially baked goods enabling them to turn out a more uniform, higher quality product. The war period had been characterized by a general scarcity of materials, and the post-war period offered the first major opportunity to the industry for improving existing equipment and extending the degree of automatic handling. By 1950, in the plants which incorporated the most modern equipment, bread production was a scientifically controlled mechanical process. From the receipt of flour to the loading of delivery vehicles, raw materials moved swiftly through a series of high-powered, precision-engineered machines; only the fermentation stage of dough preparation interrupted an otherwise completely mechanized process. While most bakeries were not so fully mechanized, the trends were clearly in that direction. A possible part of these trends by 1950 was the growing use of prepared mixes in the bakery. Several of the large milling firms had devised automatic systems of premixing dry ingredients at the mill with the idea of making baking formulas more accurate and eliminating many handling and scaling operations in the bakery. While bakers had been using prepared mixes of one sort or another for many years, they now held promise of an accelerated use in the future.

Technological progress by 1950 was further evidenced by the possibility of complete automation in bread production. One such method, the John C. Baker Do-Maker Process, involved continuous mixing of bread dough. It eliminated the usual fermentation, dividing, rounding, intermediate proofing, and moulding steps in bread production by automatically mixing the dough and extruding it into baking pans. The dough was then given a pan proof and carried directly to the oven for baking. By 1950 this technique of bread production had been developed to the point of experimental commercial application, but even today it is still too early to judge its potential use.

The production of variety goods, while still not as mechanized as that of bread, also improved after the war. Because of the very nature of such bakery products, however, their production involved more handwork and preparatory operations, largely on account of hand scaling of ingredients and cooking of fillings and icings. But with respect to production flow, the assembly line principle was clearly established by 1950. Cake production, for example, was greatly simplified with the use of continuous mixers, not unlike the one used in the bread making experiment. In principle these units pre-mixed all ingredients, then, under sustained air pressure, effectively whipped them into a fine batter and automatically deposited the correct amounts into baking pans. Pie machinery and other special product equipment, while not as revolutionary as the automatic cake mixers, were also developed in the later post-war years. Together with better wrapping machines and the wider use of automatic conveyor equipment, they helped to make variety good production a more mechanical operation, applicable to the large-scale production techniques so necessary to meet the rising consumer demand.

In a less apparent manner than was true of other factors, the enrichment program of the baking industry in the last few years of the 1940s continually enforced the established reputation of commercial bakers and contributed to the increased acceptance of bakers' products. The very fact that enrichment was taken for granted by consumers is evidence of its continued importance. Actually bakers were still enriching their bread products on a voluntary basis as of 1950.[30] The government hearings on bread standards which had been postponed during the war were resumed again in 1948, but it was not until 1953 that final standards emerged. By 1950, however, largely due to the bakers' own efforts, 90 per cent of all bread sold at wholesale and 80 per cent of all bread commercially produced was enriched.[31] The benefits of enriched bread, widely publicized to consumers, have been heralded by all nutritionists. Surveys made by the Bureau of Home Economics and Home Nutrition indicate that the use of enriched flour and bread has resulted in an increased intake of 30 per cent more thiamine, 16 per cent more riboflavin, 21 per cent more niacin, and 19 per cent more iron than would be consumed had ordinary flour and bread been continued. In other

[30] Some states had enacted mandatory enrichment laws, but most flour and bread producers took it upon themselves to add the synthetic compounds suggested.

[31] W. B. Bradley, "Nutritionally Improved Bread to the American Consumer," *Baking Industry Magazine*, April 12, 1952, p. 378.

A Modern Horizontal Mixer

A Modern Slicing and Wrapping Machine

Courtesy of Baker Perkins, Inc.

Bulk Flour Storage Bins with 45-Inch Pneumatic Flour Dump Hopper

A Modern Dough Divider, Rounder, and Automatic
Overhead Loaf Proofer

A Modern Traveling-Tray Oven with Automatic Loader and Unloader

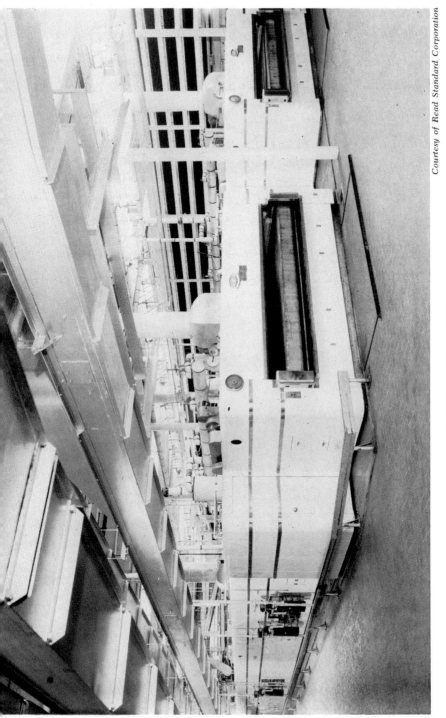

A Modern Tunnel Oven

Courtesy of Continental Baking Company

Delivery Trucks of the Late 1920's

Courtesy of BAKING INDUSTRY Magazine

A Modern Fleet of Bakery Trucks at Loading Platform

Automatic Conveyor System

studies enriched bread has been singularly credited with eliminating B vitamin deficiencies among clinic patients throughout the entire country.[32]

Conclusion

The baking industry as of 1950 reflected the postwar market
primarily built upon the continuing high demand of the preceding war years. As had been true throughout the entire history of the industry, the nation's bakers owed their high level
of consumer demand primarily to the successive inroads which
had been made in the home baking market. Industry structure
was unchanged from its 1947 counterpart with all segments
of the industry having shared in the gradual expansion. Indeed, structure was relatively little changed from its 1929
level, as most segments had come through both the depression
and war with no major shifts in relative importance. More
pronounced competitive activities were apparent by 1950,
especially by the chain-store bakers and the large multi-plant
operators, and there were increasing pressures toward larger
operations; but the smaller independent bakers were still
holding their relative positions.

As for the long-run prospects for the future of the baking
industry, they included both encouraging aspects of further
expansion and less promising ones of a general leveling-off of
output. On the plus side there were the expectations of an increasing population and a rising national income. Population
growth obviously meant a greater demand for baked foods.
Increasing income implied the continued prospect of capturing more of the home baking market. In the case of bread,
bakers were already producing more than 85 per cent of all
bread consumed, but there is no reason to believe that this
proportion could not be increased to as much as 95 per cent.
Because of the tremendous absolute consumption of bread,
even a relatively small shift away from home baking would
mean a significant increase in commercial production. In the

---

[32] *Ibid.,* p. 226.

case of variety baked foods, the market potentials were perhaps greater. With 60 per cent of such goods still being made
in the home, bakers had only begun to exploit their possibil-
ities in this area. Moreover, the consumer trend toward an increased per capita consumption of variety goods meant that
bakers would be taking a larger share of a market that was
increasing absolutely.

On the less promising side of the picture the baking industry faced the still gloomy prospect of a further drop in the per
capita consumption of flour and its implication of a decline in
per capita bread consumption. The relationship between flour
and bread consumption is somewhat uncertain, but with the
consumption of other baked goods continuing to increase over
the years, the probability is that per capita bread consumption
will decline. There are, however, two bright aspects to this
not so promising prediction. For one thing, population increases might be sufficient in the future to offset the bread decline. This was the case, for example, in the flour milling industry wherein total production between 1910 and 1950 increased by 4 per cent despite a 37 per cent decrease in the per
capita consumption of flour. Thus total commercial bread
production might increase slightly with an increasing population even without a further decline in home baking. Secondly,
there is the possibility, not altogether remote, that the increased per capita consumption of variety baked goods might
arrest or even reverse to some degree the downward trend of
flour consumption.

In general, therefore, the future trends in the baking industry seem to be an increasing level of output with variety
baked foods progressively becoming more important. In terms
of industry structure, such trends should do relatively little
to upset the established positions among the various segments
of bakery operations. Even the small-scale independent retailers who historically have become relatively less important
in the industry seem to have settled into their market niche;
moreover, the indicated trends in the industry should help

Today's Air Conditioned Bakery

to maintain their position. The larger firms, of course, with their tremendous multi-plant capacity, should easily be able to continue to make any necessary adjustments. The major question mark involves the smaller independent industrial bakers increasingly facing the stepped-up competition of the chain-store bakers and the larger consolidated bakeries. While baking is not a heavily concentrated industry, these smaller firms must greatly improve their methods of operation if they are not to fall by the wayside.

BIBLIOGRAPHY

BOOKS

Alderfer, F. B., and Michl, H. E. *Economics of American Industry*. New York: McGraw-Hill Book Company, Inc., 1950.

Alsberg, Carl L. *Combination in the American Bread Baking Industry*. Food Research Institute, Misc. Pub. No. 3. Stanford University, Calif.: Stanford University Press, 1926.

American Medical Association, *Handbook of Nutrition*. New York: The Blakiston Company, 1951.

Ashley, William. *The Bread of Our Forefathers*. Oxford: The Clarendon Press, 1928.

Barnes, Harry E. *An Economic History of the Western World*. New York: Harcourt, Brace and Company, 1937.

Breasted, James H. *Ancient Times, A History of the Early World*. Boston: Ginn and Company, 1916.

Carcopine, Jerome. *Daily Life in Ancient Rome*. Translated by E. O. Lorimer. New Haven: Yale University Press, 1940.

Carmen, Harry J., and Syrett, Harold C. *A History of the American People*. New York: Alfred A. Knopf, 1952.

Casey, Robert J. *Chicago Medium Rare*. Indianapolis: Bobbs-Merrill Book Company, 1949.

Cash, W. J. *The Mind of the South*. New York: Doubleday and Company (Doubleday Anchor Books, 1954). Albert A. Knopf, 1941.

Clark, Thomas D. *Pills, Petticoats, and Plows*. New York: Bobbs-Merrill Book Company, 1944.

Cummings, R. O. *The American and His Food*. Revised ed. Chicago: University of Chicago Press, 1941.

Duddy, E. A., and Revzan, D. A. *Marketing, an Institutional Approach*, Second ed. New York: McGraw-Hill Book Company, Inc., 1953.

[245]

Earle, A. M. *Home Life in Colonal Days.* New York: The Macmillan Company, 1899.

General Managers Conference, 1926–1950. Chicago: W. E. Long Company.

Homan, E. P. *The American Whaleman.* New York: Longmans, Green, and Company, 1928.

Jacob, H. E. *Six Thousand Years of Bread, Its Holy and Unholy History.* Garden City: Doubleday, Doran and Company, Inc., 1944.

Jacobs, Morris B. (ed.). *The Chemistry and Technology of Food and Food Products.* New York: Interscience Publications, Inc., 1944. Also, 2nd ed., 1951.

Kennedy, F. A. "The Biscuit Industry," *One Hundred Years of American Commerce, 1795–1895.* Vol. II. C. M. Depew (ed.). New York: D. O. Haynes and Company, 1895.

Kuhlmann, Charles B. *The Development of the Flour Milling Industry in the United States.* Boston: Houghton Mifflin Co., 1929.

Kyrk, H., and Davis, J. S. *The American Baking Industry, 1849–1923.* Misc. Pub. No. 2, Food Research Institute, Stanford, Calif.: Stanford University Press, 1925.

Martin, Edgar W. *The Standard of Living 1860.* Chicago: University of Chicago Press, 1942.

Martin, Robert F. *National Income in the United States, 1799–1938.* New York: National Industrial Conference Board, 1939.

Moore, Mary K. *The Baking Industry.* Boston: Bellman Publishing Company, Inc., 1946.

Morrison, Samuel Eliot, and Commager, Henry Steele. *The Growth of the American Republic.* New York: Oxford University Press, 1942. Also, Vol. II, 4th ed., 1950.

Pirenne, Henri. *Economic and Social History of Medieval Europ.* Translated by I. E. Clegg. New York: Harcourt, Brace and Company, no date.

Presbrey, F. *The History and Development of Advertising.* Garden City: Doubleday, Doran, and Company, Inc., 1929.

Pyler, E. *Baking Science and Technology.* Chicago: Siebel Publishing Company, 1952.

Reid, Margaret G. *Food for People.* New York: John Wiley and Sons, Inc., 1943.

Robertson, Ross M. *History of the American Economy.* New York: Harcourt, Brace and Company, 1955.

Shannon, F. A. *America's Economic Growth.* New York: The Macmillan Co., 1940. Also, 3rd ed., 1951.

Sperry, E. J. *Bread Brands.* Chicago: E J. Sperry—Industrial Publications, 1949.

"The Stale Bread Problem," *Wheat Studies of the Food Research Institute.* Stanford University, Calif.: Stanford University Press, 1936.

Stone, R. W., and V. B. *The Baking Industry Under NRA.* Studies in Business Administration, Vol. I, No. 3. Chicago: University of Chicago Press, 1936.

Storck, J., and Teague, W. D. *Flour for Man's Bread.* Minneapolis: University of Minnesota Press, 1952.

Taylor, Alonzo E. *War Bread.* New York: The Macmillan Co., 1918.

Tinley, J. M. *Control of Food Prices.* Berkeley, Calif.: University of California Press, 1942.

———: *Rationing and Control of Food Supplies.* Berkeley, Calif.: University of California Press, 1942.

Wilder, Russel M., and Williams, Robert R. *Enrichment of Flour and Bread, A History of the Movement.* Bulletin No. 110. Washington: National Research Council, National Academy of Sciences, 1944.

PERIODICAL AND JOURNAL ARTICLES

Albright, J. M. "How the Bakers and Equipment Manufacturers Co-operated to Build Better Bread-Making Machinery," *Baking Industry,* XCV (April 12, 1952).

The Bakers Journal and Deutsche-Amerikanischer Baeker Zeitung, September 9, 1933. Also April 28, 1934.

Bradley, W. B. "Nutritionally Improved Bread to the American Consumer," *Baking Industry,* April 12, 1952.

"Bread in the Ancient World," *Baking Industry,* April 12, 1952.

Business Week, September 13, 1941.

Chicago Daily News, December 30, 1954.

Clissold, Walter N. "Washington—Capitol of the World," *Baking Industry,* April, 1942.

Custis, Vendever. "Throwing the Spotlight on Bakery Mergers," *General Managers Conference, 1926.* Chicago: W. E. Long Company, 1926.

"The Enrichment Program—How It Grew," *Journal of Home Economics,* September, 1945.

"The Fabulous Market for Food," *Fortune,* October, 1953.

Galbraith, J. K. "The Disequilibrium System," *The American Economic Review.* XXXVII, No. 3 (June, 1947).

Graf, G. N. "The Years Teach Much Which the Days Never Know," *Baking Industry*, April 12, 1952.

Journal of Home Economics, September, 1945.

Joyce, Arthur T. "America's Changing Food Habits," *Bakers' Weekly*, September 17, 1954.

Kennedy, Lou. "Continental, the Wonder Bakery," *Bakers Helper* (reprinted), November 26, 1949.

Long, W. E. "Solving the Bakers' Advertising and Merchandising Problems," *Bakers Helper*, April 17, 1937.

McCollum, E. V. "Half-Baked Program" (To Enrich or Not to Enrich: A Symposium), *Journal of Home Economics*. XXXVII, No. 6 (June, 1945).

Mendel, L. B. "The Changing Diet of the American People," *Journal of the American Medical Association*, XCIX (July 9, 1932).

Mitchell, Helen S. "A First Step," *Journal of Home Economics*, American Home Economics Association, October, 1929.

Morgan, Agnes Fay. "Education the Key" (To Enrich or Not to Enrich: A Symposium). *Journal of Home Economics*, September, 1945.

"The Organizing Era, 1897–1904," *Bakers Helper*, April 17, 1937.

Sherwood, R. C. "Accomplishments in Cereal Fortification," *American Journal of Public Health*, XXXIII, No. 5 (May, 1943).

"Sixty Centuries of Bakers and Baking," *Bakers' Weekly*. A series of articles appearing from Vol. 31, July 30, 1921 through Volume 47, August 8, 1925, not running consecutively.

Slater, Charles C. "Price Control 1942 vs. 1952," *Bakers Helper*, December, 1951.

Sperry, E. J. "Sixty-Five Years of Bakery Advertising," *Baking Industry*, April 12, 1952.

Webb, Sidney and Beatrice. "The Assize of Bread," *Economic Journal*. XIV (June, 1904).

Williams, Robert R. "Bread Enrichment," *Science*, Vol. 102, No. 2641 (August 16, 1945).

"The Wonders of the Diet," *Fortune*, May, 1936.

PUBLICATIONS OF THE UNITED STATES GOVERNMENT

Bureau of the Census. *Catalog of U. S. Census Publications, 1790–1945*. Washington: Government Printing Office, 1950.

———. *Census of Business, Vol. V, Distribution of Manufacturers' Sales, 1939*. Washington: Government Printing Office, 1942.

———. *Census of Business: 1948*. Retail Trade, U. S. Summary,

Bulletin No. 1-R-O. Washington: Government Printing Office, 1950.

———. *Census of Manufactures, Bakery Products,* 1849, 1859, 1869, 1879, 1889, 1899, 1904, 1909, 1914, 1919, 1921, 1923, 1925, 1927, 1929, 1931, 1933, 1935, 1937, 1939, 1947. Washington: Government Printing Office.

———. *Census of Manufactures, General Statistics for all Manufacturing Industries, 1849–1939.* Washington: Government Printing Office, 1940.

———. *Census of Manufactures, 1947, Product Supplement.* Washington: Government Printing Office, 1950.

———. *Census of Distribution, 1930, Vol. II, Distribution of Sales of Manufacturing Plants.* Washington: Government Printing Office, 1932.

———. *Fifteenth Census of U. S. (1930).* Census of Distribution, Agricultural Commodity Series. Washington: Government Printing Office, 1934.

———. *Fifteenth Census of U. S. (1930).* Vol. 1 Retail Distribution and Vol. 2 Wholesale Distribution, Summary for U. S. Washton: Government Printing Office, 1933.

———. *Historical Statistics of the U. S. 1789–1945.* Washington: Government Printing Office, 1949.

Bureau of Human Nutrition and Home Economics. Burk, Marguerite C. and Clark, Faith. *Nutritive Value of the Per Capita Food Supply 1909–1945.* Misc. Pub. 616. Washington: Government Printing Office, 1947.

Department of Agriculture. Bureau of Agricultural Economics. *Consumption of Food in the United States, 1909–1952.* Agricultural Handbook No. 62. Washington: Government Printing Office, 1953.

———. Means, Gardner C. *NRA, AAA and Making of Industrial Policy.* Washington: Government Printing Office, 1935.

———. *Price Spreads between Consumers and Farmers for Food Products, 1913–1944.* Misc. Pub. No. 576. Washington: Government Printing Office, September, 1945.

Department of Commerce. *National Income Supplement to Survey of Current Business.* Washington: Government Printing Office, 1954.

Department of Labor, Bureau of Labor Statistics. *Average Retail Price per Pound of White Bread, 1913–1949.* Washington: Government Printing Office, 1950.

———. *Changes in Cost of Living in Large Cities in the U. S., 1913–*

1941. Bulletin No. 699. Washington: Government Printing
Office, 1941.

————. *Retail Prices and Cost of Living* (Retail Prices 1890 to December 1926). Bulletin No. 495, Washington: Government
Printing Office, August, 1929.

————. *Wholesale Prices, 1890–1923.* Bulletin No. 357. Washington:
Government Printing Office, 1924.

————. *Job Descriptions for the Bakery Products Industry. June 1939,*
Washington: Government Printing Office, 1941.

Federal Trade Commission. *Bakery Combines and Profits.* Senate Doc.
No. 212, 69th Congress, 2nd Session. Washington: Government
Printing Office, 1927.

————. *Bread and Bakery Products Manufacturing Corporations.*
Industrial Corporation Reports. Washington: Federal Trade
Commission, October, 1940.

————. *Chain Stores: Chain Store Manufacturing.* Washington: Government Printing Office, 1933.

————. *Competition and Profits in Bread and Flour.* Senate Doc. No.
98, 70th Congress, 1st Session. Washington: Government Printing Office, 1928.

————. *Distributon Methods and Costs.* Parts 1, 2 and 5. Washington:
Government Printing Office, 1944.

————. *Wholesale Baking Industry.* Parts I, II and Summary. Costs,
Prices, and Profits. Washington: Government Printing Office,
1946.

National Recovery Administration. *The Baking Industry: Distribution and Marketing of Bakery Products.* Washington: National
Archives and Record Service, 1955.

————. *Code of Fair Competition for the Baking Industry.* Washington: Government Printing Office, 1934.

UNPUBLISHED MATERIAL

Collins, Edward C. *History of the Bakery Section,* Cereals, Feeds and
Agricultural Branch, Food Price Division, Office of Price Administration, December, 1941–December, 1946. Unpublished
manuscript.

Eggert, H. F. "Interesting Facts about Nabisco—National Biscuit Company." Privately printed pamphlet. (Mimeographed.)

"Study of the Flour and Baking Industries in the United States." A
report prepared by the Research Department. J. Walter Thompson Company. Chicago: January, 1924. (Typewritten.)

Talbott, Philip. History of the Code of Fair Competition for the Baking Industry. Unpublished manuscript.

Taggart, III, A. L. "Collective Bargaining in the Bread Baking Industry of Middle Western United States." Unpublished senior thesis, Department of Economics, Princeton University, 1948.

"Wages, Hours and Employment in the Baking Industry." A brief submitted at code hearing by Bakery and Confectionary Workers' International Union, January, 1934.

What Is the Baker's Toughest Competition? Minneapolis: Pillsbury Mills, Inc., 1953. Privately printed brochure.